Christus: The Messiah of Israel

The History of Early Christianity

by

Fernando Klein

Christus: The Messiah of Israel

The History of Early Christianity

Copyright © 2011 by **Fernando Klein**

Printed in the United States of America. No part of this book may be used or reproduced in any manner whatsoever without written permission except in the case of brief quotations embodied in critical articles and reviews.

Fifth Estate,
Blountsville, AL 35031

First Edition

Cover Designed by An Quigley

Printed on acid-free paper

Library of Congress Control No: 2011943715
ISBN: 9781936533206

Fifth Estate, 2011

www.fifthestatepub.com

**To my wife and daughter who,
of all that walk the earth,
are most precious to me...**

Author's preface

This book was made with the propose of being a suitable tool for the student and people in general to reach the very beginning for a certain religion, in this case, the Christianity.

The life of Jesus Christ, his family, disciples, his Ministry and Sayings, his trial and Death, will be considered; after reviewing Jesus life, there will be a multi focal approach to early Christendom from its foundation until the moment it became the religion of the Roman Empire.

My principal aim, in a word, is to make this approaching from the "witness" point of view: the history will be show through the eyes of the people who lived different times in Christianity history.

There will be several sources for such an approaching: Greek and Roman historians and writers (Suetonius, Tito Livius, Tacitus), Jewish historian and writers (Flavius Josephus), early Christian theologians (Tertullian, Origen), apocrypha, documents and edicts from the Roman empire rulers and so on.

Looking at the diverse source materials available, from the earliest New Testament texts and the complex treaties of third century authors such as Lactantius, to archaeology, epigraphy and papyrology, the book examines what is needed to study the subject, what materials were available, how useful they were, and how the study of the subject may be approached.

The imposition of "correct belief," religious uniformity, and an institutional framework that enforced orthodoxy were both consolidating and stifling. Uncovering the difficulties in establishing the Christian church, the relationship with Judaism, Gnosticism, Greek philosophy and Greco-Roman society would be examined.

Christianity not only made history but was modified and shaped by history. No genetic study of Christianity will ever explain Christianity, yet ignorance of its antecedents and of the contemporary spiritual forces and mentality renders a true appreciation impossible. There is a more excellent way of magnifying Christianity than by ignoring or decrying Paganism, or disparaging the rival systems which Christianity overcame and laid under tribute.

Hellenistic-Oriental syncretism cannot be overlooked by students of the history and evolution of Christianity. The Christian Ecclesia is best appreciated when observed at work in an intensely religious world in competition with the Synagogues of the Dispersion, the Guilds of the Mystery-Religions, and the Schools of Greek philosophy.

Fernando Klein is Professor of Middle East Religions and Chair of the Religious Studies Department at Complutense University, Madrid, Spain. He has published several books on the Bible, Judaism and Christendom, including "The Naked Bible", "The Gnostic Gospels", "The Church of Paper", and so on.

Contents

Author's preface

1. Life of Jesus Christ

1.1. Context

- Description of the Jerusalem Temple
- Tacitus. Histories (on the war of the Jews)
- Sects of the Jews (Antiquities of the Jews, Book XVIII, Flavius Josephus)
- The Theodotus Inscription in Jerusalem

1.2 Cannonical and Apocrypha

The Apocryphal Works

- Infancy Gospels
- Essene-Nazarene Gospels
- Gnostic Esoterica (some from the Nag Hammadi library)
- Ritual Diagrams
- Fate of Mary
- Acts of the Apostles
- Epistles
- Visions and Channeled Works
- Miscellany
- Fragments
- Lost Works

1.3. The Birth, Infancy and Childhood of Jesus

- The Infancy Gospel of Thomas

1.4 Jesus and John the Baptist

1.5 Saying of Jesus

- Gospel of Thomas

1.6 Miracles of Jesus

- The Signs Gospel

1.7. Messiah and Messianism in Israel

Qumran's two Messiahs
Later developments: from Messiah to Christ

Messianic Candidates

- Judas, son of Hezekiah (4 BCE)
- Simon of Peraea (4 BCE)
- Athronges, the shepherd (4 BCE)
- Judas the Galilean (6 CE)
- The Samaritan prophet (36 CE)
- Theudas (about 45 CE)
- The Egyptian prophet (between 52 and 58 CE)
- Menahem (66 CE)
- Judas the Galilean (6 CE)
- Simon bar Giora (69-70 CE)
- Jonathan the weaver (73 CE)
- Simon ben Kosiba (132-135 CE)

1.8. The Disciples of Jesus

- The Gospel of Judas

1.9 Jesús and Mary Magdalene

- The Gospel According to Mary Magdalene

1.10. The Trial and Death of Jesus Christ

- The Acts of Pilate

1.11 Historical and Archaeological Evidence

- The Pilate Inscription
- The Testimonium Flavianum (Josephus, Antiquities 18.63)
- Celsus on Jesus
- Tertullian Passage (De Spetaculis 100.30)
- Yeshu and Joshua (Sanhedrin 107b)
- Baraitha Bab. Sanhedrin 43a
- Jesus' Students/Disciples

2. Early Church: First Century

2.1 Saul of Tarsus (d.c.65 CE, Paul, the Apostle of the Heathen)

- Anti-Jewish Attitude.
- Jewish Proselytism and Paul.
- Paul's Christ.
- The Crucified Messiah.
- His Missionary Travels.
- Paul's Church versus the Synagogue.
- Influence of the Greek Mysteries.
- The Mystery of the Cross
- Conflict with Judaism and the Law.
- Antinomianism and Jew-Hatred.
- The Old Testament and the New One
- Spurious Writings Ascribed to Paul.
- His System of Faith.

2.2 Simon Cephas (Saint Peter)

- He Pronounces Jesus the Messiah.
- Head of the Church.
- Peter and Paul.

- His Supposed Writings.
- The Apocalypse of Peter.

2.3 Christians Beginnings. The Persecution of the Christians

2.4 The Didache (Teaching of the Twelve Apostles)

2.5 The Oxyrhynchus Hymn

2.6 Eusebius (c.260-340 CE) and the Early Church (Ecclesiastical History)

2.7 Pagan Influences in Early Christianity

    a. Mithras
    b. Attis

- Hymn to Demeter
- The Eleusinian Mysteries
- Death and Initiation in the Mysteries
- The Worship of Cybele (Lucretius (98-c.55 BCE)
- Initiation into the Mysteries of Cybele. The Taurobolium
- Isis, Queen of Heaven

3. Early Church: 2nd-3rd Centuries

    a. Persecution and Survival

- Letters of Pliny the Younger and the Emperor Trajan
- The Martyrdom of Saints Perpetua and Felicitas
- Tertullian (Apology)
- The Ritual Cannabilism Charge Against Christians (Minucius Felix. Octavius)
- Hippolytus. Apostolic Tradition
- Deeds of Zenophilus. How the Romans Tried to Seize Christian Books, c. 395 CE

- Celsus' view of Christians and Christianity (Contra Celsus, Origen)

   b. Church Organization

- St. Jerome. Letter to a Soldier
- Gregory Nazianzus. On divorce
- Codex Justinianus. On the Lex Julia Relating to Adultery and Fornication
- Ambrose, Bishop of Milan. On the characteristics suitable for a bishop

4. The Emergence of Theologies

- Heresy in Early Chruch. Early Christendom Sects
- Against Heresies (St. Irenaeus)
- Herejías. Contra las Herejias. Irineus. Sectas Cristianas Primitivas
- The Muratorian Canon (170 AD)
- Origen
- Gnostic Marcion (2nd Cent CE): Gospel of the Lord c. 220 CE
- Orthodoxy: Tertullian: On Pagan Learning, c. 220 CE

5. The "Triumph" of the Church

- The List of Popes.
- Las listas papales, el papa.
- Eusebius (c.260-340 CE): Ecclesiastical History - Conversion of Constantine
- Edit of Galerius and the "Edict of Milan" 311/313
- The Nicene Creed (325) Jesus, God and the Holy Spirit. The Trinity
- The 'Decretum gelasianum´

✠ **Codex Theodosianus: On Religion, 4th Cent CE.**

Bibliography

1. Life of Jesus Christ

1.1 Context

Description of the Jerusalem Temple
War of the Jews (Book 5 Chapter 5) by Flavius Josephus

1. Now this temple, as I have already said, was built upon a strong hill. At first the plain at the top was hardly sufficient for the holy house and the altar, for the ground about it was very uneven, and like a precipice; but when king Solomon, who was the person that built the temple, had built a wall to it on its east side, there was then added one cloister founded on a bank cast up for it, and on the other parts the holy house stood naked. But in future ages the people added new banks, and the hill became a larger plain. They then broke down the wall on the north side, and took in as much as sufficed afterward for the compass of the entire temple. And when they had built walls on three sides of the temple round about, from the bottom of the hill, and had performed a work that was greater than could be hoped for, (in which work long ages were spent by them, as well as all their sacred treasures were exhausted, which were still replenished by those tributes which were sent to God from the whole habitable earth,) they then encompassed their upper courts with cloisters, as well as they [afterward] did the lowest [court of the] temple. The lowest part of this was erected to the height of three hundred cubits, and in some places more; yet did not the entire depth of the foundations appear, for they brought earth, and filled up the valleys, as being desirous to make them on a level with the narrow streets of the city; wherein they made use of stones of forty cubits in magnitude; for the great plenty of money they then had, and the liberality of the people, made this attempt of theirs to succeed to an incredible degree; and what could not be so much as hoped for as ever to be accomplished, was, by perseverance and length of time, brought to perfection.

2. Now for the works that were above these foundations, these were not unworthy of such foundations; for all the cloisters were double, and the pillars to them belonging were twenty-five cubits in height, and supported the cloisters. These pillars were of one entire stone each of them, and that stone was white marble; and the roofs were adorned with cedar, curiously graven. The natural magnificence, and

excellent polish, and the harmony of the joints in these cloisters, afforded a prospect that was very remarkable; nor was it on the outside adorned with any work of the painter or engraver. The cloisters [of the outmost court] were in breadth thirty cubits, while the entire compass of it was by measure six furlongs, including the tower of Antonia; those entire courts that were exposed to the air were laid with stones of all sorts. When you go through these [first] cloisters, unto the second [court of the] temple, there was a partition made of stone all round, whose height was three cubits: its construction was very elegant; upon it stood pillars, at equal distances from one another, declaring the law of purity, some in Greek, and some in Roman letters, that "no foreigner should go within that sanctuary" for that second [court of the] temple was called "the Sanctuary," and was ascended to by fourteen steps from the first court. This court was four-square, and had a wall about it peculiar to itself; the height of its buildings, although it were on the outside forty cubits, was hidden by the steps, and on the inside that height was but twenty-five cubits; for it being built over against a higher part of the hill with steps, it was no further to be entirely discerned within, being covered by the hill itself. Beyond these thirteen steps there was the distance of ten cubits; this was all plain; whence there were other steps, each of five cubits a-piece, that led to the gates, which gates on the north and south sides were eight, on each of those sides four, and of necessity two on the east. For since there was a partition built for the women on that side, as the proper place wherein they were to worship, there was a necessity for a second gate for them: this gate was cut out of its wall, over against the first gate. There was also on the other sides one southern and one northern gate, through which was a passage into the court of the women; for as to the other gates, the women were not allowed to pass through them; nor when they went through their own gate could they go beyond their own wall. This place was allotted to the women of our own country, and of other countries, provided they were of the same nation, and that equally. The western part of this court had no gate at all, but the wall was built entire on that side. But then the cloisters which were betwixt the gates extended from the wall inward, before the chambers; for they were supported by very fine and large pillars. These cloisters were single, and, excepting their magnitude, were no way inferior to those of the lower court.

3. Now nine of these gates were on every side covered over with gold and silver, as were the jambs of their doors and their lintels; but there was one gate that was without the [inward court of the] holy house, which was of Corinthian brass, and greatly excelled those that were only covered over with silver and gold. Each gate had two doors, whose height was severally thirty cubits, and their breadth fifteen. However, they had large spaces within of thirty cubits, and had on each side rooms, and those, both in breadth and in length, built like towers, and their height was above forty cubits. Two pillars did also support these rooms, and were in circumference twelve cubits. Now the magnitudes of the other gates were equal one to another; but that over the Corinthian gate, which opened on the east over against the gate of the holy house itself, was much larger; for its height was fifty cubits; and its doors were forty cubits; and it was adorned after a most costly manner, as having much richer and thicker plates of silver and gold upon them than the other. These nine gates had that silver and gold poured upon them by Alexander, the father of Tiberius. Now there were fifteen steps, which led away from the wall of the court of the women to this greater gate; whereas those that led thither from the other gates were five steps shorter.

4. As to the holy house itself, which was placed in the midst [of the inmost court], that most sacred part of the temple, it was ascended to by twelve steps; and in front its height and its breadth were equal, and each a hundred cubits, though it was behind forty cubits narrower; for on its front it had what may be styled shoulders on each side, that passed twenty cubits further. Its first gate was seventy cubits high, and twenty-five cubits broad; but this gate had no doors; for it represented the universal visibility of heaven, and that it cannot be excluded from any place. Its front was covered with gold all over, and through it the first part of the house, that was more inward, did all of it appear; which, as it was very large, so did all the parts about the more inward gate appear to shine to those that saw them; but then, as the entire house was divided into two parts within, it was only the first part of it that was open to our view. Its height extended all along to ninety cubits in height, and its length was fifty cubits, and its breadth twenty. But that gate which was at this end of the first part of the house was, as we have already observed, all over covered with gold,

as was its whole wall about it; it had also golden vines above it, from which clusters of grapes hung as tall as a man's height. But then this house, as it was divided into two parts, the inner part was lower than the appearance of the outer, and had golden doors of fifty-five cubits altitude, and sixteen in breadth; but before these doors there was a veil of equal largeness with the doors. It was a Babylonian curtain, embroidered with blue, and fine linen, and scarlet, and purple, and of a contexture that was truly wonderful. Nor was this mixture of colors without its mystical interpretation, but was a kind of image of the universe; for by the scarlet there seemed to be enigmatically signified fire, by the fine flax the earth, by the blue the air, and by the purple the sea; two of them having their colors the foundation of this resemblance; but the fine flax and the purple have their own origin for that foundation, the earth producing the one, and the sea the other. This curtain had also embroidered upon it all that was mystical in the heavens, excepting that of the [twelve] signs, representing living creatures.

5. When any persons entered into the temple, its floor received them. This part of the temple therefore was in height sixty cubits, and its length the same; whereas its breadth was but twenty cubits: but still that sixty cubits in length was divided again, and the first part of it was cut off at forty cubits, and had in it three things that were very wonderful and famous among all mankind, the candlestick, the table [of shew-bread], and the altar of incense. Now the seven lamps signified the seven planets; for so many there were springing out of the candlestick. Now the twelve loaves that were upon the table signified the circle of the zodiac and the year; but the altar of incense, by its thirteen kinds of sweet-smelling spices with which the sea replenished it, signified that God is the possessor of all things that are both in the uninhabitable and habitable parts of the earth, and that they are all to be dedicated to his use. But the inmost part of the temple of all was of twenty cubits. This was also separated from the outer part by a veil. In this there was nothing at all. It was inaccessible and inviolable, and not to be seen by any; and was called the Holy of Holies. Now, about the sides of the lower part of the temple, there were little houses, with passages out of one into another; there were a great many of them, and they were of three stories high; there were also entrances on each side into them from the gate of the temple. But

the superior part of the temple had no such little houses any further, because the temple was there narrower, and forty cubits higher, and of a smaller body than the lower parts of it. Thus we collect that the whole height, including the sixty cubits from the floor, amounted to a hundred cubits.

6. Now the outward face of the temple in its front wanted nothing that was likely to surprise either men's minds or their eyes; for it was covered all over with plates of gold of great weight, and, at the first rising of the sun, reflected back a very fiery splendor, and made those who forced themselves to look upon it to turn their eyes away, just as they would have done at the sun's own rays. But this temple appeared to strangers, when they were coming to it at a distance, like a mountain covered with snow; for as to those parts of it that were not gilt, they were exceeding white. On its top it had spikes with sharp points, to prevent any pollution of it by birds sitting upon it. Of its stones, some of them were forty-five cubits in length, five in height, and six in breadth. Before this temple stood the altar, fifteen cubits high, and equal both in length and breadth; each of which dimensions was fifty cubits. The figure it was built in was a square, and it had corners like horns; and the passage up to it was by an insensible acclivity. It was formed without any iron tool, nor did any such iron tool so much as touch it at any time. There was also a wall of partition, about a cubit in height, made of fine stones, and so as to be grateful to the sight; this encompassed the holy house and the altar, and kept the people that were on the outside off from the priests. Moreover, those that had the gonorrhea and the leprosy were excluded out of the city entirely; women also, when their courses were upon them, were shut out of the temple; nor when they were free from that impurity, were they allowed to go beyond the limit before-mentioned; men also, that were not thoroughly pure, were prohibited to come into the inner [court of the] temple; nay, the priests themselves that were not pure were prohibited to come into it also.

7. Now all those of the stock of the priests that could not minister by reason of some defect in their bodies, came within the partition, together with those that had no such imperfection, and had their share with them by reason of their stock, but still made use of none except their own private garments; for nobody but he that officiated had on

his sacred garments; but then those priests that were without any blemish upon them went up to the altar clothed in fine linen. They abstained chiefly from wine, out of this fear, lest otherwise they should transgress some rules of their ministration. The high priest did also go up with them; not always indeed, but on the seventh days and new moons, and if any festivals belonging to our nation, which we celebrate every year, happened. When he officiated, he had on a pair of breeches that reached beneath his privy parts to his thighs, and had on an inner garment of linen, together with a blue garment, round, without seam, with fringe work, and reaching to the feet. There were also golden bells that hung upon the fringes, and pomegranates intermixed among them. The bells signified thunder, and the pomegranates lightning. But that girdle that tied the garment to the breast was embroidered with five rows of various colors, of gold, and purple, and scarlet, as also of fine linen and blue, with which colors we told you before the veils of the temple were embroidered also. The like embroidery was upon the ephod; but the quantity of gold therein was greater. Its figure was that of a stomacher for the breast. There were upon it two golden buttons like small shields, which buttoned the ephod to the garment; in these buttons were enclosed two very large and very excellent sardonyxes, having the names of the tribes of that nation engraved upon them: on the other part there hung twelve stones, three in a row one way, and four in the other; a sardius, a topaz, and an emerald; a carbuncle, a jasper, and a sapphire; an agate, an amethyst, and a ligure; an onyx, a beryl, and a chrysolite; upon every one of which was again engraved one of the forementioned names of the tribes. A mitre also of fine linen encompassed his head, which was tied by a blue ribbon, about which there was another golden crown, in which was engraven the sacred name [of God]: it consists of four vowels. However, the high priest did not wear these garments at other times, but a more plain habit; he only did it when he went into the most sacred part of the temple, which he did but once in a year, on that day when our custom is for all of us to keep a fast to God. And thus much concerning the city and the temple; but for the customs and laws hereto relating, we shall speak more accurately another time; for there remain a great many things thereto relating which have not been here touched upon.

8. Now as to the tower of Antonia, it was situated at the corner of two

cloisters of the court of the temple; of that on the west, and that on the north; it was erected upon a rock of fifty cubits in height, and was on a great precipice; it was the work of king Herod, wherein he demonstrated his natural magnanimity. In the first place, the rock itself was covered over with smooth pieces of stone, from its foundation, both for ornament, and that any one who would either try to get up or to go down it might not be able to hold his feet upon it. Next to this, and before you come to the edifice of the tower itself, there was a wall three cubits high; but within that wall all the space of the tower of Antonia itself was built upon, to the height of forty cubits. The inward parts had the largeness and form of a palace, it being parted into all kinds of rooms and other conveniences, such as courts, and places for bathing, and broad spaces for camps; insomuch that, by having all conveniences that cities wanted, it might seem to be composed of several cities, but by its magnificence it seemed a palace. And as the entire structure resembled that of a tower, it contained also four other distinct towers at its four corners; whereof the others were but fifty cubits high; whereas that which lay upon the southeast corner was seventy cubits high, that from thence the whole temple might be viewed; but on the corner where it joined to the two cloisters of the temple, it had passages down to them both, through which the guard (for there always lay in this tower a Roman legion) went several ways among the cloisters, with their arms, on the Jewish festivals, in order to watch the people, that they might not there attempt to make any innovations; for the temple was a fortress that guarded the city, as was the tower of Antonia a guard to the temple; and in that tower were the guards of those three. There was also a peculiar fortress belonging to the upper city, which was Herod's palace; but for the hill Bezetha, it was divided from the tower Antonia, as we have already told you; and as that hill on which the tower of Antonia stood was the highest of these three, so did it adjoin to the new city, and was the only place that hindered the sight of the temple on the north. And this shall suffice at present to have spoken about the city and the walls about it, because I have proposed to myself to make a more accurate description of it elsewhere…

Tacitus. Histories (on the war of the jews)

Fragments

1 The Jews, being closely besieged and given no opportunity to make peace or to surrender, were finally dying of starvation, and the streets began to be filled with corpses everywhere, for they were now unequal to the duty of burying their dead; moreover, made bold to resort to every kind of horrible food, they did not spare even human bodies — save those of which they had been robbed by the wasting that such food had caused.

2 It is said that Titus first called a council and deliberated whether he should destroy such a mighty temple. For some thought that a consecrated shrine, which was famous beyond all other works of men, ought not to be razed, arguing that its preservation would bear witness to the moderation of Rome, while its destruction would for ever brand her cruelty. Yet others, including Titus himself, opposed, holding the destruction of this temple to be a prime necessity in order to wipe out more completely the religion of the Jews and the Christians; for they urged that these religions, although hostile to each other, nevertheless sprang from the same sources; the Christians had grown out of the Jews: if the root were destroyed, the stock would easily perish.

3 That six hundred thousand Jews were killed in that war is stated by Cornelius and Suetonius.1

4 Next, to quote the words of Cornelius Tacitus, "the gate of Janus, that had been opened when Augustus was old, remained so while on the very boundaries of the world new peoples were being attacked, often to our profit and sometimes to our loss, even down to the reign of Vespasian." Thus far Cornelius.

5 Gordianus ... opened the gates of Janus:2 as to the question whether anyone closed them after Vespasian and Titus, I can recall no statement by any historian; yet Cornelius Tacitus reports that they were opened after a year by Vespasian himself.

6 For the mighty battles of Diurpaneus, king of the Dacians, with the Roman general Fuscus,3 and the mighty losses of the Romans I should now set forth at length, if Cornelius Tacitus, who composed the history of these times with the greatest care, had not said that

Sallustius Crispus and very many other historians had approved of passing over in silence the number of our losses, and that he for his own part had chosen the same course before all others.

7 Those vast Scythian peoples whom all our ancestors and even the famous Alexander the Great had feared and avoided according to the testimony of Pompeius4 and Cornelius ... I mean the Alans, the Huns, and the Goths, Theodosius attacked without hesitation and defeated in many great battles.

8 But these (Locrians) who live near Delphi are called the Ozolians..; however, those who moved to Libya have the name of Nasamones,° as Cornelius Tacitus reports, being sprung from the Narycii.

Sects of the Jews (Antiquities of the Jews, Book XVIII, Flavius Josephus)

Chapter 1.

How Cyrenius Was Sent By Caesar To Make A Taxation Of Syria And Judea; And How Coponius Was Sent To Be Procurator Of Judea; Concerning Judas Of Galilee And Concerning The Sects That Were Among The Jews.

1. Now Cyrenius, a Roman senator, and one who had gone through other magistracies, and had passed through them till he had been consul, and one who, on other accounts, was of great dignity, came at this time into Syria, with a few others, being sent by Caesar to he a judge of that nation, and to take an account of their substance. Coponius also, a man of the equestrian order, was sent together with him, to have the supreme power over the Jews. Moreover, Cyrenius came himself into Judea, which was now added to the province of Syria, to take an account of their substance, and to dispose of Archelaus's money; but the Jews, although at the beginning they took the report of a taxation heinously, yet did they leave off any further opposition to it, by the persuasion of Joazar, who was the son of Beethus, and high priest; so they, being over-pesuaded by Joazar's words, gave an account of their estates, without any dispute about it. Yet was there one Judas, a Gaulonite, (1) of a city whose name was

Gamala, who, taking with him Sadduc, (2) a Pharisee, became zealous to draw them to a revolt, who both said that this taxation was no better than an introduction to slavery, and exhorted the nation to assert their liberty; as if they could procure them happiness and security for what they possessed, and an assured enjoyment of a still greater good, which was that of the honor and glory they would thereby acquire for magnanimity. They also said that God would not otherwise be assisting to them, than upon their joining with one another in such councils as might be successful, and for their own advantage; and this especially, if they would set about great exploits, and not grow weary in executing the same; so men received what they said with pleasure, and this bold attempt proceeded to a great height. All sorts of misfortunes also sprang from these men, and the nation was infected with this doctrine to an incredible degree; one violent war came upon us after another, and we lost our friends which used to alleviate our pains; there were also very great robberies and murder of our principal men. This was done in pretense indeed for the public welfare, but in reality for the hopes of gain to themselves; whence arose seditions, and from them murders of men, which sometimes fell on those of their own people, (by the madness of these men towards one another, while their desire was that none of the adverse party might be left,) and sometimes on their enemies; a famine also coming upon us, reduced us to the last degree of despair, as did also the taking and demolishing of cities; nay, the sedition at last increased so high, that the very temple of God was burnt down by their enemies' fire. Such were the consequences of this, that the customs of our fathers were altered, and such a change was made, as added a mighty weight toward bringing all to destruction, which these men occasioned by their thus conspiring together; for Judas and Sadduc, who excited a fourth philosophic sect among us, and had a great many followers therein, filled our civil government with tumults at present, and laid the foundations of our future miseries, by this system of philosophy, which we were before unacquainted withal, concerning which I will discourse a little, and this the rather because the infection which spread thence among the younger sort, who were zealous for it, brought the public to destruction.

2. The Jews had for a great while had three sects of philosophy peculiar to themselves; the sect of the Essens, and the sect of the

Sadducees, and the third sort of opinions was that of those called Pharisees; of which sects, although I have already spoken in the second book of the Jewish War, yet will I a little touch upon them now.

3. Now, for the Pharisees, they live meanly, and despise delicacies in diet; and they follow the conduct of reason; and what that prescribes to them as good for them they do; and they think they ought earnestly to strive to observe reason's dictates for practice. They also pay a respect to such as are in years; nor are they so bold as to contradict them in any thing which they have introduced; and when they determine that all things are done by fate, they do not take away the freedom from men of acting as they think fit; since their notion is, that it hath pleased God to make a temperament, whereby what he wills is done, but so that the will of man can act virtuously or viciously. They also believe that souls have an immortal rigor in them, and that under the earth there will be rewards or punishments, according as they have lived virtuously or viciously in this life; and the latter are to be detained in an everlasting prison, but that the former shall have power to revive and live again; on account of which doctrines they are able greatly to persuade the body of the people; and whatsoever they do about Divine worship, prayers, and sacrifices, they perform them according to their direction; insomuch that the cities give great attestations to them on account of their entire virtuous conduct, both in the actions of their lives and their discourses also.

4. But the doctrine of the Sadducees is this: That souls die with the bodies; nor do they regard the observation of any thing besides what the law enjoins them; for they think it an instance of virtue to dispute with those teachers of philosophy whom they frequent: but this doctrine is received but by a few, yet by those still of the greatest dignity. But they are able to do almost nothing of themselves; for when they become magistrates, as they are unwillingly and by force sometimes obliged to be, they addict themselves to the notions of the Pharisees, because the multitude would not otherwise bear them.

5. The doctrine of the Essens is this: That all things are best ascribed to God. They teach the immortality of souls, and esteem that the rewards of righteousness are to be earnestly striven for; and when

they send what they have dedicated to God into the temple, they do not offer sacrifices (3) because they have more pure lustrations of their own; on which account they are excluded from the common court of the temple, but offer their sacrifices themselves; yet is their course of life better than that of other men; and they entirely addict themselves to husbandry. It also deserves our admiration, how much they exceed all other men that addict themselves to virtue, and this in righteousness; and indeed to such a degree, that as it hath never appeared among any other men, neither Greeks nor barbarians, no, not for a little time, so hath it endured a long while among them. This is demonstrated by that institution of theirs, which will not suffer any thing to hinder them from having all things in common; so that a rich man enjoys no more of his own wealth than he who hath nothing at all. There are about four thousand men that live in this way, and neither marry wives, nor are desirous to keep servants; as thinking the latter tempts men to be unjust, and the former gives the handle to domestic quarrels; but as they live by themselves, they minister one to another. They also appoint certain stewards to receive the incomes of their revenues, and of the fruits of the ground; such as are good men and priests, who are to get their corn and their food ready for them. They none of them differ from others of the Essens in their way of living, but do the most resemble those Dacae who are called Polistae (4) [dwellers in cities].

6. But of the fourth sect of Jewish philosophy, Judas the Galilean was the author. These men agree in all other things with the Pharisaic notions; but they have an inviolable attachment to liberty, and say that God is to be their only Ruler and Lord. They also do not value dying any kinds of death, nor indeed do they heed the deaths of their relations and friends, nor can any such fear make them call any man lord. And since this immovable resolution of theirs is well known to a great many, I shall speak no further about that matter; nor am I afraid that any thing I have said of them should be disbelieved, but rather fear, that what I have said is beneath the resolution they show when they undergo pain. And it was in Gessius Florus's time that the nation began to grow mad with this distemper, who was our procurator, and who occasioned the Jews to go wild with it by the abuse of his authority, and to make them revolt from the Romans. And these are the sects of Jewish philosophy.

The Theodotus Inscription in Jerusalem: The Functions of the Synagogue

This inscription, of the mid-first century C.E., not only introduces us to a family of archisynagogues but explains some of the purposes of the synagogue itself. The early date of this inscription testifies to the presence of a synagogue in Jerusalem even before the destruction of the Second Temple. Inscriptions from Egypt c. 230 B.C.E.: Proseuché. Originated in Hellenistic Diaspora because of distance from Temple. Not mentioned again until First-Century Palestine

"Theodotus, son of Vettenus, priest and archisynagogue, son of an archisynagogue, grandson of an archisynagogue, built the synagogue for the reading of the Law and the teaching of the commandments, and guest-house and the rooms and the water supplies for the lodging of strangers in need, which his fathers founded and the Elders and Simonides."

1.2 Cannonical and Apocrypha

The New Testament is composed of the 4 Gospels, the Book of Acts, 21 Epistles (letters), and the Book of Revelation (John). The four Gospels are actually anonymously written. They do not purport to have been written by Matthew, Mark, Luke and John and their titles do not affirm it. The Epistles are:

- Romans - Paul
- 1 and 2 Corinthians - Paul
- Galatians - Paul
- Ephesians - Paul
- Philippians - Paul
- Colossians - Paul

- 1 and 2 Thessalonians - Paul
- 1 and 2 Timothy - attributed to Paul but considered forgeries
- Titus - Paul
- Philemon - Paul
- Hebrews - probably Paul
- James
- 1 and 2 Peter
- 1, 2 and 3 John
- Jude

The gospels of Matthew, Mark, and Luke are known as the **Synoptic Gospels** because they include many of the same stories, often in the same sequence, and sometimes exactly the same wording. This degree of parallelism in content, narrative arrangement, language, and sentence structures can only be accounted for by literary interdependence. Many scholars believe that these gospels share the same point of view and are clearly linked. The term synoptic comes from the Greek syn, meaning "together", and optic, meaning "seen". According to the majority viewpoint, Mark was the first gospel written. Matthew and Luke then used Mark as a source, as well as a hypothetical **sayings gospel known as Q.** Matthew and Luke also included unique material, and the sources for this material are designated M and L, respectively.

The synoptic gospels are the primary source for historical information about Jesus. Apocryphal gospels, as well as the canonical Gospel of John, differ greatly from the Synoptic Gospels. Of the many gospels written in antiquity, only the four gospels came to be accepted as part of the New Testament, or **canonical.**

The **Apocrypha**: Medieval Latin, from Late Latin, neuter plural of apocryphus secret, from Greek apokryphos obscure, from apokryptein to hide away, from apo- + kryptein to hide.
1: books included in the Septuagint and Vulgate but excluded from the Jewish and Protestant canons of the Old Testament.
2: early Christian writings not included in the New Testament.

Gnosticism is a set of religious beliefs and spiritual practices common to early Christianity, Hellenistic Judaism, Greco-Roman mystery religions, Zoroastrianism and Neoplatonism. A common characteristic of some of these groups was the teaching that the realisation of Gnosis (intuitive knowledge), is the way to salvation of the soul from the material world. They saw the material world as created through an intermediary being (demiurge) rather than directly by God. In most of the systems, this demiurge was seen as imperfect, in others even as evil. Some apocryphal work are gnostic ones.

The Apocryphal Works

It is important to note that while this list is lengthy, it is by no means final or complete. Many of the books listed here were considered heretical (especially those belonging to the gnostic tradition).

Infancy Gospels

- The Gospel of Pseudo-Matthew (Birth of Mary and Infancy of the Saviour)
- The Protevangelion of James (Gospel of James)
- The Infancy Gospel of Thomas (not to be confused with the Gospel of Thomas)
- The Life of John the Baptist
- The History of Joseph the Carpenter
- The Arabic Infancy Gospel
- The Libellus de Nativitate Sanctae Mariae (Nativity of Mary)
- The Latin Infancy Gospel

Essene-Nazarene Gospels

- The Gospel of the Hebrews
- The Gospel of the Nazarenes (Gospel of the Holy Twelve)
- The Gospel of the Ebionites
- The Essene Gospels of Peace

Gnostic Esoterica (some from the Nag Hammadi library)

Sethian Gnostic Texts

- The Apocalypse of Adam
- The Apocryphon of John (also called the "Secret Gospel of John")
- The Thought of Norea
- The Trimorphic Protennoia
- The Coptic Gospel of the Egyptians (wholly independent of its namesake, the Greek Gospel of the Egyptians)
- The Coptic Apocalypse of Paul (wholly independant of its namesake, the Apocalypse of Paul)
- Three Steles of Seth
- Allogenes
- Zostrianos
- Marsenes

Rival Versions of Canonical Gospels

- Gospel of Cerinthus (Cerinthus' version)
- Gospel of Basilides (Basilides' version)
- Gospel of Marcion (Marcion's version)
- Gospel of Appelles (Appelles' version)
- Gospel of Bardesanes (Bardesanes' version)
- Gospel of Mani (Mani's version)

Sayings Gospels

- The Gospel of Thomas (not to be confused with the Infancy Gospel of Thomas)
- The Gospel of Philip

Morality Gospels

- Greek Gospel of the Egyptians (wholly independent of the Coptic Gospel of the Egyptians)
- Book of Thomas the Contender ("Book of Thomas", "Epistle of the Contender", and "Letter of the contender")

Passion Gospels

- The Gospel of Peter

- The Gospel of Nicodemus (also called the "Acts of Pilate")
- The Gospel of Bartholomew
- The Questions of Bartholomew
- The Resurrection of Jesus Christ (which claims to be according to Bartholomew)

General Gnostic Texts

- Gnostic Apocalypse of Peter (it is not to be confused with the Apocalypse of Peter)
- The Wisdom of Jesus Christ ("Sophia of Jesus Christ" and the "Sophia Jesu Christi")
- The Epistle of Eugnostos ("Letter of Eugnostos")
- The Dialogue of the Saviour
- The Gospel of Mary Magdalene ("Gospel of Mary")
- Interpretation of Knowledge
- The Gospel of Truth
- Pistis Sophia

Cainite Gnostic Texts

- The Gospel of Judas

Ritual Diagrams

- The Ophite Diagrams
- The First and Second Books of Jeu

Fate of Mary

- The Home Going of Mary
- The Falling asleep of the Mother of God

Acts of the Apostles

- The Acts of John
- The Acts of Peter (with the Martyrdom of Peter)
- The Acts of Andrew (Gospel of Andrew)

- The Acts of Thomas
- The Acts of Paul, which contained within it texts which were sometimes found separately including:
- The Third Epistle to the Corinthians
- The Acts of Paul and Thecla
- The Acts of Peter and Andrew

- The Acts of Peter and the Twelve
- The Acts of Peter and Paul
- The Nine Books of Clement
- The Acts of Phillip
- The Acts of Xanthippe, Polyxena, and Rebecca featuring Paul, Peter, Philip, and Andrew

Epistles

- The Epistle of Barnabas ("Gospel of Barnabas", it is not the same Gospel of Barnabas)
- 1 and 2 Clement
- The Epistle of the Corinthians to Paul
- The Epistle to the Laodiceans, found only in some manuscripts of the Latin Vulgate apocrypha
- The Third Epistle to the Thessalonians (an epistle in the name of Paul)
- The Epistle to the Ionians (an epistle in the name of Paul)
- The Epistle to Seneca the Younger (an epistle in the name of Paul)
- The Epistles of Jesus Christ and Abgarus King of Edessa
- The Third Epistle to the Corinthians

Visions and Channeled Works

- Apocalypse of Peter (very different to the Gnostic Apocalypse of Peter)
- Apocalypse of Thomas (also called the Revelation of Thomas)
- Apocalypse of Stephen (also called the Revelation of Stephen')
- First Apocalypse of James (also called the First Revelation of James)

- Second Apocalypse of James (also called the Second Revelation of James)
- Apocalypse of Paul (with a change of visionary, this becomes the Apocalypse of the Virgin)

Miscellany

- The Physiologus of Ambrose
- The Foundation
- The Treasure
- The Didache
- The Apocryphon of James (also named Secret Gospel of James)
- The Prayer of Paul
- The Sermon of Paul
- The Preaching of Peter (also named Clementine Literature and Pseudo-Clementines)
- The Penitence of Origen
- The Sentences of Sextus
- The Book of Nepos
- The Canons of the Apostles

Fragments

- The Unknown Berlin Gospel
- The Naassene Fragment
- The Fayum Fragment
- The Secret Gospel of Mark
- The Oxyrhynchus Gospels
- The Egerton Gospel

Lost Works

- The Gospel of Matthias (probably not to be confused with the Gospel of Matthew)
- The Gospel of the Four Heavenly Realms
- The Gospel of Perfection
- The Gospel of Eve
- The Gospel of the Holy

- Memoria Apostolorum
- The Gospel of the Seventy
- The Grave-plate of the Apostles
- The Book of spells of serpents
- The Portion of the Apostles

1.3. The Birth, Infancy and Childhood of Jesus

	Matthew	Mark	Luke	John
Prologue	...0	...0	1:1-4	1:1-18
Annunciation to Zachary in the Temple in Jerusalem	...0	...0	1:5-25	...0
Annunciation to Mary in Nazareth	...0	...0	1:26-38	...0
The Incarnation	1:18-25	...0	...0	...0
The visit of Mary to Elizabeth at Ain Karim	...0	...0	1:39-56	...0
Birth of John the Baptist at Ain Karim	...0	...0	1:57-80	...0
Marriage of Mary and Joseph	...0	...0	...0	...0
The Genealogies	1:1-17	...0	3:23-38	...0
The Birth of Christ in Bethlehem	...0	...0	2:1-7	...0
Adoration by Shepherds from the neighbouring hills	...0	...0	2:8-20	...0
Circumcision of Jesus on the eight day	...0	...0	2:21	...0
Presentation in the Temple at Jerusalem	...0	...0	2:22-38	...0
Adoration of the Maji from the East	2:1-12	...0	...0	...0
Flight into Egypt	2:13-15	...0	...0	...0
Slaughter of the Innocents by Herod	2:16-18	...0	...0	...0
The Holy Family leave Egypt	2:19-21	...0	...0	...0
Return to Nazareth	2:22-23	...0	2:39-40	...0
Finding the Child Jesus in the Temple in Jerusalem	...0	...0	2:41-52	...0

The Infancy Gospel of Thomas
Range of Dating: 140-170 A.D.

Here beginneth a treatise of the Boyhood of Jesus according to Thomas.

I. How Mary and Joseph fled with him into Egypt.

When there was a tumult because search was made by Herod for our Lord Jesus Christ, that he might slay him, then said an angel unto Joseph: Take Mary and her child and flee into Egypt from the face of them that seek to slay him. Now Jesus was two years old when he entered into Egypt. And as he walked through a sown field he put forth his hand and took of the ears and put them upon the fire and ground them and began to eat. [And he gave such favour unto that field that year by year when it was sown it yielded unto the lord of it so many measures of wheat as the number of the grains which he had taken from it.] Now when they had entered into Egypt they took lodging in the house of a certain widow, and abode in the same place one year. And Jesus became three years old. And seeing boys playing he began to play with them. And he took a dried fish and put it into a basin and commanded it to move to and fro, and it began to move. And again he said to the fish: Cast out thy salt that is in thee and go into the water. And it came to pass. But when the neighbours saw what was done they told it to the widow woman in whose house his mother Mary dwelt. And she when she heard it hasted and cast them out of her house.

II. How a Master cast him out of the city.
1 And as Jesus walked with Mary his mother through the midst of the marketplace of the city, he looked about and saw a master teaching his pupils. And behold twelve sparrows which were quarrelling one with another fell from the wall into the lap of the master who taught the boys. And when Jesus saw it he laughed and stood still. 2 Now when that teacher saw him laughing, he said to his pupils in great anger: Go, bring him hither unto me. And when they had brought him, the master took hold on his ear and said: What sawest thou that thou didst laugh? And he said unto him: Master, see, my hand is full of corn, and I shewed it unto them, and scattered the corn, which they are carrying away in danger: for this cause they fought with one another that they might partake of the corn. 3 And Jesus left not the place until it was accomplished. And for this cause the master laboured to cast him out of the city together with his mother.

III. How Jesus came out of Egypt.
1 And behold, an angel of the Lord met with Mary and said unto her: Take the child and return into the land of the Jews: for they are dead

which sought his life. So Mary arose with Jesus, and they went into the city Nazareth, which is in the inheritance of his (her?) father. 2 But when Joseph departed out of Egypt after the death of Herod, he took Jesus into the wilderness until there was quiet in Jerusalem from them that sought the life of the child. And he gave thanks to God for that he had given him understanding, and because he had found grace before the Lord God. Amen.

or, And Mary arose with Jesus, and they went unto the city of Capernaum which is of Tiberias, unto the inheritance of her father. 2 But when Joseph heard that Jesus was come out of Egypt after the death of Herod, he took him, &c.

or, After these things an angel of the Lord came unto Joseph and unto Mary the mother of Jesus and said unto them: Taketh he child, return into the land of Israel, for they are dead that sought the life of the child. And they arose and went to Nazareth where Joseph possessed the goods of his father. 2 And when Jesus was seven years old, there was quiet in the realm of Herod from all them that sought the life of the child. And they returned unto Bethlehem and abode there.

IV. What Jesus did in the city of Nazareth.

It is a glorious work for Thomas the Israelite (Ismaelite) the apostle of the Lord to tell of the works of Jesus after he came out of Egypt unto Nazareth. Hear (understand) therefore all of you beloved brethren, the signs which the Lord Jesus did when he was in the city of Nazareth: as it is said in the first chapter.

1 Now when Jesus was five years old there was a great rain upon the earth, and the child Jesus walked about therein. And the rain was very terrible: and he gathered the water together into a pool and commanded with a word that it should become clear: and forthwith it did so.

2 Again, he took of the clay which came of that pool and made thereof to the number of twelve sparrows. Now it was the Sabbath day when Jesus did this among the children of the Hebrews: and the children of the Hebrews went and said unto Joseph his father: Lo, thy son was playing with us and he took clay and made sparrows which it was not right to do upon the Sabbath, and he hath broken it. And Joseph went to the child Jesus, and said unto him: Wherefore hast thou done this which it was not right to do on the Sabbath? But Jesus spread forth (opened) his hands and commanded the sparrows, saying:

Go forth into the height and fly: ye shall not meet death at any man's hands. And they flew and began to cry out and praise almighty God. But when the Jews saw what was done they marvelled and departed, proclaiming the signs which Jesus did.

3 But a Pharisee which was with Jesus took a branch of an olive tree and began to empty the pool which Jesus had made. And when Jesus saw it he was vexed and said to him: O thou of Sodom, ungodly and ignorant, what hurt did the fountain of water do thee, which I made? Lo, thou shalt become like a dry tree which hath neither roots nor leaf nor fruit. And straightway he was dried up and fell to the earth and died: but his parents carried him away dead and reviled Joseph, saying: Behold what thy son hath done: teach thou him to pray and not to blaspheme.

V. How the people of the city were grieved against Joseph because of that which Jesus did.

1 And after some days as Jesus walked with Joseph through the city, there ran one of the children and smote Jesus on the arms: but Jesus said unto him: So finish thou thy course. And immediately he fell to the earth and died. But they when they saw this wonder, cried out saying: From whence cometh this child? And they said unto Joseph: It is not right that such a child should be among us. And he departed and took him with him. And they said to him: Depart out of this place; and if thou must be with us, teach him to pray and not to blaspheme: for our sons are put to death by him (lit. lose their senses). 2 And Joseph called Jesus and began to admonish him, saying: Wherefore blasphemest thou? They that dwell in this place conceive hatred against us. But Jesus said: I know that these words are not mine but thine: yet for thy sake I will hold my peace: But let them see (? bear) their own foolishness. And straightway they that spake against Jesus were made blind, and as they walked to and fro they said: Every word that cometh out of his mouth hath fulfillment. 3 And when Joseph saw what Jesus had done he took hold on him by his ear in anger: but Jesus was vexed and said unto Joseph: It sufficeth thee to see me and not to touch me. For thou knowest not who I am, which if thou knewest, thou wouldest not grieve me. And albeit I am with thee now, yet was I made before thee.

VI. How Jesus was treated by the Master.

1 There was therefore a man named Zacheus who heard all that Jesus said unto Joseph, and he marvelled in himself and said: I have never beheld such a child that spake so. And he came near unto Joseph and said to him: Thou hast a wise child: deliver him to me to learn letters, and when he is learned in the study of the letters, I will teach him reverently that he become not foolish. Joseph answered and said unto him: No man is able to teach him but God only. Think you that this young child will be the occasion unto us of little torment, my brother? [There should be mention of a cross in this sentence. Syriac has, Thinkest thou that he is worthy to receive a little cross? See below.]

2 But when Jesus heard Joseph saying these things, he said unto Zacheus: Verily, O master, all things that proceed out of my mouth are true. And I am before all men, and I am Lord, but ye are the children of strangers: for unto me is given the glory of them (or of the worlds) but unto you nothing is given: for I am before all worlds. And I know how many are the years of thy life, and when thou shalt raise that standard (i. e. the cross) whereof my father spake, then shalt thou understand that all things that proceed out of my mouth are true.

3 But the Jews which stood by and heard the words which Jesus spake, marvelled and said: Now have we seen such wonders and heard such words from this child, as we have never heard neither shall hear from any other man, neither from the chief priests nor the doctors nor the Pharisees. 4 Jesus answered and said unto them: Wherefore marvel ye? Do ye think it a thing incredible that I have told you the truth? I know when ye were born, and your fathers: and if I should say more unto you, I know when the world was created, and who sent me unto you.

When the Jews heard the word which the child spake, they were wroth because they were not able to answer him. And the child turned himself about and rejoiced and said: I spake unto you a proverb; but I know that ye are weak and know not anything.

5 Now that master said unto Joseph: Bring him unto me and I will teach him letters. And Joseph took the child Jesus and brought him to the house [of a certain master] where other children also were taught. But the master began to teach him the letters with sweet speech, and wrote for him the first line which goeth from A unto T, and began to flatter him and to teach him (and commanded him to say the letters:) but the child held his peace. 6 Then that teacher smote the child on the head and when the child received the blow, he said unto him: I ought

to teach thee and not thou to teach me. I know the letters which thou wouldest teach me, and I know that ye are unto me as vessels out of which cometh nought but sound, and neither wisdom nor salvation of the soul. And beginning the line he spake all the letters from A even unto T fully with much quickness: and he looked upon the master and said: But thou knowest not how to interpret A and B: how wouldest thou teach others? Thou hypocrite, if thou knowest and canst tell me concerning A, then will I tell thee concerning B. But when the teacher began to expound concerning the first letter, he was not able to give any answer.

7 Then said Jesus unto Zacheus: Hearken unto me, O master and understand the first letter. Give ear unto me, how that it hath two lines (eight quite unintelligible descriptive phrases follow).

8 Now when Zacheus saw that he so divided the first letter he was confounded at such names, and at his teaching, and cried out and said: Woe is me, for I am confounded: I have hired shame unto myself by means of this child. And he said unto Joseph: I beseech thee earnestly, my brother, take him away from me: for I cannot look upon his face nor hear his mighty words. For this child is able to subdue the fire and to restrain the sea, for he was born before the worlds. What womb bare him or what manner of mother brought him up I know not. 10 O my friends, I am astray in my wits, I am mocked, wretched man that I am. I said that I had a disciple, but he is found to be my master. I cannot overcome my shame, for I am old, and I cannot find wherewithal to answer him, so that I am like to fall into heavy sickness and depart out of the world or go away from this city, for all men have seen my shame, that a child hath ensnared me. What can I answer any man, or what words can I speak, for he hath overcome me at the first letter! I am confounded, O ye my friends and acquaintances, and I can find neither first nor last to answer him. 11 And now I beseech thee brother Joseph, remove him from me and take him unto thine house, for either he is a sorcerer or a god (Lord) or an angel, and what to say I know not.

12 And Jesus turned himself unto the Jews that were with Zacheus and said unto them: Now let all them that see not see and let them understand which understand not, and let the deaf hear, and let them arise which have died by my means, and let me call them that are high unto that which is higher, even as he that sent me unto you hath commanded me. And when the child Jesus ceased speaking, all the

afflicted were made whole, as many as had been afflicted at his word. And they durst not speak unto him.

VII. How Jesus raised up a boy.
1 Now on a day, when Jesus climbed up upon an house with the children, he began to play with them: but one of the boys fell down through the door out of the upper chamber and died straightway. And when the children saw it they fled all of them, but Jesus remained alone in the house. 2 And when the parents of the child which had died came they spake against Jesus saying: Of a truth thou madest him fall. But Jesus said: I never made him fall: nevertheless they accused him still. Jesus therefore came down from the house and stood over the dead child and cried with a loud voice, calling him by his name: Zeno, Zeno, arise and say if I made thee fall. And on a sudden he arose and said: Nay, Lord. And when his parents saw this great miracle which Jesus did, they glorified God, and worshipped Jesus.

VIII. How Jesus healed the foot of a boy.
1 And aft er a few days a certain boy of that village was cleaving wood, and smote his foot. 2 And when much people came unto him, Jesus also came with them. And he touched the foot which was hurt, and forthwith it was made whole. And Jesus said unto him: Arise and cleave the wood and remember me. But when the multitude that were with him saw the signs which were done they worshipped Jesus and said: of a truth we believe surely that thou art God.

IX. How Jesus bare water in his cloak.
1 And when Jesus was six years old, his mother sent him to draw water. And when Jesus was come unto the well there was much people there and they brake his pitcher. 2 But he took the cloak which he had upon him and filled it with water and brought it to Mary his mother. And when his mother saw the miracle that Jesus did she kissed him and said: Lord, hearken unto me and save my son.

X. How Jesus sowed wheat.
1 Now when it was seed time, Joseph went forth to sow corn, and Jesus followed after him. And when Joseph began to sow, Jesus put forth his hand and took of the corn so much as he could hold in his

hand, and scattered it. 2 Joseph therefore came at the time of harvest to reap his harvest. And Jesus also came and gathered the ears which he had sown, and they made an hundred measures of good corn: and he called the poor and the widows and fatherless and gave them the corn which he had gained, save that Joseph took a little thereof unto his house for a blessing [of Jesus].

XI. How Jesus made a short beam even with a long one.
1 And Jesus came to be eight years old. Now Joseph was a builder and wrought ploughs and yokes for oxen. And on a day a certain rich man said unto Joseph: Sir, make me a bed serviceable and comely. But Joseph was troubled because the beam which he had made ready for the work was short. 2 Jesus said unto him: Be not troubled, but take thou hold of this beam by the one end and I by the other, and let us draw it out. And so it came to pass, and forthwith Joseph found it serviceable for that which he desired. And he said unto Joseph: Behold, fashion that thou wilt. But Joseph when he saw what was done embraced him and said: Blessed am I for that God hath given me such a son.

XII. How Jesus was delivered over to learn letters.
1 And when Joseph saw that he had so great grace and that he increased in stature, he thought to deliver him over to learn letters. And he delivered him to another doctor that he should teach him. Then said that doctor unto Joseph: What manner of letters wouldest thou teach this child? Joseph answered and said: Teach him first the letters of the Gentiles and after that the Hebrew. Now the doctor knew that he was of an excellent understanding, and received him gladly. And when he had written for him the first line, that is to say A and B, he taught him for the space of some hours: but Jesus held his peace and answered nothing. 2 At the last Jesus said unto the master: If thou be verily a master and indeed knowest the letters, tell me the power of A and I will tell thee the power of B. Then was the master filled with indignation and smote him on the head. But Jesus was wroth and cursed him, and on a sudden he fell down and died. 3 But Jesus returned unto his own home. And Joseph enjoined Mary his mother that she should not let him go out of the court of the house.

XIII. How he was delivered unto another master.
1 After many days there came another doctor which was a friend of Joseph and said unto him: Deliver him to me and I will teach him letters with much gentleness. And Joseph said unto him: If thou art able, take him and teach him, and it shall be done gladly. And when the doctor received Jesus, he went with fear and great boldness and took him rejoicing. 2 And when he was come unto the house of the doctor, he found a book lying in that place and took it and opened it, and read not those things which were written therein, but opened his mouth and spake by the Holy Ghost and taught the law: and all that stood by hearkened attentively, and the teacher sat by him and heard him gladly and entreated him to continue teaching. And much people gathered together and heard all the holy doctrine which he taught and the beloved words which proceeded out of his mouth marvelling that he being a little child spake such things. 3 But when Joseph heard, he was afraid and ran unto the place where Jesus was; and the master said unto Joseph: Know my brother, that I received thy child to teach him and instruct him, but he is filled with great grace and wisdom. Therefore behold now, take him unto thy house with joy, because the grace which he hath is given him of the Lord. 4 And when Jesus heard the master speak thus he was joyful and said: Lo, now thou hast well said, O master: for thy sake shall he rise again who was dead. And Joseph took him unto his own home.

XIV. How Jesus made James whole of the bite of a serpent.
Now Joseph sent James to gather straw, and Jesus followed after him. And as James gathered straw, a viper bit him and he fell to the earth as dead by means of the venom. But when Jesus saw that, he breathed upon his wound and forthwith James was made whole, and the viper died.

XV. How Jesus raised up a boy.
After a few days a child that was his neighbour died, and his mother mourned for him sore; and when Jesus heard, he went and stood over the child, and smote him on the breast and said: Child, I say unto thee, die not, but live. And immediately the child arose: and Jesus said unto the mother of the child: Take up thy son and give him suck, and remember me. 2 But the multitudes when they saw that miracle said: Of a truth this child is from heaven, for now hath he set free many

souls from death and hath saved all them that hoped in him. 3 The Scribes and Pharisees said unto Mary: Art thou the mother of this child? and Mary said: Of a truth I am. And they said unto her: Blessed art thou among women, because God hath blessed the fruit of thy womb in that he hath given thee a child so glorious: for so great gifts of wisdom we have never seen nor heard in any. 4 And Jesus arose and followed his mother. But Mary kept in her heart all the great signs which Jesus wrought among the people, in healing many that were sick. And Jesus increased in stature and wisdom, and all that saw him glorified God the Father Almighty: Who is blessed for ever and ever. Amen.

All these things have I, Thomas the Israelite (Ismaelite), written and recorded for the Gentiles and for our brethren, and likewise many other things which Jesus did, which was born in the land of Juda. Behold, the house of Israel hath seen all these from the first even unto the last, even how great signs and wonders Jesus did among them, which were good exceedingly. And this is he which shall judge the world according to the will of his Father, immortal and invisible, as the holy Scripture declareth and as the prophets have testified of his works among all the peoples of Israel: for he is the Son of God throughout all the World. And unto him belongeth all glory and honour everlastingly, who liveth and reigneth God, world without end. Amen.

1.4 Jesus and John the Baptist

John was an Essene saint and preacher that flourished between 20 and 30 C.E.; fore-runner of Jesus of Nazareth and originator of the Christian movement. Of his life and character Josephus ("Ant." xviii. 5, § 2) says:

"He was a good man, who admonished the Jews to practise abstinence [ἀρετὴν = "Pharisaic virtue" = "perishut"; comp. "B. J." ii. 8, § 2], lead a life of righteousness toward one another and of piety [εὐσέβειαν = "religious devotion"] toward God, and then join him in the rite of bathing [baptism]; for, said he, thus would baptism be acceptable to Him [God] if they would use it not simply for the putting away of certain sins [comp. II. Sam. xi. 4] or in the case of proselytes [see Soṭah 12b; comp. Gen. R. i.], but for the sanctification of the body after the soul had beforehand been thoroughly purified by righteousness. The people flocked in crowds to him, being stirred by his addresses. King Herod Antipas, fearing lest the great influence John had over the people might be used by him to raise a rebellion, sent him to the fortress of Macherus as a prisoner, and had him put to death.

"The people in their indignation over this atrocious act beheld in the destruction which came soon afterward upon the army of Herod a divine punishment."

John the Baptist was made the subject of a legendary narrative embodied in Luke i. 5-25, 57-80, and iii. 1-20, according to which he was the son of Zacharias, a priest of the section of Abia, and of Elisabeth, also of priestly descent, and was born in their old age. The angel Gabriel announced John's birth to Zacharias while that priest stood at the altar offering incense, and told him that this child would be a Nazarite for life ("nezir 'olam"; Nazir i. 2); filled with the Holy Spirit from his mother's womb, he would be called upon to convert the children of Israel to God, and with the power of Elijah would turn the hearts of the fathers to the children while preparing the people for the Lord (Mal. iii. 24 [A. V. iv. 6]). Zacharias, hesitating to believe the message, was struck dumb, and his mouth was opened again only after the birth of the child, when at the circumcision a name was to be given him; then he answered simultaneously with his wife that he should be called "John," as the angel had foretold. Zacharias, filled with the Holy Spirit, blessed God for the redemption of the people of Israel from the hand of their enemies (the Romans) through the house of David (a Messianic view altogether at variance with the New Testament conception), and prophesied that the child John should be called "Prophet of the Highest," one that would show how salvation should be obtained by remission of sins (through baptism; comp. Midr. Teh. to Ps. cxix. 76), so that through him a light from on high would be brought to "those that sit in darkness."

John remained hidden in the desert until, in the fifteenth year of Tiberius, the word of God came to him, and he stepped forth, saying in the words of Isa. xl. 2-5: "Repent ye: for the kingdom of heaven is at hand" (Matt. iii. 2), and preaching to the people to undergo baptism in repentance for the remission of their sins, and instead of relying on the merit of their father Abraham like hypocrites ("many-colored vipers"; see Hypocrisy), to prepare for the coming day of judgment and its fiery wrath by fruits of righteousness, sharing their coats and their meat with those that had none. To the publicans also he preached the same, telling them to exact no moretaxes than those prescribed; to the soldiers he declared that they should avoid violence and calumny (as informers) and be content with their wages. (The sermon of John the Baptist given here is obviously original with him, and the similar one of Jesus, Matt. xii. 33-34, xxiii. 33, is based thereon.) When asked whether he was the Messiah, he answered that with his baptism of repentance he would only prepare the people for the time when the Messiah would come as judge to baptize them with fire, to winnow them and burn the chaff with fire unquenchable (the fire of Gehenna; comp. Sibyllines, iii. 286; Enoch, xlv. 3, lv. 4, lxi. 8)—a conception of the Messiah which is widely different from the one which saw the Messiah in Jesus.

Among the many that came to the Jordan to undergo the rite of baptism in response to the call of John, was Jesus of Nazareth, and the influence wrought through him created a new epoch in those circles among which Christianity arose, so that henceforth the whole life-work of John the Baptist was given a new meaning—as if in his Messianic expectations he had Jesus in view as the true Messiah (see Matt. iii. 14; John i. 26-36).
His Appearance.

John the Baptist was regarded by the multitude as a great prophet (Matt. xiv. 5; Mark xi. 32). His powerful appeal (see Matt. xi. 12) and his whole appearance reminded the people forcibly of Elijah the prophet; "he wore raiment of camel's hair, and a leathern girdle about his loins; and his meat was locusts and wild honey" (Matt. iii. 4; comp. xi. 7-8). He stationed himself near some water-fountain to baptize the people, at Bethabara (John i. 28) or Ænon (John iii. 23). While he "preached good tidings unto the people" (Luke iii. 18), that is, announced to them that the redemption was at hand, he made his disciples prepare for it by fasting (Matt. ix. 14, xi. 18, and parallel passages). The prayer he taught his disciples was probably similar to the so-called Lord's Prayer (Luke xi. 1). John, however, provoked the wrath of King Herod because in his addresses he reproached the king for having married Herodias, his brother Philip's wife, and for all the evil things he had done. Herod therefore sent for him and put him in prison. It was while in prison that John heard of the work of preaching or healing done by Jesus (Matt. xi. 2-19; Luke vii. 18-35). Herod was afraid of the multitude and would not put John to death; but Herodias, says the legend (Matt. xiv. 6; Mark vi. 19.), had plotted revenge, and when on Herod's birthday a feast was given at which Herodias' daughter ingratiated herself into his favor by her dancing, she, at the instigation of her mother, asked that the head of John the Baptist be given her on a charger, and the cruel petition was granted. John's disciples came and buried his body.

The influence and power of John continued after his death, and his fame was not obscured by that of Jesus, who was taken by Herod to be John risen from the dead (Matt. xiv. 1-2 and parallel passages). His teaching of righteousness (Matt. xxi. 32) and his baptism (Luke vii. 29) created a movement which by no means ended with the appearance of Jesus. There were many who, like Apollos of Alexandria in Ephesus, preached only the baptism of John, and their little band gradually merged into Christianity (Acts xviii. 25, xix. 1-7). Some of the disciples of John placed their master above Jesus. John had thirty apostles, of whom Simon Magus claimed to be the chief (Clementine, Recognitions, i. 60, ii. 8; ib. Homilies, ii. 23). No doubt along the Jordan the work begun by John the Baptist was continued by his disciples, and later the Mandæans, called also "Sabians" (from "ẓaba'" = "to baptize") and "Christians according to John," retained many traditions about him.

1.5 Saying of Jesus

	Matthew	Mark	Luke	John
Preaching of John the Baptist near the Jordan	3:1-6	1:1-6	3:1-6	...0
His denunciation of Pharisees and Sadducces	3:7-20	...0	3:7-14	...0
Baptism of Christ in the Jordan	3:11-17	1:7-11	3:15-23	...0
The temptation of Christ on a mountain near Jericho	4:1-11	1:12-13	4:1-13	...0
Deputation of Jesus to the Baptist	...0	...0	...0	1:19-28
The Baptist's testimony to Christ	...0	...0	...0	1:29-34
Christ's first disciples, Andrew and Peter	...0	...0	...0	1:35-42
Calling of Philip and Nathanael	...0	...0	...0	1:43-51
The Marriage feast at Cana				2:1-11
Sojourn at Capharnaum				2:12

Gospel of Thomas
Range of Dating: 50-140 A.D.

These are the secret sayings that the living Jesus spoke and Didymos Judas Thomas recorded.

1 And he said, "Whoever discovers the interpretation of these sayings will not taste death."
2 Jesus said, "Those who seek should not stop seeking until they find. When they find, they will be disturbed. When they are disturbed, they will marvel, and will reign over all. [And after they have reigned they will rest.]"
3 Jesus said, "If your leaders say to you, 'Look, the (Father's) kingdom is in the sky,' then the birds of the sky will precede you. If they say to you, 'It is in the sea,' then the fish will precede you. Rather, the kingdom is within you and it is outside you.
When you know yourselves, then you will be known, and you will understand that you are children of the living Father. But if you do not know yourselves, then you live in poverty, and you are the poverty."
4 Jesus said, "The person old in days won't hesitate to ask a little child seven days old about the place of life, and that person will live.
For many of the first will be last, and will become a single one."

5 Jesus said, "Know what is in front of your face, and what is hidden from you will be disclosed to you.
For there is nothing hidden that will not be revealed. [And there is nothing buried that will not be raised."]
6 His disciples asked him and said to him, "Do you want us to fast? How should we pray? Should we give to charity? What diet should we observe?"
Jesus said, "Don't lie, and don't do what you hate, because all things are disclosed before heaven. After all, there is nothing hidden that will not be revealed, and there is nothing covered up that will remain undisclosed."
7 Jesus said, "Lucky is the lion that the human will eat, so that the lion becomes human. And foul is the human that the lion will eat, and the lion still will become human."
8 And he said, The person is like a wise fisherman who cast his net into the sea and drew it up from the sea full of little fish. Among them the wise fisherman discovered a fine large fish. He threw all the little fish back into the sea, and easily chose the large fish. Anyone here with two good ears had better listen!
9 Jesus said, Look, the sower went out, took a handful (of seeds), and scattered (them). Some fell on the road, and the birds came and gathered them. Others fell on rock, and they didn't take root in the soil and didn't produce heads of grain. Others fell on thorns, and they choked the seeds and worms ate them. And others fell on good soil, and it produced a good crop: it yielded sixty per measure and one hundred twenty per measure.
10 Jesus said, "I have cast fire upon the world, and look, I'm guarding it until it blazes."
11 Jesus said, "This heaven will pass away, and the one above it will pass away.
The dead are not alive, and the living will not die. During the days when you ate what is dead, you made it come alive. When you are in the light, what will you do? On the day when you were one, you became two. But when you become two, what will you do?"
12 The disciples said to Jesus, "We know that you are going to leave us. Who will be our leader?"
Jesus said to them, "No matter where you are you are to go to James the Just, for whose sake heaven and earth came into being."

13 Jesus said to his disciples, "Compare me to something and tell me what I am like."

Simon Peter said to him, "You are like a just messenger."

Matthew said to him, "You are like a wise philosopher."

Thomas said to him, "Teacher, my mouth is utterly unable to say what you are like."

Jesus said, "I am not your teacher. Because you have drunk, you have become intoxicated from the bubbling spring that I have tended."

And he took him, and withdrew, and spoke three sayings to him. When Thomas came back to his friends they asked him, "What did Jesus say to you?"

Thomas said to them, "If I tell you one of the sayings he spoke to me, you will pick up rocks and stone me, and fire will come from the rocks and devour you."

14 Jesus said to them, "If you fast, you will bring sin upon yourselves, and if you pray, you will be condemned, and if you give to charity, you will harm your spirits.

When you go into any region and walk about in the countryside, when people take you in, eat what they serve you and heal the sick among them.

After all, what goes into your mouth will not defile you; rather, it's what comes out of your mouth that will defile you."

15 Jesus said, "When you see one who was not born of woman, fall on your faces and worship. That one is your Father."

16 Jesus said, "Perhaps people think that I have come to casy peace upon the world. They do not know that I have come to cast conflicts upon the earth: fire, sword, war.

For there will be five in a house: there'll be three against two and two against three, father against son and son against father, and they will stand alone.

17 Jesus said, "I will give you what no eye has seen, what no ear has heard, what no hand has touched, what has not arisen in the human heart."

18 The disciples said to Jesus, "Tell us, how will our end come?"

Jesus said, "Have you found the beginning, then, that you are looking for the end? You see, the end will be where the beginning is.

Congratulations to the one who stands at the beginning: that one will know the end and will not taste death."

19 Jesus said, "Congratulations to the one who came into being before coming into being.

If you become my disciples and pay attention to my sayings, these stones will serve you.

For there are five trees in Paradise for you; they do not change, summer or winter, and their leaves do not fall. Whoever knows them will not taste death."

20 The disciples said to Jesus, "Tell us what Heaven's kingdom is like."

He said to them, It's like a mustard seed, the smallest of all seeds, but when it falls on prepared soil, it produces a large plant and becomes a shelter for birds of the sky.

21 Mary said to Jesus, "What are your disciples like?"

He said, They are like little children living in a field that is not theirs. when the owners of the field come, they will say, "Give us back our field." They take off their clothes in front of them in order to give it back to them, and they return their field to them.

For this reason I say, if the owners of a house know that a thief is coming, they will be on guard before the thief arrives and will not let the thief break into their house (their domain) and steal their possessions.

As for you, then, be on guard against the world. Prepare yourselves with great strength, so the robbers can't find a way to get to you, for the trouble you expect will come.

Let there be among you a person who understands.

When the crop ripened, he came quickly carrying a sickle and harvested it. Anyone here with two good ears had better listen!

22 Jesus saw some babies nursing. He said to his disciples, "These nursing babies are like those who enter the kingdom."

They said to him, "Then shall we enter the kingdom as babies?"

Jesus said to them, "When you make the two into one, and when you make the inner like the outer and the outer like the inner, and the upper like the lower, and when you make male and female into a single one, so that the male will not be male nor the female be female, when you make eyes in place of an eye, a hand in place of a hand, a foot in place of a foot, an image in place of an image, then you will enter [the kingdom]."

23 Jesus said, "I shall choose you, one from a thousand and two from ten thousand, and they will stand as a single one."

24 His disciples said, "Show us the place where you are, for we must seek it."
He said to them, "Anyone here with two ears had better listen! There is light within a person of light, and it shines on the whole world. If it does not shine, it is dark."
25 Jesus said, "Love your friends like your own soul, protect them like the pupil of your eye."
26 Jesus said, "You see the sliver in your friend's eye, but you don't see the timber in your own eye. When you take the timber out of your own eye, then you will see well enough to remove the sliver from your friend's eye."
27 "If you do not fast from the world, you will not find the kingdom. If you do not observe the sabbath as a sabbath you will not see the Father."
28 Jesus said, "I took my stand in the midst of the world, and in flesh I appeared to them. I found them all drunk, and I did not find any of them thirsty. My soul ached for the children of humanity, because they are blind in their hearts and do not see, for they came into the world empty, and they also seek to depart from the world empty.
But meanwhile they are drunk. When they shake off their wine, then they will change their ways."
29 Jesus said, "If the flesh came into being because of spirit, that is a marvel, but if spirit came into being because of the body, that is a marvel of marvels.
Yet I marvel at how this great wealth has come to dwell in this poverty."
30 Jesus said, "Where there are three deities, they are divine. Where there are two or one, I am with that one."
31 Jesus said, "No prophet is welcome on his home turf; doctors don't cure those who know them."
32 Jesus said, "A city built on a high hill and fortified cannot fall, nor can it be hidden."
33 Jesus said, "What you will hear in your ear, in the other ear proclaim from your rooftops.
After all, no one lights a lamp and puts it under a basket, nor does one put it in a hidden place. Rather, one puts it on a lampstand so that all who come and go will see its light."
34 Jesus said, "If a blind person leads a bind person, both of them will fall into a hole."

35 Jesus said, "One can't enter a strong person's house and take it by force without tying his hands. Then one can loot his house."

36 Jesus said, "Do not fret, from morning to evening and from evening to morning, [about your food--what you're going to eat, or about your clothing--] what you are going to wear. [You're much better than the lilies, which neither card nor spin.

As for you, when you have no garment, what will you put on? Who might add to your stature? That very one will give you your garment.]"

37 His disciples said, "When will you appear to us, and when will we see you?"

Jesus said, "When you strip without being ashamed, and you take your clothes and put them under your feet like little children and trample then, then [you] will see the son of the living one and you will not be afraid."

38 Jesus said, "Often you have desired to hear these sayings that I am speaking to you, and you have no one else from whom to hear them. There will be days when you will seek me and you will not find me."

39 Jesus said, "The Pharisees and the scholars have taken the keys of knowledge and have hidden them. They have not entered nor have they allowed those who want to enter to do so.

As for you, be as sly as snakes and as simple as doves."

40 Jesus said, "A grapevine has been planted apart from the Father. Since it is not strong, it will be pulled up by its root and will perish."

41 Jesus said, "Whoever has something in hand will be given more, and whoever has nothing will be deprived of even the little they have."

42 Jesus said, "Be passersby."

43 His disciples said to him, "Who are you to say these things to us?"
"You don't understand who I am from what I say to you.

Rather, you have become like the Judeans, for they love the tree but hate its fruit, or they love the fruit but hate the tree."

44 Jesus said, "Whoever blasphemes against the Father will be forgiven, and whoever blasphemes against the son will be forgiven, but whoever blasphemes against the holy spirit will not be forgiven, either on earth or in heaven."

45 Jesus said, "Grapes are not harvested from thorn trees, nor are figs gathered from thistles, for they yield no fruit.

Good persons produce good from what they've stored up; bad persons produce evil from the wickedness they've stored up in their hearts, and say evil things. For from the overflow of the heart they produce evil."

46 Jesus said, "From Adam to John the Baptist, among those born of women, no one is so much greater than John the Baptist that his eyes should not be averted.

But I have said that whoever among you becomes a child will recognize the kingdom and will become greater than John."

47 Jesus said, "A person cannot mount two horses or bend two bows. And a slave cannot serve two masters, otherwise that slave will honor the one and offend the other.

"Nobody drinks aged wine and immediately wants to drink young wine. Young wine is not poured into old wineskins, or they might break, and aged wine is not poured into a new wineskin, or it might spoil.

An old patch is not sewn onto a new garment, since it would create a tear."

48 Jesus said, "If two make peace with each other in a single house, they will say to the mountain, 'Move from here!' and it will move."

49 Jesus said, "Congratulations to those who are alone and chosen, for you will find the kingdom. For you have come from it, and you will return there again."

50 Jesus said,

"If they say to you, 'Where have you come from?' say to them, 'We have come from the light, from the place where the light came into being by itself, established [itself], and appeared in their image.'

If they say to you, 'Is it you?' say, 'We are its children, and we are the chosen of the living Father.'

If they ask you, 'What is the evidence of your Father in you?' say to them, 'It is motion and rest.'"

51 His disciples said to him, "When will the rest for the dead take place, and when will the new world come?"

He said to them, "What you are looking forward to has come, but you don't know it."

52 His disciples said to him, "Twenty-four prophets have spoken in Israel, and they all spoke of you."

He said to them, "You have disregarded the living one who is in your presence, and have spoken of the dead."

53 His disciples said to him, "is circumcision useful or not?"
He said to them, "If it were useful, their father would produce children already circumcised from their mother. Rather, the true circumcision in spirit has become profitable in every respect."
54 Jesus said, "Congratulations to the poor, for to you belongs Heaven's kingdom."
55 Jesus said, "Whoever does not hate father and mother cannot be my disciple, and whoever does not hate brothers and sisters, and carry the cross as I do, will not be worthy of me."
56 Jesus said, "Whoever has come to know the world has discovered a carcass, and whoever has discovered a carcass, of that person the world is not worthy."
57 Jesus said, The Father's kingdom is like a person who has [good] seed. His enemy came during the night and sowed weeds among the good seed. The person did not let the workers pull up the weeds, but said to them, "No, otherwise you might go to pull up the weeds and pull up the wheat along with them." For on the day of the harvest the weeds will be conspicuous, and will be pulled up and burned.
58 Jesus said, "Congratulations to the person who has toiled and has found life."
59 Jesus said, "Look to the living one as long as you live, otherwise you might die and then try to see the living one, and you will be unable to see."
60 He saw a Samaritan carrying a lamb and going to Judea. He said to his disciples, "that person ... around the lamb." They said to him, "So that he may kill it and eat it." He said to them, "He will not eat it while it is alive, but only after he has killed it and it has become a carcass."
They said, "Otherwise he can't do it."
He said to them, "So also with you, seek for yourselves a place for rest, or you might become a carcass and be eaten."
61 Jesus said, "Two will recline on a couch; one will die, one will live."
Salome said, "Who are you mister? You have climbed onto my couch and eaten from my table as if you are from someone."
Jesus said to her, "I am the one who comes from what is whole. I was granted from the things of my Father."
"I am your disciple."

"For this reason I say, if one is whole, one will be filled with light, but if one is divided, one will be filled with darkness."

62 Jesus said, "I disclose my mysteries to those [who are worthy] of [my] mysteries.

Do not let your left hand know what your right hand is doing."

63 Jesus said, There was a rich person who had a great deal of money. He said, "I shall invest my money so that I may sow, reap, plant, and fill my storehouses with produce, that I may lack nothing." These were the things he was thinking in his heart, but that very night he died. Anyone here with two ears had better listen!

64 Jesus said, A person was receiving guests. When he had prepared the dinner, he sent his slave to invite the guests. The slave went to the first and said to that one, "My master invites you." That one said, "Some merchants owe me money; they are coming to me tonight. I have to go and give them instructions. Please excuse me from dinner." The slave went to another and said to that one, "My master has invited you." That one said to the slave, "I have bought a house, and I have been called away for a day. I shall have no time." The slave went to another and said to that one, "My master invites you." That one said to the slave, "My friend is to be married, and I am to arrange the banquet. I shall not be able to come. Please excuse me from dinner." The slave went to another and said to that one, "My master invites you." That one said to the slave, "I have bought an estate, and I am going to collect the rent. I shall not be able to come. Please excuse me." The slave returned and said to his master, "Those whom you invited to dinner have asked to be excused." The master said to his slave, "Go out on the streets and bring back whomever you find to have dinner."

Buyers and merchants [will] not enter the places of my Father.

65 He said, A [...] person owned a vineyard and rented it to some farmers, so they could work it and he could collect its crop from them. He sent his slave so the farmers would give him the vineyard's crop. They grabbed him, beat him, and almost killed him, and the slave returned and told his master. His master said, "Perhaps he didn't know them." He sent another slave, and the farmers beat that one as well. Then the master sent his son and said, "Perhaps they'll show my son some respect." Because the farmers knew that he was the heir to the vineyard, they grabbed him and killed him. Anyone here with two ears had better listen!

66 Jesus said, "Show me the stone that the builders rejected: that is the keystone."
67 Jesus said, "Those who know all, but are lacking in themselves, are utterly lacking."
68 Jesus said, "Congratulations to you when you are hated and persecuted;
and no place will be found, wherever you have been persecuted."
69 Jesus said, "Congratulations to those who have been persecuted in their hearts: they are the ones who have truly come to know the Father.
Congratulations to those who go hungry, so the stomach of the one in want may be filled."
70 Jesus said, "If you bring forth what is within you, what you have will save you. If you do not have that within you, what you do not have within you [will] kill you."
71 Jesus said, "I will destroy [this] house, and no one will be able to build it [...]."
72 A [person said] to him, "Tell my brothers to divide my father's possessions with me."
He said to the person, "Mister, who made me a divider?"
He turned to his disciples and said to them, "I'm not a divider, am I?"
73 Jesus said, "The crop is huge but the workers are few, so beg the harvest boss to dispatch workers to the fields."
74 He said, "Lord, there are many around the drinking trough, but there is nothing in the well."
75 Jesus said, "There are many standing at the door, but those who are alone will enter the bridal suite."
76 Jesus said, The Father's kingdom is like a merchant who had a supply of merchandise and found a peal. That merchant was prudent; he sold the merchandise and bought the single pearl for himself.
So also with you, seek his treasure that is unfailing, that is enduring, where no moth comes to eat and no worm destroys."
77 Jesus said, "I am the light that is over all things. I am all: from me all came forth, and to me all attained.
Split a piece of wood; I am there.
Lift up the stone, and you will find me there."
78 Jesus said, "Why have you come out to the countryside? To see a reed shaken by the wind? And to see a person dressed in soft clothes,

[like your] rulers and your powerful ones? They are dressed in soft clothes, and they cannot understand truth."

79 A woman in the crowd said to him, "Lucky are the womb that bore you and the breasts that fed you."

He said to [her], "Lucky are those who have heard the word of the Father and have truly kept it. For there will be days when you will say, 'Lucky are the womb that has not conceived and the breasts that have not given milk.'"

80 Jesus said, "Whoever has come to know the world has discovered the body, and whoever has discovered the body, of that one the world is not worthy."

81 Jesus said, "Let one who has become wealthy reign, and let one who has power renounce ."

82 Jesus said, "Whoever is near me is near the fire, and whoever is far from me is far from the kingdom."

83 Jesus said, "Images are visible to people, but the light within them is hidden in the image of the Father's light. He will be disclosed, but his image is hidden by his light."

84 Jesus said, "When you see your likeness, you are happy. But when you see your images that came into being before you and that neither die nor become visible, how much you will have to bear!"

85 Jesus said, "Adam came from great power and great wealth, but he was not worthy of you. For had he been worthy, [he would] not [have tasted] death."

86 Jesus said, "[Foxes have] their dens and birds have their nests, but human beings have no place to lay down and rest."

87 Jesus said, "How miserable is the body that depends on a body, and how miserable is the soul that depends on these two."

88 Jesus said, "The messengers and the prophets will come to you and give you what belongs to you. You, in turn, give them what you have, and say to yourselves, 'When will they come and take what belongs to them?'"

89 Jesus said, "Why do you wash the outside of the cup? Don't you understand that the one who made the inside is also the one who made the outside?"

90 Jesus said, "Come to me, for my yoke is comfortable and my lordship is gentle, and you will find rest for yourselves."

91 They said to him, "Tell us who you are so that we may believe in you."

He said to them, "You examine the face of heaven and earth, but you have not come to know the one who is in your presence, and you do not know how to examine the present moment.
92 Jesus said, "Seek and you will find.
In the past, however, I did not tell you the things about which you asked me then. Now I am willing to tell them, but you are not seeking them."
93 "Don't give what is holy to dogs, for they might throw them upon the manure pile. Don't throw pearls [to] pigs, or they might ... it [...]."
94 Jesus [said], "One who seeks will find, and for [one who knocks] it will be opened."
95 [Jesus said], "If you have money, don't lend it at interest. Rather, give [it] to someone from whom you won't get it back."
96 Jesus [said], The Father's kingdom is like [a] woman. She took a little leaven, [hid] it in dough, and made it into large loaves of bread. Anyone here with two ears had better listen!
97 Jesus said, The [Father's] kingdom is like a woman who was carrying a [jar] full of meal. While she was walking along [a] distant road, the handle of the jar broke and the meal spilled behind her [along] the road. She didn't know it; she hadn't noticed a problem. When she reached her house, she put the jar down and discovered that it was empty.
98 Jesus said, The Father's kingdom is like a person who wanted to kill someone powerful. While still at home he drew his sword and thrust it into the wall to find out whether his hand would go in. Then he killed the powerful one.
99 The disciples said to him, "Your brothers and your mother are standing outside."
He said to them, "Those here who do what my Father wants are my brothers and my mother. They are the ones who will enter my Father's kingdom."
100 They showed Jesus a gold coin and said to him, "The Roman emperor's people demand taxes from us."
He said to them, "Give the emperor what belongs to the emperor, give God what belongs to God, and give me what is mine."
101 "Whoever does not hate [father] and mother as I do cannot be my [disciple], and whoever does [not] love [father and] mother as I do cannot be my [disciple]. For my mother [...], but my true [mother] gave me life."

102 Jesus said, "Damn the Pharisees! They are like a dog sleeping in the cattle manger: the dog neither eats nor [lets] the cattle eat."

103 Jesus said, "Congratulations to those who know where the rebels are going to attack. [They] can get going, collect their imperial resources, and be prepared before the rebels arrive."

104 They said to Jesus, "Come, let us pray today, and let us fast."
Jesus said, "What sin have I committed, or how have I been undone? Rather, when the groom leaves the bridal suite, then let people fast and pray."

105 Jesus said, "Whoever knows the father and the mother will be called the child of a whore."

106 Jesus said, "When you make the two into one, you will become children of Adam, and when you say, 'Mountain, move from here!' it will move."

107 Jesus said, The kingdom is like a shepherd who had a hundred sheep. One of them, the largest, went astray. He left the ninety-nine and looked for the one until he found it. After he had toiled, he said to the sheep, 'I love you more than the ninety-nine.'

108 Jesus said, "Whoever drinks from my mouth will become like me; I myself shall become that person, and the hidden things will be revealed to him."

109 Jesus said, The (Father's) kingdom is like a person who had a treasure hidden in his field but did not know it. And [when] he died he left it to his [son]. The son [did] not know about it either. He took over the field and sold it. The buyer went plowing, [discovered] the treasure, and began to lend money at interest to whomever he wished.

110 Jesus said, "Let one who has found the world, and has become wealthy, renounce the world."

111 Jesus said, "The heavens and the earth will roll up in your presence, and whoever is living from the living one will not see death."
Does not Jesus say, "Those who have found themselves, of them the world is not worthy"?

112 Jesus said, "Damn the flesh that depends on the soul. Damn the soul that depends on the flesh."

113 His disciples said to him, "When will the kingdom come?"
"It will not come by watching for it. It will not be said, 'Look, here!' or 'Look, there!' Rather, the Father's kingdom is spread out upon the earth, and people don't see it."

1.6 Miracles of Jesus

	Matthew	Mark	Luke	John
Christ in Judea	...0	...0	...0	...0
	...0	...0	...0	
Cure at the Pool of Bethsaida	...0	...0	...0	5:1-16
The Christologic discourse with the Jews in Jerusalem	...0	...0	...0	5:17-47
Christ in Galilee				
The disciples pluck corn	12:1-8	2:23-28	6:1-5	...0
Cure of a withered hand	12:9-14	3:1-6	6:6-11	...0
Other cures in Galilee	12:15-21	3:7-12	6:17-19	...0
Choosing of the Apostles	10:1-4	3:13-19	6:12-16	...0
Sermon on the Mount	5:1-8	...0	6:20-49	...0
Cure of the centurion's servant at Capharnaum	8:5-13	...0	7:1-10	...0
Raising of the widow's son to life at Naim	...0	...0	7:11-17	...0
The Baptist's embassy to Christ	11:2-19	...0	7:18-35	...0
Annointing of Christ by the sinful woman	...0	...0	7:36-50	...0
Second tour of Galilee	...0	...0	8:1-3	...0
Christ's friends attempt to seize Him	...0	3:20-21	...0	...0
Cure of a blind man and dumb man in Capharnaum	12:22-23	...0	11:14	...0
Charge of diabolism	12:24-30	3:22-27	11:15-23	...0
Blasphemy against the Holy Spirit	12:31-32	3:28-30	...0	...0
The tree and its fruit	12:33-37	...0	...0	...0
Christ's mother is praised	...0	...0	11:27-28	...0
Rebuke to those who demanded a sign	12:38-42	...0	11:29-36	...0
The wicked generation	12:43-45	...0	11:24-26	...0
The true family of Christ	12:46-50	3:31-35	8:19-21	...0

The Signs Gospel
Estimated Range of Dating: 50-90 A.D.

It is now rather widely agreed that the Jhon Evangelist drew upon a miracle tradition or written source(s) substantially independent of the synoptics, whether or not he had any knowledge of one or more of those gospels. The hypothesis of a semeia- (or miracle) source has gained rather wide acceptance. A number of things in the gospel contribute to the effort to reconstruct such a source: The presence of the series of wonder stories in the narrative, the unique use of the word, semeia ("signs"), to designate such wonders, the numbering of the signs in 2:11 and 4:54, and the reference to signs in the conclusion of the gospel. It is further proposed that the delicate and complicated attitude toward the role of signs in nurturing faih found throughout the gospel is explained by the fact that the evangelist was using a collection of wonder stories which purported a view of signs about which there was some reservation on the part of the author of the gospel. What is proposed is that there was a collection of the wonders of Jesus circulating within the Johannine community prior to the writing of the gospel. Efforts to reconstruct such a signs source from the gospel vary. At one extreme is the argument that it contained not only the wonders narrated in the gospel, but also the calling of the disciples in 1:19-51 and a passion story. At the other extreme is the suggestion that the collection was little more than seven wonder stories told consecutively. Some such theory is embraced by a large number of Johannine scholars, but by no means has agreement been reached on such a proposal.

Thus, to many scholars there has seemed to lie behind the present text a protogospel that presented only Jesus' signs, and a series of them, and did so wholly affirmatively. They were significations (that is, demonstrations) of his messianic status, on the basis of which his first disciples and then many others believed in him; those who "came and saw" (1:39) immediately recognized him as the one so long hoped for in Jewish expectation.On the contents of the Signs Gospel, the following deeds of Jesus, less the Johannine insertions they now contain, would have comprised the bulk of SQ: changing water into wine (2:1-11), healing an official's son (4:46-54) and a lame man (5:2-9), feeding the multitude (6:1-14) - probably together with crossing the sea (6:15-25), giving sight to a blind man (9:1-8), and raising Lazarus (11:1-45). (Some would also include the catch of fish now found at 21:1-14.) An articulated series emerges from the reconstruction, not merely a gather of miracle stories, and a few other passages are also to be included: part of chap. 1 (at least the gathering of the first disciples in vv 35-49) as introduction and, as conclusion, 20:30-31a, and perhaps also parts of 12:37-41.

There is considerable debate over whether the Signs Gospel may have contained a passion narrative or instead contained only a collection of seven miracle stories. In the reconstruction offered by Fortna, a passion story is included. On the dating of the Signs Gospel, there is little to go on. The reference to the Pool of Bethesda as still standing in 5:2, even though it was destroyed by the Romans in 70 CE, suggests a dating before the year 70 CE or not too long afterwards. The latest possible date is set by its incorporation into the Gospel of John.

This is a reconstruction of the hypothetical source employed by the author of the fourth gospel.

John 1   (6) There was a man sent from God, whose name was John. (7) He came as a witness, so that all might believe through him.

(19) This is the testimony given by John when priests and Levites *came* to ask him, "Who are you?"

(20) *He* confessed, "I am not the Messiah."

(21) And they asked him, "What then? Are you Elijah?"

He said, "I am not."

"Are you the prophet?"

He answered, "No."

(22) Then they said to him, "Who are you? What do you say about yourself?"

(23) He said, "I am the voice of one crying out in the wilderness, 'Make straight the way of the Lord,' " as the prophet Isaiah said. I baptize with water. Among you stands (27) the one who is coming after me; I am not worthy to untie the thong of his sandal."

(28) He saw Jesus coming toward him and declared, "Here is the Lamb of God. I came for this reason, that he might be revealed to Israel. I saw the Spirit descending from heaven like a dove on him. (34) And I myself have seen and have testified that this is the Son of God."

(35) *Now* John was standing with two of his disciples *who* heard him say this, and they followed Jesus. (38) They said to him, "Rabbi, where are you staying?"

(39) He said to them, "Come and see." They came and saw where he was staying, and they remained with him that day. It was about four o'clock in the afternoon.

(40) One of the two who heard John speak and followed him was Andrew. (41) He first found his brother Simon and said to him, "We have found the Messiah." (42)

He brought Simon to Jesus, who looked at him and said, "You are Simon son of John. You are to be called Cephas."

He found Philip and *Jesus* said to him, "Follow me." (44) Now Philip was from Bethsaida, the city of

Andrew and Peter.

(45) Philip found Nathanael and said to him, "We have found him about whom Moses in the law wrote, Jesus son of Joseph from Nazareth."

(46) Nathanael said to him, "Can anything good come out of Nazareth?"

Philip said to him, "Come and see."

(47) When Jesus saw Nathanael coming toward him, he said of him, "Here is truly an Israelite."

(49) Nathanael replied, "Rabbi, you are the Son of God! You are the King of Israel!"

John 2 (1) There was a wedding in Cana, and the mother of Jesus was there. (2) Jesus and his disciples had also been invited to the wedding. (3) When the wine gave out, the mother of Jesus said to the servants, "Do whatever he tells you." (6) Now standing there were six stone water jars, each holding twenty or thirty gallons.

(7) Jesus said to them, "Fill the jars with water." And they filled them up to the brim.

(8) He said to them, "Now draw some out, and take it to the chief steward." So they took it.

(9) When the steward tasted the water that had become wine, the steward called the bridegroom (10) and said to him, "Everyone serves the good wine first, and then the inferior wine after the guests have become drunk. But you have kept the good wine until now."

(11) Jesus did this, the first of his signs; and his

disciples believed in him.

(12) After this he went down to Capernaum with his disciples.

John 4

(46) Now there was a royal official whose son lay ill in Capernaum. (47) He went and said to him, "Sir, come down before my little boy dies."

(50) Jesus said, "Go; your son will live."

The man started on his way. (51) As he was going down, his slaves met him and told him that his child was alive. (52) So he asked them the hour when he began to recover, and they said to him, "Yesterday at one in the afternoon the fever left him." (53) So he himself believed, along with his whole household.

(54) Now this was the second sign that Jesus did.

John 21

(2) Gathered there together were Simon Peter, Thomas called the Twin, Nathanael of Cana, the sons of Zebedee. (3) Simon Peter said to them, "I am going fishing."

They said to him, "We will go with you."

They went out and got into the boat, but that night they caught nothing.

(4) Just after daybreak, Jesus stood on the beach. (6) He said to them, "Cast the net to the right side of the boat, and you will find some."

So they cast it, and now they were not able to haul it in because there were so many fish. (7) Simon Peter put on some clothes and jumped into the sea (8) for they were not far from the land, only about a hundred yards off. (11) So Simon Peter went *ashore* and hauled the net ashore, full of large fish, a hundred fifty-three of them; and though there were so many, the net was not torn. (14) This was now the third *sign* that Jesus *did before* the disciples.

John 6

(1) After this Jesus went to the other side of the Sea of Tiberias. (3) *He* went up the mountain and sat down there with his disciples. (5) When he looked up and saw a large crowd coming toward him, Jesus said to Philip, "Where are we to buy bread for these people to eat?"

(7) Philip answered him, "Six months' wages would not buy enough bread for each of them to get a little."

(8) One of his disciples said to him, (9) "There is a boy here who has five barley loaves and two fish. But what are they among so many people?"

(10) Jesus said, "Make the people sit down." Now there was a great deal of grass in the place; so they sat down, about five thousand in all. (11) Then Jesus took the loaves, and when he had given thanks, he distributed them to those who were seated; so also the fish, as much as they wanted.

(13) And from the fragments of the five barley loaves, left by those who had eaten, they filled twelve baskets. (14) When the people saw the sign that he had done, they began to say, "This is indeed the prophet who is to come into the world."

(15) *Jesus* withdrew again to the mountain by himself. (16) When evening came, his disciples went down to the sea, (17) got into a boat, and started across the sea to Capernaum. (18) The sea became rough because a strong wind was blowing. (19) When they had rowed about three or four miles, they saw Jesus walking on the sea, and they were terrified. (20) But he said to them, "It is I; do not be afraid." (21) And immediately

the boat reached the land toward which they were going.

John 11　(1) Now a certain Mary; (2) her brother Lazarus was ill. (3) *She* sent a message to Jesus, "Lord, he whom you love is ill."

(7) He said to the disciples, "Our friend Lazarus has fallen asleep. Let us go to him."

(17) When Jesus arrived, he found that Lazarus had already been in the tomb four days. (32) When Mary saw him, she knelt at his feet and said to him, "Lord, if you had been here, my brother would not have died."

(33) When Jesus saw her weeping, he was greatly disturbed in spirit and deeply moved. (34) He said, "Where have you laid him?"

They said to him, "Lord, come and see."

(38) Then Jesus came to the tomb. It was a cave, and a stone was lying against it. (39) Jesus said, "Take away the stone." *Then* he cried with a loud voice, "Lazarus, come out!"

(44) The dead man came out, his hands and feet bound with strips of cloth, and his face wrapped in a cloth. Jesus said to them, "Unbind him, and let him go."

(45) *Those who* had seen what Jesus did, believed in him.

John 9　(1) As he walked along, he saw a man blind from birth. (6) He spat on the ground and made mud with the saliva and spread the mud on the man's eyes, (7) saying to him, "Go, wash in the pool of Siloam." Then he went and washed and came back able to see. (8) The neighbors and those who had seen him before as a beggar began to ask, "Is this not the man who used to

John 5	sit and beg?" (2) Now in Jerusalem by the Sheep Gate there is a pool, called in Hebrew Beth-zatha, which has five porticoes. (3) In these lay many invalids—blind, lame, and paralyzed. (5) One man was there who had been ill for thirty-eight years. (6) When Jesus saw him lying there and knew that he had been there a long time, he said to him, "Do you want to be made well?" (7) The sick man answered him, "Sir, I have no one to put me into the pool when the water is stirred up; and while I am making my way, someone else steps down ahead of me." (8) Jesus said to him, "Stand up, take your mat and walk." (9) At once the man was made well, and he took up his mat and began to walk.
John 2	(14) In the temple *Jesus* found people selling cattle, sheep, and doves, and the money changers seated at their tables. (15) Making a whip of cords, he drove all of them out of the temple, both the sheep and the cattle. He also poured out the coins of the money changers and overturned their tables. (16) He told those who were selling the doves, "Take these things out of here! Stop making my Father's house a marketplace!" (18) The Jews then said to him, "What sign can you show us for doing this?" 19 Jesus answered them, "Destroy this temple, and in three days I will raise it up."
John 11	(47) So the chief priests called a meeting of the council, and said, "This man is performing many signs.

(48) If we let him go on like this, everyone will believe in him, and the Romans will come and destroy our nation."

(49) But one of them, Caiaphas, who was high priest that year, said to them, (50) "It is better for you to have one man die for the people than to have the whole nation destroyed." (53) So from that day on they planned to put him to death.

John 12

(37) Although he had performed so many signs, they did not believe in him. (38) This was to fulfill the word spoken by the prophet Isaiah: "Lord, who has believed our message, and to whom has the arm of the Lord been revealed?" (39) And so they could not believe, because Isaiah also said, (40) "He has blinded their eyes and hardened their heart, so that they might not look with their eyes, and understand with their heart and turn— and I would heal them."

(1) Six days before the Passover Jesus came to Bethany, the home of Lazarus, whom he had raised from the dead. (2) There they gave a dinner for him. Martha served, and Lazarus was one of those at the table with him. (3) Mary took a pound of costly perfume made of pure nard, anointed Jesus, and wiped them with her hair. The house was filled with the fragrance of the perfume.

(4) But Judas Iscariot, one of his disciples, said, (5) "Why was this perfume not sold for three hundred denarii and the money given to the poor?"

(7) Jesus said, "She bought it so that she might keep it for the day of my burial. (8) You always have the poor with you, but you do not always have me."

(12) The next day the great crowd that had come to the festival heard that Jesus was coming to Jerusalem. (13)

So they took branches of palm trees and went out to meet him, shouting, "Hosanna! Blessed is the one who comes in the name of the Lord— the King of Israel!"

(14) Jesus found a young donkey and sat on it; as it is written: (15) "Do not be afraid, daughter of Zion. Look, your king is coming, sitting on a donkey's colt!"

John 13   (1) Now before the festival of the Passover, Jesus knew that his hour had come to depart from this world and go to the Father. Having loved his own who were in the world, he loved them to the end. (2) The devil had already put it into the heart of Judas son of Simon Iscariot to betray him. And during supper (3) Jesus, knowing that the Father had given all things into his hands, and that he had come from God and was going to God, (4) got up from the table, took off his outer robe, and tied a towel around himself. (5) Then he poured water into a basin and began to wash the disciples' feet and to wipe them with the towel that was tied around him. (6) He came to Simon Peter, who said to him, "Lord, are you going to wash my feet?"

(7) Jesus answered, "You do not know now what I am doing, but later you will understand."

(8) Peter said to him, "You will never wash my feet."

Jesus answered, "Unless I wash you, you have no share with me."

(9) Simon Peter said to him, "Lord, not my feet only but also my hands and my head!"

(10) Jesus said to him, "One who has bathed does not need to wash, except for the feet, but is entirely clean. And you are clean, though not all of you." (11) For he

knew who was to betray him; for this reason he said, "Not all of you are clean."

(12) After he had washed their feet, had put on his robe, and had returned to the table, he said to them, "Do you know what I have done to you? (13) You call me Teacher and Lord—and you are right, for that is what I am. (14) So if I, your Lord and Teacher, have washed your feet, you also ought to wash one another's feet. (15) For I have set you an example, that you also should do as I have done to you. (16) Very truly, I tell you, servants are not greater than their master, nor are messengers greater than the one who sent them. (17) If you know these things, you are blessed if you do them. (18) I am not speaking of all of you; I know whom I have chosen. But it is to fulfill the scripture, 'The one who ate my bread has lifted his heel against me.' (19) I tell you this now, before it occurs, so that when it does occur, you may believe that I am he. (20) Very truly, I tell you, whoever receives one whom I send receives me; and whoever receives me receives him who sent me."

John 18

(1) Jesus went out with his disciples across the Kidron valley to a place where there was a garden. (2) Now Judas, who betrayed him, also knew the place, because Jesus often met there with his disciples. (3) So Judas brought a detachment of soldiers together with police from the chief priests, and they came there with lanterns and torches and weapons. (4) Then Jesus asked them, "Whom are you looking for?"

(5) They answered, "Jesus of Nazareth."

Jesus replied, "I am he."

(10) Then Simon Peter, who had a sword, drew it, struck the high priest's slave, and cut off his right ear.

The slave's name was Malchus.

(11) Jesus said to Peter, "Put your sword back into its sheath. Am I not to drink the cup that the Father has given me?" (12) So the soldiers, their officer, and the Jewish police arrested Jesus and bound him.

(13) First they took him to Annas, who was the father-in-law of Caiaphas, the high priest that year. (15) Simon Peter and another disciple followed Jesus. Since that disciple was known to the high priest, he went with Jesus into the courtyard of the high priest, (16) but Peter was standing outside at the gate. So the other disciple, who was known to the high priest, went out, spoke to the woman who guarded the gate, and brought Peter in.

(17) The woman said to Peter, "You are not also one of this man's disciples, are you?"

He said, "I am not."

(18) Now the slaves and the police had made a charcoal fire because it was cold, and they were standing around it and warming themselves. Peter also was standing with them and warming himself.

(19) Then the high priest questioned Jesus about his teaching. (20) Jesus answered, "I have always taught in the temple, where all come together. (21) Why do you ask me?"

(22) When he had said this, one of the police standing nearby struck Jesus on the face, saying, "Is that how you answer the high priest?"

(24) Then Annas sent him bound to Caiaphas the high priest. (25)They asked him, "You are not also one of

his disciples, are you?"

He denied it and said, "I am not."

(26) One of the slaves of the high priest, a relative of the man whose ear Peter had cut off, asked, "Did I not see you in the garden with him?"

(27) Again Peter denied it, and at that moment the cock crowed.

(28) Then they took Jesus from Caiaphas to Pilate's headquarters. It was early in the morning. (29) Pilate said, "What accusation do you bring against this man?"

(33) Then Pilate summoned Jesus and asked him, "Are you the King of the Jews?"

Jesus answered, "You say that I am a king."

(38) He told them, "I find no case against him. (39) But you have a custom that I release someone for you at the Passover. Do you want me to release for you the King of the Jews?"

(40) They shouted in reply, "Not this man, but Barabbas!" Now Barabbas was a bandit.

John 19 (1) Then Pilate took Jesus and had him flogged. (2) And the soldiers wove a crown of thorns and put it on his head, and they dressed him in a purple robe. (3) They kept coming up to him, saying, "Hail, King of the Jews!" and striking him on the face.

(6) And the police saw him, they shouted, "Crucify him! Crucify him!"

Pilate said to them, "I find no case against him."

(13) Pilate brought Jesus outside and sat on the judge's bench at a place called The Stone Pavement, or in Hebrew Gabbatha. (14) Now it was the day of Preparation; and it was about noon. (16) Then he handed him over to them to be crucified.

So they took Jesus. (17) He went out to what is called The Place of the Skull, which in Hebrew is called Golgotha. (18) There they crucified him, and with him two others, one on either side. (19) *And there was written*, "Jesus of Nazareth, the King of the Jews." (20) And it was written in Hebrew, in Latin, and in Greek.

(23) When the soldiers had crucified Jesus, they took his clothes and divided them into four parts, one for each soldier. They also took his tunic; now the tunic was seamless, woven in one piece from the top. (24) So they said to one another, "Let us not tear it, but cast lots for it to see who will get it." This was to fulfill what the scripture says, "They divided my clothes among themselves, and for my clothing they cast lots."

(25) And that is what the soldiers did. Meanwhile, standing near the cross of Jesus were his mother, and his mother's sister, Mary the wife of Clopas, and Mary Magdalene. (28) After this, he said (in order to fulfill the scripture), "I am thirsty."

(29) A jar full of sour wine was standing there. So they put a sponge full of the wine on a branch of hyssop and held it to his mouth.

(30) When Jesus had received the wine, he said, "It is finished." Then he bowed his head and gave up his spirit.

(31) Since it was the day of Preparation, the Jews did not want the bodies left on the cross during the

sabbath. So they asked Pilate to have the legs of the crucified men broken and the bodies removed. (32) Then the soldiers came and broke the legs of the first and of the other who had been crucified with him. (33) But when they came to Jesus and saw that he was already dead, they did not break his legs. (34) Instead, one of the soldiers pierced his side with a spear, and at once blood and water came out. (36) These things occurred so that the scripture might be fulfilled, "None of his bones shall be broken."

(37) And again another passage of scripture says, "They will look on the one whom they have pierced." (38) After these things, Joseph of Arimathea, who was a disciple of Jesus, asked Pilate to let him take away the body of Jesus. Pilate gave him permission; so he came and removed his body and wrapped it with the spices in linen cloths.

(41) Now there was a garden in the place where he was crucified, and in the garden there was a new tomb in which no one had ever been laid. (42) And so, because it was the day of Preparation, and the tomb was nearby, they laid Jesus there.

John 20   (1) Early on the first day of the week, Mary Magdalene came to the tomb and saw that the stone had been removed from the tomb. (2) So she ran and went to Simon Peter and said, "They have taken the Lord out of the tomb, and we do not know where they have laid him."

(3) Then Peter set out and went toward the tomb and went into the tomb. (9) For as yet they did not understand the scripture, that he must rise from the dead. (10) Then *he* returned to *his* home.

(11) But Mary stood weeping outside the tomb. As she wept, she bent over to look into the tomb; (12) and she

saw two angels in white, sitting where the body of Jesus had been lying, one at the head and the other at the feet. (14) She turned around and saw Jesus standing there.

(15) Jesus said to her, "Whom are you looking for, Mary?"

She said to him in Hebrew, "Rabbouni!."

(17) Jesus said to her, "Do not hold on to me. But go to my brothers."

(18) Mary Magdalene went and announced to the disciples, "I have seen the Lord."

(19) When it was evening on that day and the doors of the house where the disciples had met were locked, Jesus came and stood among them and said, "Peace be with you." (20) He showed them his hands and his side. Then the disciples rejoiced when they saw the Lord.

(22) He breathed on them and said to them, "Receive the Holy Spirit."

(30) Now Jesus did many other signs in the presence of his disciples, which are not written in this book. (31) But these are written so that you may come to believe that Jesus is the Messiah, the Son of God.

1.7 Messiah and Messianism in Israel

	Matthew	Mark	Luke	John
Christ in Galilee	...0	...0	...0	...0
Pharasaic formalism	15:1-20	7:1-23	...0	...0
Christ in Pagan Lands	...0	...0	...0	...0
Cure of the daughter of the Syrophoenician woman	15:21-28	7:24-30	...0	...0
Many other cures	15:29-31	...0	...0	...0
Cure of a deaf mute	...0	7:31-37	...0	...0
Second multiplication of loaves	15:32-39	8:1-10	...0	...0
Christ Back in Galilee	...0	...0	...0	...0
Pharisees ask for a sign at Magdala	16:1-4	8:11-13	...0	...0
The leaven of the Pharisees	16:5-12	8:14-21	...0	...0
Cure of a blind man at Bethsaida Julias	...0	8:23-26	...0	...0
Christ again in Pagan Lands	...0	...0	...0	...0
Peter's confession	16:13-19	8:27-29	9:18-20	...0
Injunction of silence	16:20	8:30	9:21	...0
First prediction of the passion	16:21	8:31-32	9:22	...0
Peter's rebuke	16:22-23	8:32-33	...0	...0
Need of self-denial	16:24-28	8:34-39	9:23-27	...0
The Transfiguration on Mount Hermon	17:1-9	9:1-9	9:28-36	...0
Question about Elias	17:10-13	9:10-12	...0	...0
Cure of a possessed boy	17:14-17	9:13-26	9:37-44	...0
Reasons why the Apostles failed to cure the possesed boy	17:18-20	9:27-28	...0	...0
Christ Back in Galilee	...0	...0	...0	...0
Second prediction of the Passion	17:21-22	9:21-31	9:44-45	...0
The tax of the didrachma	17:23-25	...0	...0	...0
A lesson in humility	18:1-5	9:32-36	9:46-48	...0
A lesson in tolerance	...0	9:37-40	9:49-50	...0
Scandals	18:6-9	...0	...0	...0
The value of souls	18:10-14	...0	...0	...0
Fraternal correction	...0	...0	...0	...0
Forgiveness of injuries	...0	...0	...0	...0
Parable of the unjust debtor	...0	...0	...0	...0

		18:15-20	9:41-49		
		18:21-22	...0		
		18:23-35	...0		

The Hebrew word *mâšîah* means 'anointed one' and may indicate Jewish priests, prophets and kings. During the sixth century BCE, the exiled Jews in Babylonia started to hope for a special Anointed One who was to bring them home; several written prophecies were fulfilled when the Persian king Cyrus the Great did in fact allow them to return. In the second century BCE, the Jews were again suffering from repression, and the old prophecies became relevant again. Some people were looking forward to a military leader who would defeat the Seleucid or Roman enemies and establish an independent Jewish kingdom; others, like the author of the *Psalms of Solomon*, stated that the Messiah was a charismatic teacher who gave the correct interpretation of Mosaic law, was to restore Israel and would judge mankind. Jesus of Nazareth was considered a Messiah; a century later, Simon bar Kochba. The idea of an eschatological king has been present in Judaism ever since.

The word Messiah renders the Aramaic word *mešîhâ'*, which in turn renders the Hebrew *mâšîah*. In Antiquity, these words were usually translated into Greek as *Christos* and into Latin as *Christus*, whence the English word *Christ*. All these words mean simply 'anointed one', anointment being a way to show that a Jewish leader had received God's personal help. Take, for example, the anointment of the high priest:

Bring Aaron and his sons to the Tent of Meeting and wash them with water. Take the garments and dress Aaron with the tunic, the robe of the ephod, the ephod itself and the breastpiece. Fasten the ephod on him by its skillfully woven waistband. Put the turban on his head and attach the sacred diadem to the turban. Take the anointing oil and anoint him by pouring it on his head.

[*Exodus* 29.4-8]

Then they acknowledged Solomon son of David as king [...], anointing him before the Lord to be ruler and Zadok to be priest.

[*1 Chronicles* 29.22b]

In the figure of the Messiah we can see several motifs found in Psalms, Micah, Isaiah, Ezekiel, 2. Isaiah, Haggai and Zecharias:

- Davidic descent
- King, prince
- Ruler of the world
- Defeat of enemies
- A Priest
- Restoration of Israel
- Cultic reforms
- Age of peace
- A Servant of God
- Anointment

The authors of these texts all describe some kind of ideal ruler. Except for Second Isaiah, they expect him to come from the house of David; except for the authors of the Psalms, they all connect this special ruler with the restoration of Israel. But there are also important differences. Most authors describe the descendant of David as a successful commander, an element that is absent from Ezekiel, Zechariah and (probably) Haggai. Some prophets speak about an age of peace, others don't. The image of the servant is an innovation that may have been a reaction to the failure of Josiah. An interesting difference is also that the prophets who lived after Josiah were interested in the pure cult in the Temple, something that earlier authors had ignored.

After Antiochus' persecution and the end of Judaism as a political force (after the revolt of Bar Kochba), between 170 BCE and 140 CE., modern scholars distinguish four types of Messiah:

- The Messiah as military leader
- The Messiah as sage
- The Messiah as high-priest

- The 'prophet like Moses'

Qumran's two Messiahs

The Dead Sea scrolls were part of a library, a simple fact that is easy to ignore. But it means that there is not one, single messianology to be found in the texts from Qumran. Instead, we must accept that there are several theories about the Messiah. In the War scroll the Messiah is a prophet and takes no part in the war between the 'children of light' against the 'children of darkness' although the Messiah can be identified with the 'prince of the community'. In other texts, the Messiah is a war leader (e.g., 4QFlorilegium and 4Q458).

However, there were clear contradictions. Sometimes, the Messiah is a warrior, sometimes he is a man of peace. Daniel 7:14 describes the triumphant son of man coming with power, but Isaiah 42.3 states that he does not even break a bruised read. Daniel 7:13 has him arriving over the clouds, but Zechariah 9:9 states that he will be riding a donkey.

After the destruction of Jerusalem in 70, some changes take place. The first of these was, as could be expected, the idea that the Messiah would restore the Temple. This is best documented in the Aramaic translations of the Bible. For example, Targum Isaiah 53.5 states 'and the Messiah will build the sanctuary'.

The most extensive discussion of messianism after the second century can be found in the Babylonian Talmud, Sanhedrin 96b-99a. This is an overview of many rabbinical opinions and diverse points of view, but what the participants have in common is that they believe that the Messiah will be the sage who will teach the correct interpretation of the Law of Moses. A selection of ideas:

- the Messiah will be called, Bar Niphile; this is a reference to the 'fallen tent' of Daniel 7.13 (nofeler) and the Greek word nephele, 'cloud', a reference to the theory that the son of man would be coming over the clouds;
- the age before the coming of the Messiah will be very hard; there will be no teachers, synagogues will be used as brothels

and there will be an evil occupant of the land of Israel; some rabbis think that the world has to be completely full of sin before the son of David will appear; the length of this period is estimated at 1000 or 2000 years;
- after this troublesome period, the Jewish sinners will feel true guilt and can truly repent; Israel will be restored by the people's righteousness (and not by the Messiah!);
- the Messiah's name will be Shiloh, Chanina, Yinnon or Menahem.

These ideas are ascribed to several rabbis from the second, third, fourth and fifth centuries. Among the later developments belongs the idea that the Messiah will convert the Christians and Muslims, so that they will become Jews. This was the opinion of Abu'lafia and Sabbathai Zwi. Other messianic ideas were influenced by christology; one may think of the Yemenite Messiah, who believed that he would rise from death.

Later developments: from Messiah to Christ

Until the end of the first century CE, there is no evidence that the Messiah was ever considered a superhuman being. This must be stressed, because it is often said that the Messiah was some sort of demi-god; those who say so, define Jewish messianism in terms of Christian theology.

It is likely that the idea that the Messiah was a superhuman being is a Christian innovation. The *Gospel* of Mark calls Jesus the 'son of God', a title that had probably not been used to describe the Messiah before, and John's *Gospel* opens with the famous hymn that

In the beginning was the Word, and the Word was with God, and the Word was God. He was in the beginning with God; all things were made through him, and without him was not anything made that was made. In him was life, and the life was the light of men. [...] And the Word became flesh and dwelt among us, full of grace and truth; we have beheld his glory, glory as of the only Son from the Father.

[

Joh

The incarnated Word is of course Jesus of Nazareth, who is, in other words, not only the son of God, but is God. How these conflicting statements -Jesus as God and as son of God, Jesus as divine and human- could be harmonized, was the subject of an intense christological debate that culminated in the discussion on the Creed of Nicaea (325).

For this development is not a single antecedent in the Jewish literature. However, two texts from Qumran suggest otherwise.

- 4Q246 seems to describe a 'son of God'. However, as we have already seen, it is not likely that this was a messianic text at all. The title that Mark uses to describe the Messiah, is unique. It may, however be added that the way he used the title is not unique. He describes Jesus seven times as 'son of God' (once in the title of the gospel and six times in other people's mouths) but never in the narrative. The indirect way of using this title can also be found in a romance called *Joseph and Aseneth*, where Joseph is indirectly called 'son of God'.
- The two additional hymns on the *Thanksgiving-scroll*, written in the last quarter of the first century BCE, can be read as if the Messiah has suffered on earth, has died an is now in heaven, higher than the angels; the Messiah will one day come to judge mankind (go here for discussion). This antedates Christianity with at least half a century, and it is possible that these ideas about a superhuman Messiah have influenced christology. However, contact between the Qumran sect and the disciples of Jesus can not be proven; moreover, the ideas in these two hymns are exceptional.

We may therefore assume that the idea that the Messiah was a superhuman being is a Christian innovation, although there may be one or two antecedents.

Another innovation is the link between messianism and apocalypticism. In the fifties, this can be found in the epistles of Paul; in the last quarter of the first century in the gospels and in the nineties in the *Book of Revelation*. It is possible that there was a parallel development in the Jewish world; the *Book of similitudes* (a part of the *First book of Enoch*) interprets the apocalyptic *Book of Daniel* in a messianic way, but we do not known when the *Similitudes* were composed.

Summarizing, we can say that Christology was a revolutionary innovation within messianology. It introduced the superhuman status of the Messiah and the idea that he was one of the actors in the apocalyptic drama. Both ideas may not have been completely new, but if they were already present in Judaism, they were extremely rare.

Messianic Candidates

Some people that were momentaneously considered Messiah by the people of Israel.

Judas, son of Hezekiah (4 BCE)

There was Judas, the son of that Hezekiah who had been head of the robbers. (This Hezekiah had been a very strong man, and had with great difficulty been caught by Herod.) Judas, having gotten together a multitude of men of a profligate character about Sepphoris in Galilee, made an assault upon the palace there, and seized upon all the weapons that were laid up in it, and with them armed every one of those that were with him, and carried away what money was left there. He became terrible to all men, by tearing and rending those that came near him; and all this in order to raise himself, and out of an ambitious desire of the royal dignity, for he hoped to obtain that as the reward not of his virtuous skill in war, but of his extravagance in doing injuries.

[Flavius Josephus, *Jewish Antiquities* 17.271-272]

Simon of Peraea (4 BCE)

There was also Simon, who had been a slave of king Herod, but in other respects a comely person, of a tall and robust body; he was one that was much superior to others of his order, and had had great things committed to his care. This man was elevated at the disorderly state of things, and was so bold as to put a diadem on his head, while a certain number of the people stood by him, and by them he was declared to be a king, and he thought himself more worthy of that dignity than any one else. He burnt down the royal palace at Jericho, and plundered what was left in it. He also set fire to many other of the king's houses in several places of the country, utterly destroyed them, and permitted those that were with him to take what was left in them for a prey. He would have done greater things, but care was taken to repress him immediately. [*The commander of Herod's infantry*] Gratus joined himself to some Roman soldiers, took the forces he had with him, and met Simon. And after a great and a long fight, no small part of those that had come from Peraea (a disordered body of men, fighting rather in a bold than in a skillful manner) were destroyed. Although Simon had saved himself by flying away through a certain valley, Gratus overtook him, and cut off his head.

[Flavius Josephus, *Jewish Antiquities* 17.273-276]

Athronges, the shepherd (4 BCE)

Athronges, a person neither eminent by the dignity of his progenitors, nor for any great wealth he possessed. For he had been a mere shepherd, not known by anybody. But because he was a tall man, and excelled others in the strength of his hands, he was so bold as to set up for king. This man thought it so sweet a thing to do more than ordinary injuries to others, that, although he risked his life, he did not much care if he lost it in so great a design. He had four brothers, who were tall men themselves, and were believed to be superior to others in the strength of their hands, and thereby were encouraged to aim at great things, and thought that strength of theirs would support them in retaining the kingdom. Each of these ruled over a band of men of their own (for those that got together to them were very numerous). They were every one of them also commanders; but when they came to fight, they were subordinate to him, and fought for him. After he had put a diadem about his head, he assembled a council to debate about what things should be done, and all things were done according to his pleasure. So, this man retained his power a great while; he was also called king, and had nothing to hinder him from doing what he pleased. Together with his brothers, he slew a great many of both of Roman and of the king's forces, and managed matters with the like hatred to each of them. They fell upon the king's soldiers because of the licentious conduct they had been allowed under Herod's government; and they fell upon the Romans, because of the injuries they had so lately received from them. But in process of time they grew more cruel to all sorts of men, nor could anyone escape from one or other of these seditions, since they slew some out of the hopes of gain, and others from a mere custom of slaying men.

Once, they attacked a Roman company at Emmaus, soldiers who were bringing grain and weapons to the army, and fell upon Arius, the centurion, who commanded the company, and shot forty of the best of his foot soldiers. The other Romans panicked after this slaughter, left their dead behind them, and were saved by Gratus, who came to their assistance with the king's troops that he commanded. Now these four brethren continued the war a long while by such sort of expeditions, and they much grieved the Romans; but they did their own nation also a great deal of mischief. Afterwards they were subdued; one of them in a fight with Gratus, another with Ptolemy; Herod Archelaus took the eldest of them prisoner; while the last of them was so dejected at the other's misfortune, and saw so plainly that he had no way now left to save himself, his army being worn away with sickness and continual labors, that he also delivered himself up to Archelaus, upon his promise and oath to God to preserve his life. But these things came to pass a good while afterward.

[Flavius Josephus, Jewish Antiquities 17.278-284]

Judas the Galilean (6 CE)

There was one Judas, a Galilean, of a city whose name was Gamala, who, taking with him Zadok, a Pharisee, became zealous to draw them to a revolt. Both said that this taxation was no better than an introduction to slavery, and exhorted the nation to assert their liberty; as if they could procure them happiness and security for what they possessed, and an assured enjoyment of a still greater good, which was that of the honor and glory they would thereby acquire for magnanimity. They also said that God would not otherwise be assisting to them, than upon their joining with one another in such councils as might be successful, and for their own advantage; and this especially, if they would set about great exploits, and not grow weary in executing the same. So men received what they said with pleasure, and this bold attempt proceeded to a great height.

[Flavius Josephus, *Jewish Antiquities* 18.4-6]

Judas the Galilean was the author of the fourth branch of Jewish philosophy. These men agree in all other things with the Pharisaic notions; but they have an inviolable attachment to liberty, and say that God is to be their only Ruler and Lord. They also do not value dying any kinds of death, nor indeed do they heed the deaths of their relations and friends, nor can any such fear make them call any man lord.

[Flavius Josephus, *Jewish Antiquities* 18.23]

The Samaritan prophet (36 CE)

For a man who made light of mendacity and in all his designs catered to the mob, rallied them, bidding them go in a body with him to Mount Gerizim, which in their belief is the most sacred of mountains. He assured them that on their arrival he would show them the sacred vessels which were buried there, where Moses had deposited them. His hearers, viewing this tale as plausible, appeared in arms. They posted themselves in a certain village named Tirathana, and, as they planned to climb the mountain in a great multitude, they welcomed to their ranks the new arrivals who kept coming. But before they could ascend, Pilate blocked their projected route up the mountain with a detachment of cavalry and heavily armed infantry, who in an encounter with the first comers in the village slew some in a pitched battle and put the others to flight. Many prisoners were taken, of whom Pilate put to death the principal leaders and those who were most influential among the fugitives.

[Flavius Josephus, Jewish Antiquities 18.85-87]

Theudas (about 45 CE)

It came to pass, while Fadus was procurator of Judea, that a certain charlatan, whose name was Theudas, persuaded a great part of the people to take their effects with them, and follow him to the river Jordan; for he told them he was a prophet, and that he would, by his own command, divide the river, and afford them an easy passage over it. Many were deluded by his words. However, Fadus did not permit them to make any advantage of his wild attempt, but sent a troop of horsemen out against them. After falling upon them unexpectedly, they slew many of them, and took many of them alive. They also took Theudas alive, cut off his head, and carried it to Jerusalem.

[(Flavius Josephus, Jewish Antiquities 20.97-98]

The Egyptian prophet (between 52 and 58 CE)

who deceived and deluded the people under pretense of Divine inspiration, but were in fact for procuring innovations and changes of the government. These men prevailed with the multitude to act like madmen, and went before them into the wilderness, pretending that God would there show them the signals of liberty.

[Flavius Josephus, Jewish War 2.259]

He continues with the following story.
There was an Egyptian false prophet that did the Jews more mischief than the former; for he was a cheat, and pretended to be a prophet also, and got together thirty thousand men that were deluded by him; these he led round about from the wilderness to the mount which was called the Mount of Olives. He was ready to break into Jerusalem by force from that place; and if he could but once conquer the Roman garrison and the people, he intended to rule them by the assistance of those guards of his that were to break into the city with him.

[Flavius Josephus, Jewish War 2.261-262]

In his Jewish antiquities, Josephus retold the story. The number of followers seems to be less exaggerated and the prophet's threat to use violence are ignored.
about this time, someone came out of Egypt to Jerusalem, claiming to be a prophet. He advised the crowd to go along with him to the Mount of Olives, as it was called, which lay over against the city, and at the distance of a kilometer. He added that he would show them from hence how the walls of Jerusalem would fall down at his command, and he promised them that he would procure them an entrance into the city through those collapsed walls. Now when Felix was informed of these things, he ordered his soldiers to take their weapons, and came against them with a great number of horsemen and footmen from Jerusalem, and attacked the Egyptian and the people that were with him. He slew four hundred of them, and took two hundred alive. The Egyptian himself escaped out of the fight, but did not appear any more. And again the robbers stirred up the people to make war with the Romans, and said they ought not to obey them at all; and when any persons would not comply with them, they set fire to their villages, and plundered them.

[Flavius Josephus, Jewish Antiquities 20.169-171]

Menahem (66 CE)

In the mean time, one Menahem, the son of that Judas, who was called the Galilean [...] took some of the men of note with him, and retired to Masada, where he broke open king Herod's armory, and gave arms not only to his own people, but to other robbers also. These he made use of for a guard, and returned in the state of a king to Jerusalem; he became the leader of the sedition. (Flavius Josephus, Jewish War 2.433-434)

After this, Menahem captured the governor's palace at Jerusalem, laid siege to some minor Roman fortifications and ordered the execution of the high priest. He was now the only leader of the Jewish revolt, and could boast remarkable successes. However, the son of the high priest, Eleasar, was the leader of the temple guard an Menahem's deadly enemy. The overthrow of the places of strength, and the death of the high priest Ananias, so puffed up Menahem, that he became barbarously cruel; and as he thought he had no antagonist to dispute the management of affairs with him, he was no better than an insupportable tyrant. But Eleasar and his party [...] made an assault upon him in the temple, for he went up thither to worship in a pompous manner, and adorned with royal garments, and had his followers with him in their armor. Eleasar and his party fell violently upon him, as did also the rest of the people; taking up stones to attack him withal, they threw them at the scholar, and thought, that if he were once ruined, the entire sedition would fall to the ground. Menahem and his party made resistance for a while, but when they perceived that the whole multitude were falling upon them, they fled which way every one was able; those that were caught were slain, and those that hid themselves were searched for. A few of them escaped privately to Masada [...]. As for Menahem himself, he ran away to the place called Ophla, and there lay skulking in private; but they took him alive, and drew him out before them all; they then tortured him with many sorts of torments, and after all slew him, as they did by those that were captains under him also.

[Flavius Josephus, Jewish War 2.442-448]

Judas the Galilean (6 CE)

There was one Judas, a Galilean, of a city whose name was Gamala, who, taking with him Zadok, a Pharisee, became zealous to draw them to a revolt. Both said that this taxation was no better than an introduction to slavery, and exhorted the nation to assert their liberty; as if they could procure them happiness and security for what they possessed, and an assured enjoyment of a still greater good, which was that of the honor and glory they would thereby acquire for magnanimity. They also said that God would not otherwise be assisting to them, than upon their joining with one another in such councils as might be successful, and for their own advantage; and this especially, if they would set about great exploits, and not grow weary in executing the same. So men received what they said with pleasure, and this bold attempt proceeded to a great height.

[Flavius Josephus, Jewish Antiquities 18.4-6]

Judas the Galilean was the author of the fourth branch of Jewish philosophy. These men agree in all other things with the Pharisaic notions; but they have an inviolable attachment to liberty, and say that God is to be their only Ruler and Lord. They also do not value dying any kinds of death, nor indeed do they heed the deaths of their relations and friends, nor can any such fear make them call any man lord.

[Flavius Josephus, Jewish Antiquities 18.23]

All sorts of misfortunes sprang from these men, and the nation was infected with this doctrine to an incredible degree. One violent war came upon us after another, and we lost our friends, which used to alleviate our pains. There were also very great robberies and murder of our principal men. This was done in pretense indeed for the public welfare, but in reality for the hopes of gain to themselves; whence arose seditions, and from them murders of men, which sometimes fell on those of their own people (by the madness of these men towards one another, while their desire was that none of the adverse party might be left), and sometimes on their enemies. Famine also came upon us, and reduced us to the last degree of despair, as did also the taking and demolishing of cities; nay, the sedition at last increased so high, that the very temple of God was burnt down by their enemies' fire. Such were the consequences of this, that the customs of our fathers were altered, and such a change was made, as added a mighty weight toward bringing all to destruction.

[Flavius Josephus, Jewish Antiquities 18.7-9]

Some time ago, Theudas appeared, claiming to be somebody, and about four hundred men rallied to him. He was killed, all his followers were dispersed, and it all came to nothing. After him, Judas the Galilean appeared in the days of the census and led a band of people in revolt. He too was killed, and all his followers were scattered.

[Luke, Acts of the apostles 5.36-37]

Then came the successor of Fadus, Tiberius Alexander. He was the son of Alexander, the chief customs officer of Alexandria, one of the most influential men of his age, both for his family and wealth. He was also more eminent for his piety than his son Alexander, for the latter did not continue in the religion of his country. Under this prefect a great famine happened in Judaea, and queen Helena of Adiabene bought grain in Egypt at a great expense, and distributed it to those that needed it. Besides this, the sons of Judas the Galilean were executed; I mean that they were the sons of that Judas who caused the people to revolt when Quirinius came to take an account of the estates of the Jews. The names of those sons were James and Simon, whom Alexander commanded to be crucified.

[Jewish antiquities 20.100-103]

Simon bar Giora (69-70 CE)

Simon had been in the upper city during the siege of Jerusalem, but when the Roman army had got within the walls and were laying the city waste, he then took the most faithful of his friends with him, and among them several stone-cutters, with those iron tools which belonged to their occupation. Taking with them as great a quantity of provisions as would suffice them for a long time, he let himself and all them down into a certain subterranean cavern that was not visible above ground. Now, so far as had been digged of old, they went onward along it without disturbance; but where they met with solid earth, they dug a mine under ground, and hoping that they should be able to proceed so far as to rise from underground in a safe place, and by that means escape. But when they came to make the experiment, they were disappointed of their hope; for the miners could make but small progress, and that with difficulty also because their provisions, though they distributed them by measure, began to fail them.

Simon, thinking he might be able to astonish and elude the Romans, put on a white frock, and buttoned upon him a purple cloak, and appeared out of the ground in the place where the temple had formerly been. At the first, indeed, those that saw him were greatly astonished, and stood still where they were; but afterward they came nearer to him, and asked him who he was. Now Simon would not tell them, but bid them call for their captain; and when they ran to call him, Terentius Rufus (who was left to command the army there) came to Simon, and learned of him the whole truth, and kept him in bonds, and let Titus know that he was taken. Thus did God bring this man to be punished for what bitter and savage tyranny he had exercised against his countrymen.

[Flavius Josephus, Jewish War 7.26-32]

Jonathan the weaver (73 CE)

The madness of the Sicarii, like a disease, reached as far as the cities of Cyrenaica, because one Jonathan, a vile person, and by trade a weaver, came thither and prevailed with no small number of the poorer sort to give ear to him. He led them into the desert, upon promising them that he would show them signs and apparitions. [...] Those of the greatest dignity among the Jews of Cyrene informed Catullus, the governor of the Libyan Pentapolis, of Jonathan's march into the desert, and of the preparations he had made for it. So Catullus sent out after him both horsemen and footmen, and easily overcame them, because they were unarmed. Many were slain in the fight, but some were taken alive, and brought to Catullus. As for Jonathan, the head of this plot, he fled away at that time; but upon a great and very diligent search, which was made all the country over for him, he was at last taken.

[Flavius Josephus, Jewish War 7.437-441]

In the next months, governor Catullus used Jonathan to incriminate several important Jewish men, but the new emperor, Vespasian, grew suspicious and in the end, Catullus was reprimanded and Jonathan was burned alive.

Lukuas (115 CE)

In the course of the eighteenth year of the reign of the emperor Trajan, a rebellion of the Jews broke out and destroyed a great multitude of them. For both in Alexandria and in the rest of Egypt and especially in Cyrenaica, as though they had been seized by some terrible spirit of rebellion, they rushed into sedition against their Greek fellow citizens, and -increasing the scope of the rebellion- in the following year started a great war while Lupus was governor of all Egypt. In the first engagement they happened to overcome the Greeks, who fled to Alexandria and captured and killed the Jews in the city, but though losing the help of the townsmen, the Jews of Cyrene continued to plunder the country of Egypt and to ravage the districts in it under their leader Lukuas. The emperor sent against them Marcius Turbo with land and sea forces including cavalry. He waged war vigorously against them in many battles for a considerable time and killed many thousands of Jews, not only those of Cyrene but also those of Egypt who had rallied to Lukuas, their king. The emperor suspected that the Jews in Mesopotamia would also attack the inhabitants and ordered Lusius Quietus to clean them out of the province. He organized a force and murdered a great multitude of the Jews there, and for this reform was appointed governor of Judaea by the emperor.

[Eusebius, History of the church 4.2.1-5]

Simon ben Kosiba (132-135 CE)

Rabbi Simeon ben Yohai taught: 'Aqiba, my master, used to interpret a star goes forth from Jacob as a Kozeba goes forth from Jacob.' Rabbi Aqiba, when he saw Ben Kozeba, said: 'This is the King Messiah.' Rabbi Yohanan ben Torta said to him: 'Aqiba! Grass will grow on your cheeks and still the Son of David does not come!' (Palestinian Talmud, Ta`anit 4.5)

This text contradicts itself. In the first line, rabbi Aqiba (the president of the rabbinical academy at Yavne and the official religious leader of the Judaean Jews) expresses that he is disappointed in Simon ben Kosiba, but in the second line he is very enthusiastic. The only way to solve this inconsistency, is to accept that the editor of the Palestinian Talmud has changed the text on two places. Because there are parallel texts (e.g., Lamentations Rabbah 2.2 §4), we may assume that the text originally ran like this:
Rabbi Simeon ben Yohai taught: 'Aqiba, my master, used to interpret a star goes forth from Jacob as a Kochba goes forth from Jacob.' Rabbi Aqiba, when he saw Ben Kosiba, said: 'This is the King Messiah.' Rabbi Yohanan ben Torta said to him: 'Aqiba! Grass will grow on your cheeks and still the Son of David does not come!'

The editor of the Palestinian Talmud changed all references into 'son of the disappointment' (Kozeba), but, however the precise wording of this testimony, it is clear that Aqiba said that Simon ben Kosiba was the Messiah and was corrected by rabbi Yohanan ben Torta. If our reconstruction is sound, we know that he proposed to call him 'son of the star' (Bar Kochba). This nickname must have been very popular, because it is also used by the contemporary Christian authors Justin Martyr and Ariston of Pella:
Barchochebas, the leader of the revolt of the Jews, gave orders that Christians alone should be lead away to cruel punishments, unless they should deny Jesus as the Christ and blaspheme.

[Justin, First apology 31.6]

The Jews were lead by a certain Bar Chochebas, which means Star.

[Ariston of Pella, quoted by Eusebius, History of the Church 4.6.2]

That famed Barchochebas, the instigator of the Jewish uprising, kept fanning a lighted blade of straw in his mouth with puffs of breath so as to give the impression that he was spewing out flames.

[Jerome, Against Rufinus 3.31]

This is of course a rationalization of a miracle story. The interesting point is that this type of miracle is exactly what the Messiah was expected to do:

Behold, when he saw the onrush of the approaching multitude, he neither lifted his hand nor held a spear or any weapon of war; but I saw how he sent forth from his mouth as it were a stream of fire, and from his lips a flaming breath, and from his tongue he shot forth a storm of sparks. All these were mingled together, the stream of fire and the flaming breath and the great storm, and fell on the onrushing multitide which was prepared to fight, and burnt them all up, so that suddenly nothing was seen of the innumerable multitude but only the dust of ashes and the smell of smoke.

[4 Ezra 13.9-11]

1.8 The Disciples of Jesus

Matt 10:2	Mark 3:16	Luke 6:14	Acts 1:13
Andrew	Andrew	Andrew	Andrew
Bartholomew	Bartholomew	Bartholomew	Bartholomew
James son of Alphaeus	James son of Alphaeus	James son of Alphaeus	James son of Alphaeus
James son of Zebedee	James son of Zebedee	James	James
John	John	John	John

Judas Iscariot	Judas Iscariot	Judas Iscariot	(not named)
Matthew	Matthew	Matthew	Matthew
Philip	Philip	Philip	Philip
Simon (who is called Peter)	Simon (to whom he gave the name Peter)	Simon (whom he named Peter)	Peter
Simon the Zealot	Simon the Zealot	Simon who was called the Zealot	Simon the Zealot
Thaddaeus	Thaddaeus	Judas son of James	Judas son of James
Thomas	Thomas	Thomas	Thomas

The Gospel of Judas

This is a Gnostic gospel that purportedly documents conversations between the Disciple Judas Iscariot and Jesus Christ. It is believed to have been written by Gnostic followers of Jesus, rather than by Judas himself, and probably dates from no earlier than the 2nd century, since it contains late 2nd century theology. In 180 A.D., Irenaeus, an influential Christian priest, wrote a document in which he railed against this gospel, indicating the book was already in circulation.

Introduction: Incipit

The secret account of the revelation that Jesus spoke in conversation with Judas Iscariot during a week three days before he celebrated Passover.

The Earthly Ministry Of Jesus

When Jesus appeared on earth, he performed miracles and great wonders for the salvation of humanity. And since some [walked] in the way of righteousness while others walked in their transgressions, the twelve disciples were called.

He began to speak with them about the mysteries beyond the world and what would take place at the end. Often he did not appear to his disciples as himself, but he was found among them as a child.

SCENE 1: Jesus dialogues with his disciples: The prayer of thanksgiving or the eucharist

One day he was with his disciples in Judea, and he found them gathered together and seated in pious observance. When he [approached] his disciples, [34] gathered together and seated and offering a prayer of thanksgiving over the bread, [he] laughed.
The disciples said to [him], "Master, why are you laughing at [our] prayer of thanksgiving? We have done what is right."
He answered and said to them, "I am not laughing at you. <You> are not doing this because of your own will but because it is through this that your god [will be] praised."
They said, "Master, you are […] the son of our god."
Jesus said to them, "How do you know me? Truly [I] say to you, no generation of the people that are among you will know me."

The Disciples Become Angry

When his disciples heard this, they started getting angry and infuriated and began blaspheming against him in their hearts.
When Jesus observed their lack of [understanding, he said] to them, "Why has this agitation led you to anger? Your god who is within you and […] [35] have provoked you to anger [within] your souls. [Let] any one of you who is [strong enough] among human beings bring out the perfect human and stand before my face."
They all said, "We have the strength."
But their spirits did not dare to stand before [him], except for Judas Iscariot. He was able to stand before him, but he could not look him in the eyes, and he turned his face away.
Judas [said] to him, "I know who you are and where you have come from. You are from the immortal realm of Barbelo. And I am not worthy to utter the name of the one who has sent you."

Jesus Speaks To Judas Privately

Knowing that Judas was reflecting upon something that was exalted, Jesus said to him, "Step away from the others and I shall tell you the mysteries of the kingdom. It is possible for you to reach it, but you will grieve a great deal. [36] For someone else will replace you, in order that the twelve [disciples] may again come to completion with their god."
Judas said to him, "When will you tell me these things, and [when] will the great day of light dawn for the generation?"
But when he said this, Jesus left him.

SCENE 2: Jesus appears to the disciples again
The next morning, after this happened, Jesus [appeared] to his disciples again.
They said to him, "Master, where did you go and what did you do when you left us?"
Jesus said to them, "I went to another great and holy generation."
His disciples said to him, "Lord, what is the great generation that is superior to us and holier than us, that is not now in these realms?"
When Jesus heard this, he laughed and said to them, "Why are you thinking in your hearts about the strong and holy generation? [37] Truly [I] say to you, no one born [of] this aeon will see that [generation], and no host of angels of the stars will rule over that generation, and no person of mortal birth can associate with it, because that generation does not come from [...] which has become [...]. The generation of people among [you] is from the generation of humanity [...] power, which [... the] other powers [...] by [which] you rule."
When [his] disciples heard this, they each were troubled in spirit. They could not say a word.
Another day Jesus came up to [them]. They said to [him], "Master, we have seen you in a [vision], for we have had great [dreams ...] night [...]."
[He said], "Why have [you ... when] <you> have gone into hiding?" [38]

The Disciples See The Temple And Discuss It

They [said, "We have seen] a great [house with a large] altar [in it, and] twelve men----they are the priests, we would say----and a name;

and a crowd of people is waiting at that altar, [until] the priests [… and receive] the offerings. [But] we kept waiting."
[Jesus said], "What are [the priests] like?"
They [said, "Some …] two weeks; [some] sacrifice their own children, others their wives, in praise [and] humility with each other; some sleep with men; some are involved in [slaughter]; some commit a multitude of sins and deeds of lawlessness. And the men who stand [before] the altar invoke your [name], [39] and in all the deeds of their deficiency, the sacrifices are brought to completion […]."
After they said this, they were quiet, for they were troubled.

Jesus Offers An Allegorical Interpretation Of The Vision Of The Temple

Jesus said to them, "Why are you troubled? Truly I say to you, all the priests who stand before that altar invoke my name. Again I say to you, my name has been written on this […] of the generations of the stars through the human generations. [And they] have planted trees without fruit, in my name, in a shameful manner."
Jesus said to them, "Those you have seen receiving the offerings at the altar----that is who you are. That is the god you serve, and you are those twelve men you have seen. The cattle you have seen brought for sacrifice are the many people you lead astray [40] before that altar. […] will stand and make use of my name in this way, and generations of the pious will remain loyal to him. After hi another man will stand there from [the fornicators], and another [will] stand there from the slayers of children, and another from those who sleep with men, and those who abstain, and the rest of the people of pollution and lawlessness and error, and those who say, 'We are like angels'; they are the stars that bring everything to its conclusion. For to the human generations it has been said, 'Look, God has received your sacrifice from the hands of a priest'----that is, a minister of error.
But it is the Lord, the Lord of the universe, who commands, 'On the last day they will be put to shame.'" [41]
Jesus said [to them], "Stop sac[rificing …] which you have […] over the altar, since they are over your stars and your angels and have already come to their conclusion there. So let them be [ensnared] before you, and let them go [----about 15 lines missing----]

generations [...]. A baker cannot feed all creation [42] under [heaven]. And [...] to them [...] and [...] to us and [...].
Jesus said to them, "Stop struggling with me. Each of you has his own star, and every[body----about 17 lines missing----] [43] in [...] who has come [... spring] for the tree [...] of this aeon [...] for a time [...] but he has come to water God's paradise, and the [generation] that will last, because [he] will not defile the [walk of life of] that generation, but [...] for all eternity."

Judas Asks Jesus About That Generation And Human Generations

Judas said to [him, "Rabb]i, what kind of fruit does this generation produce?"
Jesus said, "The souls of every human generation will die. When these people, however, have completed the time of the kingdom and the spirit leaves them, their bodies will die but their souls will be alive, and they will be taken up."
Judas said, "And what will the rest of the human generations do?"
Jesus said, "It is impossible [44] to sow seed on [rock] and harvest its fruit. [This] is also the way [...] the [defiled] generation [...] and corruptible Sophia [...] the hand that has created mortal people, so that their souls go up to the eternal realms above. [Truly] I say to you, [...] angel [...] power will be able to see that [...] these to whom [...] holy generations [...]."
After Jesus said this, he departed.

SCENE 3: Judas recounts a vision and Jesus responds
Judas said, "Master, as you have listened to all of them, now also listen to me. For I have seen a great vision."
When Jesus heard this, he laughed and said to him, "You thirteenth spirit, why do you try so hard? But speak up, and I shall bear with you."
Judas said to him, "In the vision I saw myself as the twelve disciples were stoning me and [45] persecuting [me severely]. And I also came to the place where [...] after you. I saw [a house ...], and my eyes could not [comprehend] its size. Great people were surrounding it, and that house <had> a roof of greenery, and in the middle of the house was [a crowd----two lines missing----], saying, 'Master, take me in along with these people.'"

[Jesus] answered and said, "Judas, your star has led you astray." He continued, "No person of mortal birth is worthy to enter the house you have seen, for that place is reserved for the holy. Neither the sun nor the moon will rule there, nor the day, but the holy will abide there always, in the eternal realm with the holy angels. Look, I have explained to you the mysteries of the kingdom [46] and I have taught you about the error of the stars; and [...] send it [...] on the twelve aeons."

Judas Asks About His Own Fate

Judas said, "Master, could it be that my seed is under the control of the rulers?"
Jesus answered and said to him, "Come, that I [----two lines missing----], but that you will grieve much when you see the kingdom and all its generation."
When he heard this, Judas said to him, "What good is it that I have received it? For you have set me apart for that generation."
Jesus answered and said, "You will become the thirteenth, and you will be cursed by the other generations----and you will come to rule over them. In the last days they will curse your ascent to the holy [generation]."

Jesus Teaches Judas About Cosmology: The Spirit And The Self-Generated

Jesus said, "[Come], that I may teach you about [secrets] no person [has] ever seen. For there exists a great and boundless realm, whose extent no generation of angels has seen, [in which] there is [a] great invisible [Spirit], which no eye of an angel has ever seen, no thought of the heart has ever comprehended, and it was never called by any name.
"And a luminous cloud appeared there. He said, 'Let an angel come into being as my attendant.'
"A great angel, the enlightened divine Self-Generated, emerged from the cloud. Because of him, four other angels came into being from another cloud, and they became attendants for the angelic Self-Generated. The Self-Generated said, [48] 'Let [...] come into being [...],' and it came into being [...]. And he [created] the first luminary

to reign over him. He said, 'Let angels come into being to serve [him],' and myriads without number came into being. He said, '[Let] an enlightened aeon come into being,' and he came into being. He created the second luminary [to] reign over him, together with myriads of angels without number, to offer service. That is how he created the rest of the enlightened aeons. He made them reign over them, and he created for them myriads of angels without number, to assist them.

Adamas And The Luminaries

"Adamas was in the first luminous cloud that no angel has ever seen among all those called 'God.' He [49] [...] that [...] the image [...] and after the likeness of [this] angel. He made the incorruptible [generation] of Seth appear [...] the twelve [...] the twentyfour [...]. He made seventy-two luminaries appear in the incorruptible generation, in accordance with the will of the Spirit. The seventy-two luminaries themselves made three hundred sixty luminaries appear in the incorruptible generation, in accordance with the will of the Spirit, that their number should be five for each.
"The twelve aeons of the twelve luminaries constitute their father, with six heavens for each aeon, so that there are seventy-two heavens for the seventy-two luminaries, and for each [of them five] firmaments, [for a total of] three hundred sixty [firmaments ...]. They were given authority and a [great] host of angels [without number], for glory and adoration, [and after that also] virgin spirits, for glory and [adoration] of all the aeons and the heavens and their firmaments.

The cosmos, chaos, and the underworld

"The multitude of those immortals is called the cosmos---- that is, perdition----by the Father and the seventy-two luminaries who are with the Self-Generated and his seventytwo aeons. In him the first human appeared with his incorruptible powers. And the aeon that appeared with his generation, the aeon in whom are the cloud of knowledge and the angel, is called [51] El. [...] aeon [...] after that [...] said, 'Let twelve angels come into being [to] rule over chaos and the [underworld].' And look, from the cloud there appeared an [angel] whose face flashed with fire and whose appearance was defiled with blood. His name was Nebro, which means 'rebel'; others call him Yaldabaoth. Another angel, Saklas, also came from the cloud. So Nebro created six angels----as well as Saklas----to be assistants, and these produced twelve angels in the heavens, with each one receiving a portion in the heavens.

The Rulers And Angels

"The twelve rulers spoke with the twelve angels: 'Let each of you [52] [...] and let them [...] generation [----one line lost----] angels':
The first is [S]eth, who is called Christ.
The [second] is Harmathoth, who is [...].
The [third] is Galila.
The fourth is Yobel.
The fifth [is] Adonaios.
These are the five who ruled over the underworld, and first of all over chaos.

The Creation Of Humanity

"Then Saklas said to his angels, 'Let us create a human being after the likeness and after the image.' They fashioned Adam and his wife Eve, who is called, in the cloud, Zoe. For by this name all the generations seek the man, and each of them calls the woman by these names. Now, Sakla did not [53] com[mand ...] except [...] the gene[rations ...] this [...]. And the [ruler] said to Adam, 'You shall live long, with your children.'"

Judas Asks About The Destiny Of Adam And Humanity

Judas said to Jesus, "[What] is the long duration of time that the human being will live?"
Jesus said, "Why are you wondering about this, that Adam, with his generation, has lived his span of life in the place where he has received his kingdom, with longevity with his ruler?"
Judas said to Jesus, "Does the human spirit die?"
Jesus said, "This is why God ordered Michael to give the spirits of people to them as a loan, so that they might offer service, but the Great One ordered Gabriel to grant spirits to the great generation with

no ruler over it----that is, the spirit and the soul. Therefore, the [rest] of the souls [54] [----one line missing----].

Jesus Discusses The Destruction Of The Wicked With Judas And Others

"[…] light [----nearly two lines missing----] around […] let […] spirit [that is] within you dwell in this [flesh] among the generations of angels. But God caused knowledge to be [given] to Adam and those with him, so that the kings of chaos and the underworld might not lord it over them."
Judas said to Jesus, "So what will those generations do?"
Jesus said, "Truly I say to you, for all of them the stars bring matters to completion. When Saklas completes the span of time assigned for him, their first star will appear with the generations, and they will finish what they said they would do. Then they will fornicate in my name and slay their children [55] and they will […] and [----about six and a half lines missing----] my name, and he will […] your star over the [thir]teenth aeon."
After that Jesus [laughed].
[Judas said], "Master, [why are you laughing at us]?"
[Jesus] answered [and said], "I am not laughing [at you] but at the error of the stars, because these six stars wander about with these five combatants, and they all will be destroyed along with their creatures."

Jesus Speaks Of Those Who Are Baptized, And Judas's Betrayal

Judas said to Jesus, "Look, what will those who have been baptized in your name do?"
Jesus said, "Truly I say [to you], this baptism [56] […] my name [----about nine lines missing----] to me. Truly [I] say to you, Judas, [those who] offer sacrifices to Saklas […] God [----three lines missing----] everything that is evil.
"But you will exceed all of them. For you will sacrifice the man that clothes me. Already your horn has been raised, your wrath has been kindled, your star has shown brightly, and your heart has […]. [57]
"Truly […] your last […] become [----about two and a half lines missing----], grieve [----about two lines missing----] the ruler, since he will be destroyed. And then the image of the great generation of

Adam will be exalted, for prior to heaven, earth, and the angels, that generation, which is from the eternal realms, exists. Look, you have been told everything. Lift up your eyes and look at the cloud and the light within it and the stars surrounding it. The star that leads the way is your star."

Judas lifted up his eyes and saw the luminous cloud, and he entered it. Those standing on the ground heard a voice coming from the cloud, saying, [58] [...] great generation [...] ... image [...] [----about five lines missing----].

Conclusion: Judas Betrays Jesus

[...] Their high priests murmured because [he] had gone into the guest room for his prayer. But some scribes were there watching carefully in order to arrest him during the prayer, for they were afraid of the people, since he was regarded by all as a prophet. They approached Judas and said to him, "What are you doing here? You are Jesus' disciple."

Judas answered them as they wished. And he received some money and handed him over to them.

1.9 Jesús and Mary Magdalene

The notion that Mary Magdalene was special to Jesus is taken primarily from the Gospel of Mary. This Gnostic gospel is not part of the New Testament, and was written by an unknown author in the last half of the second century, or about one hundred fifty years after Jesus' death. No eyewitnesses, including Mary, would have been alive at the time it was written (about 150 A. D.). Such a late date means the Gospel of Mary could not have been written by an eyewitness of Jesus, and no one knows who wrote it.

One verse in the Gospel of Mary refers to Mary Magdalene as Jesus' favorite disciple, saying he loved Mary "more than us (meaning his disciples)." In another verse Peter supposedly told Mary, "Sister, we know the savior loved you more than any other woman." Yet nothing written in The Gospel of Mary speaks of a romance or sexual relationship between Mary Magdalene and Jesus.

In the Gnostic Gospel of Philip, Jesus and Mary were "companions". This verse reads:
"Three women always walked with the master: Mary his mother, [] sister, and Mary of Magdala, who is called his companion (koinonos). For "Mary" is the name of his sister, his mother and his companion (koinonos)."

There is also a single verse in the Gospel of Philip that says Jesus kissed Mary.

"The companion of the [] is Mary of Magdala. The [] her more than [] the disciples, [] kissed her often on her []. The other []...said to him, 'Why do you love her more than all of us?'"

It is also important to note that, aside from these few questionable passages, there is no other historical document that even insinuates Jesus and Mary had a romantic relationship. No secular historian, Jewish historian, or early Christian historian writes even one iota about such a relationship. And since both the Gospel of Mary and the Gospel of Philip were written 100-220 years after Christ by unknown authors, their statements about Jesus and Mary need to be evaluated in context of both contemporary history and the much earlier New Testament documents.

The Gospel According to Mary Magdalene
Estimated Range of Dating: 120-180 A.D.

Chapter 4

(Pages 1 to 6 of the manuscript, containing chapters 1 - 3, are lost)

. . . Will matter then be destroyed or not?
22) The Savior said, All nature, all formations, all creatures exist in and with one another, and they will be resolved again into their own roots.

23) For the nature of matter is resolved into the roots of its own nature alone.
24) He who has ears to hear, let him hear.
25) Peter said to him, Since you have explained everything to us, tell us this also: What is the sin of the world?
26) The Savior said There is no sin, but it is you who make sin when you do the things that are like the nature of adultery, which is called sin.
27) That is why the Good came into your midst, to the essence of every nature in order to restore it to its root.
28) Then He continued and said, That is why you become sick and die, for you are deprived of the one who can heal you.
29) He who has a mind to understand, let him understand.
30) Matter gave birth to a passion that has no equal, which proceeded from something contrary to nature. Then there arises a disturbance in its whole body.
31) That is why I said to you, Be of good courage, and if you are discouraged be encouraged in the presence of the different forms of nature.
32) He who has ears to hear, let him hear.
33) When the Blessed One had said this, He greeted them all, saying, Peace be with you. Receive my peace unto yourselves.
34) Beware that no one lead you astray saying Lo here or lo there! For the Son of Man is within you.
35) Follow after Him!
36) Those who seek Him will find Him.
37) Go then and preach the gospel of the Kingdom.
38) Do not lay down any rules beyond what I appointed you, and do not give a law like the lawgiver lest you be constrained by it.
39) When He said this He departed.

Chapter 5
1) But they were grieved. They wept greatly, saying, How shall we go to the Gentiles and preach the gospel of the Kingdom of the Son of Man? If they did not spare Him, how will they spare us?
2) Then Mary stood up, greeted them all, and said to her brethren, Do not weep and do not grieve nor be irresolute, for His grace will be entirely with you and will protect you.

3) But rather, let us praise His greatness, for He has prepared us and made us into Men.
4) When Mary said this, she turned their hearts to the Good, and they began to discuss the words of the Savior.
5) Peter said to Mary, Sister we know that the Savior loved you more than the rest of woman.
6) Tell us the words of the Savior which you remember which you know, but we do not, nor have we heard them.
7) Mary answered and said, What is hidden from you I will proclaim to you.
8) And she began to speak to them these words: I, she said, I saw the Lord in a vision and I said to Him, Lord I saw you today in a vision. He answered and said to me,
9) Blessed are you that you did not waver at the sight of Me. For where the mind is there is the treasure.
10) I said to Him, Lord, how does he who sees the vision see it, through the soul or through the spirit?
11) The Savior answered and said, He does not see through the soul nor through the spirit, but the mind that is between the two that is what sees the vision and it is [...]
(pages 11 - 14 are missing from the manuscript)

Chapter 8:
. . . it.
10) And desire said, I did not see you descending, but now I see you ascending. Why do you lie since you belong to me?
11) The soul answered and said, I saw you. You did not see me nor recognize me. I served you as a garment and you did not know me.
12) When it said this, it (the soul) went away rejoicing greatly.
13) Again it came to the third power, which is called ignorance.
14) The power questioned the soul, saying, Where are you going? In wickedness are you bound. But you are bound; do not judge!
15) And the soul said, Why do you judge me, although I have not judged?
16) I was bound, though I have not bound.
17) I was not recognized. But I have recognized that the All is being dissolved, both the earthly things and the heavenly.
18) When the soul had overcome the third power, it went upwards and saw the fourth power, which took seven forms.

19) The first form is darkness, the second desire, the third ignorance, the fourth is the excitement of death, the fifth is the kingdom of the flesh, the sixth is the foolish wisdom of flesh, the seventh is the wrathful wisdom. These are the seven powers of wrath.
20) They asked the soul, Whence do you come slayer of men, or where are you going, conqueror of space?
21) The soul answered and said, What binds me has been slain, and what turns me about has been overcome,
22) and my desire has been ended, and ignorance has died.
23) In a aeon I was released from a world, and in a Type from a type, and from the fetter of oblivion which is transient.
24) From this time on will I attain to the rest of the time, of the season, of the aeon, in silence.

Chapter 9
1) When Mary had said this, she fell silent, since it was to this point that the Savior had spoken with her.
2) But Andrew answered and said to the brethren, Say what you wish to say about what she has said. I at least do not believe that the Savior said this. For certainly these teachings are strange ideas.
3) Peter answered and spoke concerning these same things.
4) He questioned them about the Savior: Did He really speak privately with a woman and not openly to us? Are we to turn about and all listen to her? Did He prefer her to us?
5) Then Mary wept and said to Peter, My brother Peter, what do you think? Do you think that I have thought this up myself in my heart, or that I am lying about the Savior?
6) Levi answered and said to Peter, Peter you have always been hot tempered.
7) Now I see you contending against the woman like the adversaries.
8) But if the Savior made her worthy, who are you indeed to reject her? Surely the Savior knows her very well.
9) That is why He loved her more than us. Rather let us be ashamed and put on the perfect Man, and separate as He commanded us and preach the gospel, not laying down any other rule or other law beyond what the Savior said.
10) And when they heard this they began to go forth to proclaim and to preach.

1.10 The Trial and Death of Jesus Christ

	Matthew	Mark	Luke	John
Entry into Jerusalem	...0 21:1-11	...0 11:1-11	...0 19:29-44	...0 12:12-19
Cursing of the fig tree and	...0 21:18-20	...0 11:12-14	...0	...0
Buyers and sellers driven from the Temple	...0	11:20-21	...0 19:45-46	...0
Cures in the Temple	21:12-13	11:15-17	...0	...0
Wrath of the Chief Priests and	21:14	...0	19:47-48	...0
Power of faith	21:15-17	11:18-19	21:37-38	...0
Christ's authority questioned	...0	...0	...0	...0
Parable of the two sons	...0	...0	...0	...0
Parable of the wicked husbandmen	21:21-22	11:22-26	20:1-8	...0
The stone which the builders rejected	21:23-27	11:27-33	...0	...0
Chief Priests desire to seize Christ	21:28-32	...0	20:9-16	...0
Parable of the wedding garment	21:33-41	12:1-9	20:17-18	...0
Question of tribute to Caesar	21:42-44	12:10-11	20:19	...0
The Sadducees and the resurrection from the dead	21:45-46	12:12	20:20-26	...0
The Great Commandment	22:1-14	...0	20:27-40	12:20-22
Christ is the son of David	22:15-22	12:13-17	...0	12:23-36
Denunciation of the Scribes and Pharisees	22:23-33	12:18-27	20:41-44	12:37-50
Lamentation over Jerusalem	22:34-40	12:28-34	20:45-47	...0
The widow's mite	22:41-46	12:35-37	13:34-35	...0
Homage of the Greeks	23:1-36	12:38-40	21:1-4	...0
Christ's hour has come	23:37-39	...0	...0	...0
Unbelief of the Jews	...0	12:41-44	...0	...0
Prophesy about Jerusalem		...0	...0	
Eschatological discourse		...0	21:5-7	
Exhortation to be vigilant			21:8-33	
Parable of the ten virgins				
Parable of the talents				
The last judgement				

	Matthew	Mark	Luke	John
	...0	13:1-4	21:34-36	
	...0	13:5-31	...0	
	...0	13:32-37	...0	
	24:1-3	...0	...0	
	24:4-35	...0		
	24:36-51	...0		
	25:1-13			
	25:14-30			
	25:31-46			

	Matthew	Mark	Luke	John
	...0	...0	...0	...0
The Sanhedrin's plot	26:1-5	14:1-2	22:1-2	...0
Judas' treason	26:14-16	14:10-11	22:3-6	...0
Preparations for the Paschal Supper	26:17-19	14:12-16	22:7-13	...0
The Last Supper	26:20	14:17	22:14	...0
The strife as to precedence	...0	...0	22:24-30	...0
The washing of the feet	...0	...0	...0	13:1-17
Christ indicates the traitor	26:21-25	14:18-21	22:21-23	13:8-30
Institution of the Eucharist	26:26-29	14:22-25	22:15-20	...0
Desertion of the eleven foretold	26:31-32	14:27-28	...0	...0
Peter's denial foretold	26:33-35	14:29-31	22:31-34	13:31
Remark concerning the sword	...0	...0	22:34-38	16:33
Discourse after the Last Supper and	...0	...0	...0	17:1-26
Christ's sacerdotal prayer	26:30	14:26	22:39	18:1
The Agony at Gethsemani	...0	...0	...0	18:2-9
The Betrayal by Judas	26:36-46	14:32-42	22:40-46	18:10-11
The arrest	26:47-50	14:43-45	22:47-48	18:12-14
Christ before Annas and	26:50-	14:46-	22:49-	18:24
Christ before Caiphas				
First trial before the Sanhedrin				
Peter's denial of Christ and				
Christ is mocked				

	Matthew	Mark	Luke	John
	56	52	54	18:19-23
	...0	...0	...0	...0
	26:57-58	14:53-54	...0	18:15-18
	26:59-66	14:55-64	22:55-62	18:25-27
	26:69-75	14:66-72	...0	
	...0	...0	22:63-65	
	26:67-68	14:65		
	...0	...0	...0	...0
Second trial before the Sanhedrin	27:1	15:1	22:66-71	...0
Suicide of Judas	27:3-10	...0	...0	...0
Christ is brought to Pilate	27:2	15:1	...0	18:28
The Jews charge Christ with sedition	...0	...0	23:1	18:29-32
Pilate questions Christ privately	27:11	15:2	23:2	18:33-38
The Jews repeat their accusations	27:12-14	15:3-5	23:3	18:38
Christ is sent to Herod	...0	...0	23:4-5	...0
Pilate declares Christ's innocence	...0	...0	23:6-12	...0
Christ or Barabas	27:15-23	15:6-14	23:13-16	18:39-40
Pilate washes his hands	27:24-25	...0	23:17-23	...0
Christ is condemned and scourged	27:26	15:15	...0	19:1
He is mocked by the soldiers	27:27-30	15:16-19	23:24-25	19:2-3
The Jews demand that He be crucified	...0	...0	...0	19:4-8
Pilate again questions Christ privately	...0	...0	...0	19:9-11
The Jews repeat their demand	...0	15:20-21	...0	19:12-16
The Way of The Cross	27:31-32	15:22	...0	19:16-17
The Crucifixion	27:33-38	15:27-28	23:26-32	19:18
and	...0	15:23	23:23-34	...0
Christ is offered wine and gall	27:34	15:24-25	...0	...0
His garments are divided	27:35-36	15:26	...0	19:23-24
The inscription on the cross	27:37	15:29-32	23:34	19:19-22
Christ is insulted on the cross	27:39-43	15:32	23:38	...0
The good thief	27:44	15:33	23:35-37	...0
Mary and John at the foot of the cross	...0	15:34-37	23:39-43	19:25-27
Darkness over the earth	27:45		...0	
The death of Christ				
Marvelous happenings				
The centurion and the disciples on Calvary				
The piercing of Christ's side				

Event	Matthew	Mark	Luke	John
	27:46-50	15:38	23:44-45	...0
	27:51-53	15:39-41	23:46	19:28-30
	27:54-56	...0	23:45	...0
	...0		23:47-49	...0
			...0	19:31-37
Joseph of Arimathea obtains the body of Christ	27:57-58	15:42-45	23:50-52	19:38
The burial	27:59-61	15:46-47	23:53-56	19:39-42
The guarding of the tomb	27:62-66	...	...0	...0
The morning of the Resurrection	...0	...0	...0	...0
The holy women come to the sepulchre	...0	...00	...0	...0
The women enter the sepulchre	28:2-4	16:1-4	24:1-2	...0
Mary Magdalen calls Peter and John	28:1	16:5-8	24:3-11	...0
Peter and John go to the sepulchre	28:5-8	...0	...0	20:1-2
Christ appears to Mary Magdalen	...0	...0	...0	20:3-10
He appears to the holy women	...0	16:9-11	24:12	20:11-18
The guards report to the Chief Priests	...0	...0	...0	...0
Manifestations to the two disciples at Emmaus	28:9-10	...0	...0	...0
Christ appears to the Apostles in Jerusalem	28:11-15	16:12-13	24:13-35	...0
He appears to the Apostles with Thomas	...0	16:14	24:36-43	20:19-23
He appears to seven disciples by the Sea of Galilee	...0	...0	...0...0	20:24-29
He appears on the mountain in Galilee	...0	...0	...0	...0
His last appearance to the Apostles	28:16-20	16:15-18	...0	21:1-23
The Ascension	...0	...0	...0	...0
Conclusion	...0	...0	24:44-49	...0
	...0	16:19	24:50-52	20:30-31
	...0	16:20	24:53	21:24-25

The Acts of Pilate
Range of Dating: 150-255 A.D.

Memorials of Our Lord Jesus Christ, Done in the Time of Pontius Pilate.

Prologue.-I Ananias, of the propraetor's body-guard, being learned in the law, knowing our Lord Jesus Christ from the Holy Scriptures, coming to Him by faith, and counted worthy of the holy baptism, searching also the memorials written at that time of what was done in the case of our Lord Jesus Christ, which the Jews had laid up in the time of Pontius Pilate, found these memorials written in Hebrew, and by the favour of God have translated them into Greek for the information of all who call upon the name of our Master Jesus Christ, in the seventeenth year of the reign of our Lord Flavius Theodosius, and the sixth of Flavius Valentinianus, in the ninth indiction.1
All ye, therefore, who read and transfer into other books, remember me, and pray for me, that God may be merciful to me, and pardon my sins which I have sinned against Him.
Peace be to those who read, and to those who hear and to their households. Amen.
In the fifteenth year2 of the government of Tiberius Caesar, emperor of the Romans, and Herod being king of Galilee, in the nineteenth year of his rule, on the eighth day before the Kalends of April, which is the twenty-fifth of March, in the consulship of Rufus and Rubellio, in the fourth year of the two hundred and second Olympiad, Joseph Caiaphas being high priest of the Jews.
The account that Nicodemus wrote in Hebrew, after the cross and passion of our Lord Jesus Christ, the Saviour God, and left to those that came after him, is as follows:-

Chapter 1.
Having called a council, the high priests and scribes Annas and Caiaphas and Seines and Dathaes, and Gamaliel, Judas, Levi and Nephthalim, Alexander and Jairus,3 and the rest of the Jews, came to Pilate accusing Jesus about many things, saying: We know this man to be the son of Joseph the carpenter, born of Mary; and he says that he is the Son of God, and a king; moreover, he profanes the Sabbath, and wishes to do away with the law of our fathers. Pilate says: And

what are the things which he does, to show that he wishes to do away with it?4 The Jews say: We have a law not to cure any one on the Sabbath; but this man5 has on the Sabbath cured the lame and the crooked, the withered and the blind and the paralytic, the dumb and the demoniac, by evil practices. Pilate says to them: What evil practices? They say to him: He is a magician, and by Beelzebul prince of the demons be casts out the demons, and all are subject to him. Pilate says to them: This is not casting out the demons by an unclean spirit, but by the god Aesculapius.

The Jews say to Pilate: we entreat your highness that he stand at thy tribunal, and be heard.6 And Pilate having called them, says: Tell me how I, being a procurator, can try a king? They say to him: W do not say that he is a king, but he himself says that he is. And Pilate having called the runner, says to him: Let Jesus be brought in with respect. And the runner going out, and recognising Him, adored Him, and took his cloak into his hand, and spread it on the ground, and says to him: My lord, walk on this, and come in, for the procurator calls thee. And the Jews seeing what the runner had done, cried out against Pilate, saying: Why hast thou ordered him to come in by a runner, and not by a crier? for assuredly the runner, when he saw him, adored him, and spread his doublet on the ground, and made him walk like a king.

And Pilate having called the runner, says to him: Why hast thou done this, and spread out thy cloak upon the earth, and made Jesus walk upon it? The runner says to him: My lord procurator, when thou didst send me to Jerusalem to Alexander,7 I saw him sitting upon an ass, and the sons of the Hebrews held branches in their hands, and shouted; and other spread their clothes under him saying, Save now, thou who art in the highest: blessed is he that cometh in the name of the Lord.8

The Jews cry out, and say, to the runner: The soils of the Hebrews shouted in Hebrew; whence then hast thou the Greek? The runner says to them: I asked one of the Jews, and said, What is it they are shouting in Hebrew? And he interpreted it for me. Pilate says to them: And what did they shout in Hebrew? The Jews say to him: Hosanna Membrome Baruchamma Adonai.9 Pilate says to them: And this hosanna, etc., how is it interpreted? The Jews say to him: Save now in the highest; blessed is he; that cometh in the name of the Lord. Pilate says to them: If you bear witness to the words spoken by the children, in what has the runner done wrong? And they were silent. And the procurator says to the runner: Go out, and bring him in in what way thou wilt. And the runner going out, did in the same manner as before, and says to Jesus: My lord, come in; the procurator calleth thee.

And Jesus going in, and the standard-bearers holding their standards, the tops of the standards were bent down, and adored Jesus. And the Jews seeing the bearing of the standards, how they were bent down and adored Jesus, cried10 out vehemently against the standard-bearers. And Pilate says to the Jews: Do you not wonder how the tops of the standards were bent down, and adored Jesus? The Jews say to Pilate: We saw how the standard-bearers bent them down, and adored him. And the procurator having called the standard-bearers, says to them: Why have you done this? They say to Pilate: We are Greeks and temple-slaves, and how could we adore him? and assuredly, as we were holding them up, the tops bent down of their own accord, and adored him.

Pilate says to the rulers of the synagogue and the elders of the people: Do you choose for yourselves men strong and powerful, and let them hold up the standards, and let us see whether they will bend down with them. And the elders of the Jews picked out twelve men powerful and strong, and made them hold up the standards six by six; and they were placed in front of the procurator's tribunal. And Pilate says to the runner: Take him outside of the praetorium, and bring him in again in whatever way may please thee. And Jesus and the runner went out of the praetorium. And Pilate, summoning those who had formerly held up the standards, says to them: I have sworn by tile health of Caesar, that if the standards do not bend down when Jesus comes in, I will cut off your heads. And the procurator ordered Jesus to come in the second time. And the runner did in the same manner as before, and made many entreaties to Jesus to walk on his cloak. And He walked on it, and went ill. And as He went in, the standards were again bent down, and adored Jesus.

Chapter 2.
And Pilate seeing this, was afraid, and sought to go away from the tribunal; but when he was still thinking of going away, his wife sent to him, saying: Have nothing to do with this just man, for many things have I suffered on his account this night.11 And Pilate, summoning the Jews, says to them: You know that my wife is a worshipper of

God, and prefers to adhere to the Jewish religion along with you. They say to him: Yes; we know. Pilate says to them: Behold, my wife12 has sent to me, saying, Have nothing to do with this just man, for many things have I suffered on account of him this night. And the Jews answering, say unto Pilate: Did we not tell thee that he was a sorcerer?13 behold, he has sent a dream to thy wife.

And Pilate, having summoned Jesus, says to Him: What do these witness against thee? Sayest thou nothing? And Jesus said: Unless they had the power, they would say nothing; for every one has the power of his own mouth to speak both good and evil. They shall see to it.14

And the eiders of the Jews answered, and said to Jesus: What shall we see? first, that thou wast born of fornication; secondly, that thy birth in Bethlehem was the cause of the murder of the infants; thirdly, that thy father Joseph and thy mother Mary fled into Egypt because they had no confidence in the people.

Some of the bystanders, pious men of the Jews, say: we deny that he was born of fornication; for we know that Joseph espoused Mary, and he was not born of fornication. Pilate says to the Jews who said that he was of fornication: This story of yours is not true, because they were betrothed, as also these fellow-countrymen of yours say. Annas and Caiaphas say to Pilate: All the multitude of us cry out that he was born of fornication, and are not believed; these are proselytes, and his disciples. And Pilate, calling Annas and Caiaphas, says to them: What are proselytes? They say to him: They are by birth children of the Greeks, and have now become Jews. And those that said that He was not born of fornication, viz.-Lazarus, Asterius, Antonius, James, Atones, Zeras, Samuel, Isaac, Phinees, Crispus, Agrippas, and Judas15 -say: We are not proselytes, but are children of the Jews, and speak of the truth; for we were present at the betrothal of Joseph and Mary.

And Pilate, calling these twelve men who said that He was not born of fornication, says to them: I adjure you by the health of Caesar, to tell me whether it be true that you say, that he was not born of fornication. They say to Pilate: We have a law against taking oaths, because it is a sin; but they will swear by the health of Caesar,16 that it is not as we have said, and we are liable to death. Pilate says to Annas and Caiaphas: Have you nothing to answer to this? Annas and Caiaphas say to Pilate: These twelve are believed when they say that he was not born of fornication; all the multitude of us cry out that he was born of fornication, and that he is a sorcerer, and he says that he is the Son of God and a king, and we are not believed.

And Pilate orders all the multitude to go out, except the twelve men who said that He was not born of fornication, and he ordered Jesus to be separated from them. And Pilate says to them: For what reason do they wish to put him to death? They say to him: They are angry because he cures on the Sabbath. Pilate says: For a good work do they wish to put him to death? They say to him: Yes...

1.11 Historical and Archaeological Evidence

The Pilate Inscription

Language: Latin
Medium: limestone
Dedicator: Pontius Pilate (praefect of Judea)
Approximate Date: 26–37 CE

[DIS AUGUSTI]S TIBERIEUM
[.... PO]NTIUS PILATUS
[...PRAEF]ECTUS IUDA[EA]E
[..FECIT D]E[DICAVIT]

To the honorable gods (this) Tiberium
Pontius Pilate,
Prefect of Judea,
had dedicated

The Testimonium Flavianum (Josephus, Antiquities 18.63)

This is the only direct discussion of Jesus to be found in the writings of Josephus. Unfortunately, the text as we have it in extant copies of Josephus' Antiquities appears to have been dramatically re-written from a Christian point of view. (The writings of Josephus were brought down to us from antiquity not by the Jewish community, but by the Christians).

"About this time there lived Jesus, a wise man if indeed one ought to call him a man. For he was one who wrought surprising feats and was a teacher of such people as accept the truth gladly. He won over many Jews and many of the Greeks. He was the Messiah. When Pilate, upon hearing him accused by men of the highest standing among us, had condemned him to be crucified, those who had in the first place come to love him did not cease. On the third day he appeared to them restored to life. For the prophets of God had prophesied these and myriads of other marvellous things about him. And the tribe of the Christians, so called after him, has still up to now, not disappeared."

Celsus on Jesus (Contra Celsum 1.28)

Celsus lived in during the 2nd century, CE. Origen is refuting him in the 3rd century. Celsus' writings no longer survive in tact, but we have access to some of his work when Origen quotes passages for the purpose of refutation. The following is one such passage.

"Jesus had come from a village in Judea, and was the son of a poor Jewess who gained her living by the work of her own hands. His mother had been turned out of doors by her husband, who was a carpenter by trade, on being convicted of adultery [with a soldier named Panthéra]. Being thus driven away by her husband, and wandering about in disgrace, she gave birth to Jesus, a bastard. Jesus, on account of his poverty, was hired out to go to Egypt. While there he acquired certain (magical) powers which Egyptians pride themselves on possessing. He returned home highly elated at possessing these"

Tertullian Passage (De Spetaculis 100.30)

Tertullian wrote this passage late in the 2nd century, CE. In the context he is imagining himself, after Jesus' triumphant return, mocking the now damned Jews for their perversions of of the truth about Jesus. Much of what he accuses the Jews of saying/doing is straight out of the canonical gospels, but some, especially the last phrase, seems to reflect some of the traditions that will later be brought together in the Toldoth Yeshu.

"This is your carpenter's son, your harlot's son; your Sabbath-breaker, your Samaritan, your demon-possessed! This is he whom you bought from Judas. This is he who was struck with reeds and fists, dishonored with spittle, and given a draught of gall and vinegar! This is he whom his disciples have stolen secretly, that it may be said, 'He has risen', or the gardener abstracted that his lettuces might not be damaged by the crowds of visitors!"

Yeshu and Joshua (Sanhedrin 107b)

This story cannot be directly connected with any of the traditional events in the life of Jesus, and it is set about 100 years before Jesus presumably lived. Yeshu/Yeshua is not an uncommon name, and it may be that we simply have a story about a Jewish 'bad boy' whose name happens to be the same as Jesus'. But as the last sentence (only in the Sanhedrin version) demonstrates, whatever the original intent of the story, it came to be connected with the Yeshu/Jesus traditions in the early medieval period. Even the historical setting -- the reign of Jannai (Alexander Jannaeus, reigned 103-76 BC) -- seems to have stuck, and is clearly embedded in the Toldoth traditions.

"The Rabbis taught: The left should always be used to push away, and the right, on the other hand to draw nearer. But one should not do it as Elisha who pushed Gehazi away, nor as R. Joshua ben Perachiah, who pushed away Yeshu with both hands. What was the problem with R. Joshua ben Perachiah? When King Jannai ordered the extermination of the Rabbis, R. Joshua ben Perachiah and Yeshu fled to Alexandria. When it was safe to return, Rabbi Simeon ben Shetach sent him a letter: From me, Jerusalem the holy city, to the Alexandria in Egypt, my sister. My spouse tarries in your midst, and I sit desolate. Joshua set off at once. During the trip they happened upon an inn in which they treated him with great respect. Joshua commented, "How fair is this inn." Yeshu replied, "But Rabbi, she has unattractive eyes." Joshua replied, "You godless person, do you fill your mind with such things?" Then he had 400 trumpets sounded and anathematized him. Yeshu often came and said to him, "Receive me back." Joshua paid no attention. One day, while Joshua was reciting the Shema, Yeshu came to him, hoping for a reprieve. Joshua made a sign to him with his hand. Yeshu misunderstood, thinking he had been repulsed, so he went away set up a brick and worshipped it. Joshua said to him, "Repent!" Yeshu replied, "I learned this from you: 'Anyone who sins and causes the people to sin, is not allowed the possibility of repentance.'"

[The Teacher said: "Yeshu practiced sorcery and corrupted and misled Israel."]

Baraitha Bab. Sanhedrin 43a

"There is a tradition (in a Barraitha): They hanged Yeshu on the Sabbath of the Passover. But for forty days before that a herald went in front of him (crying), "Yeshu is to be stoned because he practiced sorcery and seduced Israel and lead them away from God. Anyone who can provide evidence on his behalf should come forward to defend him." When, however, nothing favorable about him was found, he was hanged on the Sabbath of the Passover. Ulla commented: "Do you think that he belongs among those for whom redeeming evidence is sought? Rather, he was a seducer [of whom] the All-merciful has said: 'Show them no pity... and do not shield them.' (Deut 13.8b) In Yeshu's case, however, an exception was *made because he was close to those who held [political/religious] authority.*"

Jesus' Students/Disciples

This is in the same larger context. Who, exactly, these disciples are is not clear. Mattai is likely to be Matthew. For the others scholarship has resorted to what is, at best, educated speculation. The fact that there are five rather than twelve suggests that we look elsewhere than Christian tradition to solve the problem. It may not be coincidence that both Yohanan b. Zakkai and Akiba each have five students

"There is a tradition (in a Barraitha): Yeshu had five students: Mattai, Nakkai, Netzer, Buni, and Todah. When Mattai was brought to trial, he said to the judges, "Should Mattai be executed? But scripture says,

'When [mathai] shall I come and behold the face of God?'" (Ps 42.2b RSV) They replied, "Yes, Mattai should be executed, for scripture says, 'When will he die, and his name perish?'" (Ps 41.5b) When Nakkai was brought, he said to them, "Should Nakkai be executed? But scripture says, 'Do not slay the innocent[naki] and righteous.'" (Ex 23.7b) They replied, "Yes, Nakkai should be executed, for scripture says, 'in hiding places he murders the innocent.'" (Ps 10.8b)

When Netzer was brought, he said to them, "Should Netzer be executed? But scripture says, 'a branch[netzer] shall grow out of his roots.'" (Is 11.1b) They replied, "Yes, Netzer should be executed, for scripture says, 'you are cast out, away from your sepulchre, like a loathed branch.'" (Is 14.19a) When Bunni was brought, he said to them, "Should Bunni be executed? But scripture says, 'Israel is my firstborn son[beni].'" (Ex 4.22b) They replied, "Yes, Bunni should be executed, for scripture says, 'behold, I will slay your firstborn son[benkha].'" (Ex 4.23b) When Todah was brought, he said to them, "Should Todah be executed? But scripture says, 'A psalm for Thanksgiving [todah].'" (Ps 100) They replied, "Yes, Todah should be executed, for scripture says, 'He who brings thanksgiving as his sacrifice honors me.'" (Ps 50.23a)

2. Early Church: First Century

2.1 Saul of Tarsus

The actual founder of the Christian Church as opposed to Judaism; born before 10 C.E.; died after 63. The records containing the views and opinions of the opponents of Paul and Paulinism are no longer in existence; and the history of the early Church has been colored by the writers of the second century, who were anxious to suppress or smooth over the controversies of the preceding period, as is shown in the Acts of the Apostles and also by the fact that the Epistles ascribed to Paul, as has been proved by modern critics, are partly spurious (Galatians, Ephesians, I and II Timothy, Titus, and others) and partly interpolated.

Saul (whose Roman cognomen was Paul; see Acts xiii. 9) was born of Jewish parents in the first decade of the common era at Tarsus in Cilicia (Acts ix. 11, xxi. 39, xxii. 3). The claim in Rom. xi. 1 and Phil. iii. 5 that he was of the tribe of Benjamin, suggested by the similarity of his name with that of the first Israelitish king, is, if the passages are genuine, a false one, no tribal lists or pedigrees of this kind having been in existence at that time (see Eusebius, "Hist. Eccl." i. 7, 5; Pes. 62b).

Nor is there any indication in Paul's writings or arguments that he had received the rabbinical training ascribed to him by Christian writers, ancient and modern; least of all could he have acted or written as he did had he been, as is alleged (Acts xxii. 3), the disciple of Gamaliel I., the mild Hillelite. His quotations from Scripture, which are all taken, directly or from memory, from the Greek version, betray no familiarity with the original Hebrew text. The Hellenistic literature, such as the Book of Wisdom and other Apocrypha, as well as Philo was the sole source for his eschatological and theological system. Notwithstanding the emphatic statement, in Phil. iii. 5, that he was "a Hebrew of the Hebrews"—a rather unusual term, which seems to refer to his nationalistic training and conduct (comp. Acts xxi. 40, xxii. 2), since his Jewish birth is stated in the preceding words "of the stock of Israel"—he was, if any of the Epistles that bear his name are really his, entirely a Hellenist in thought and sentiment. As such he was imbued with the notion that "the whole creation groaneth" for liberation from "the prison-house of the body," from this earthly existence, which, because of its pollution by sin and death, is intrinsically evil (Gal. i. 4; Rom. v. 12, vii. 23-24, viii. 22; I Cor. vii. 31; II Cor. v. 2, 4; comp. Philo, "De Allegoriis Legum," iii. 75; idem, "De Vita Mosis," iii. 17; idem, "De Ebrietate," § 26; and Wisdom ii.24).

As a Hellenist, also, he distinguished between an earthly and a heavenly Adam (I Cor. xv. 45-49; comp. Philo, "De Allegoriis Legum," i. 12), and, accordingly, between the lower psychic. life and the higher spiritual life attained only by asceticism (Rom. xii. 1; I Cor. vii. 1-31, ix. 27, xv. 50; comp. Philo, "De Profugis," § 17; and elsewhere). His whole state of mind shows the influence of the theosophic or Gnostic lore of Alexandria, especially the Hermes literature.

Anti-Jewish Attitude.

Whatever the physiological or psychological analysis of Paul's temperament may be, his conception of life was not Jewish. Nor can his unparalleled animosity and hostility to Judaism as voiced in the Epistles be accounted for except upon the assumption that, while born a Jew, he was never in sympathy or in touch with the doctrines of the rabbinical schools. For even his Jewish teachings came to him through Hellenistic channels, as is indicated by the great emphasis laid upon "the day of the divine wrath" (Rom. i. 18; ii. 5, 8; iii. 5; iv. 15; v. 9; ix. 22; xii. 19; I Thess. i. 10; Col. iii. 6; comp. Sibyllines, iii. 309 et seq., 332; iv. 159, 161 et seq.; and elsewhere), as well as by his ethical monitions, which are rather inconsistently taken over from Jewish codes of law for proselytes, the Didache and Didascalia. It is quite natural, then, that not only the Jews (Acts xxi. 21), but also the Judæo-Christians, regarded Paul as an "apostate from the Law" (see Eusebius, l.c. iii. 27; Irenæus, "Adversus Hæreses," i. 26, 2; Origen, "Contra Celsum," v. 65; Clement of Rome, "Recognitiones," i. 70. 73).

Jewish Proselytism and Paul.

Before the authenticity of the story of the so-called conversion of Paul is investigated, it seems proper to consider from the Jewish point of view this question: Why did Paul find it necessary to create a new system of faith for the admission of the Gentiles, in view of the fact that the Synagogue had well-nigh two centuries before opened its door to them and, with the help of the Hellenistic literature, had made a successful propaganda, as even the Gospels testify? (Matt. xxiii. 15) and others, in order that they may reserve the claim of universality for Christianity, deny the existence of uncircumcised proselytes in Judaism, and misconstrue plain Talmudic and other statements referring to God-fearing Gentiles; whereas the very doctrine of Paul concerning the universal faith of Abraham (Rom. iv. 3-18) rests upon the traditional interpretation of Gen. xii. 3 and upon the traditional view which made Abraham the prototype of a missionary bringing the heathen world under the wings of the Shekinah. As a matter of fact, only the Jewish propaganda work along the Mediterranean Sea made it possible for Paul and his associates to establish Christianity among the Gentiles, as is expressly recorded in the Acts (x. 2; xiii. 16, 26, 43, 50; xvi. 14; xvii. 4, 17; xviii. 7); and it is exactly from such synagogue manuals for proselytes as the Didache and the Didascalia that the ethical teachings in the Epistles of Paul and of Peter were derived.

Paul's Christ.

In the foreground of all of Paul's teaching stands his peculiar vision of Christ, to which he constantly refers as his only claim and title to apostleship (I Cor. ix. 1, xv. 8; II Cor. xii. 1-7; Phil. iii. 9; Gal. i. 1, 12, 16). The other apostles saw Jesus in the flesh; Paul saw him when, in a state of entrancement, he was carried into paradise to the third heaven, where he heard "unspeakable words, which it is not lawful for a man to utter" (II Cor. xii. 2-4). Evidently this picture of Christ must have occupied a prominent place in his mind before, just as Meṭaṭron (Mithra) and Akteriel did in the minds of Jewish mystics (see Angelology; Merkabah). To him the Messiah was the son of God in a metaphysical sense, "the image of God" (II Cor. iv. 4; Col. i. 15), "the heavenly Adam" (I Cor. xv. 49; similar to the Philonic or cabalistic Adam Ḳadmon), the mediator between God and the world (I Cor. viii. 6), "the first-born of all creation, for by him were all things created"

(Col. i. 15-17), identical also with the Holy Spirit manifested in Israel's history (I Cor. x. 4; II Cor. iii. 17).

It is, however, chiefly as "the king of glory" (I Cor. ii. 8), as ruler of the powers of light and life eternal, that Christ is to manifest his cosmic power. He has to annihilate Satan or Belial, the ruler of this world of darkness and death, with all his hosts of evil, physical and moral (I Cor. xv. 24-26). Paul's "gnosis" (I Cor. viii. 1, 7; II Cor. ii. 14; I Tim. vi. 20) is a revival of Persian dualism, which makes of all existence, whether physical, mental, or spiritual, a battle between light and darkness (I Thess. v. 4-5; Eph. v. 8-13; Col. i. 13), between flesh and spirit (I Cor. xv. 48; Rom. viii. 6-9), between corruption and life everlasting (I Cor. xv. 50, 53). The object of the Church is to obtain for its members the spirit, the glory, and the life of Christ, its "head," and to liberate them from the servitude of and allegiance to the flesh and the powers of earth. In order to become participants in the salvation that had come and the resurrection that was nigh, the saints were to cast off the works of darkness and to put on the armor of light, the breastplate of love, and the helmet of hope (Rom. xiii. 12; II Cor. x. 4; Eph. vi. 11. I Thess. v. 8; comp. Wisdom v. 17-18; Isa. lix. 17; "the weapons of light of the people of Israel," Pesiḳ, R. 33 [ed. Buber, p. 154]; Targ. Yer. to Ex. xxxiii. 4; "the men of the shields" ["ba'ale teresin"], a name for high-ranking Gnostics, Ber. 27b).

The Crucified Messiah.

How then can this world of perdition and evil, of sin and death, be overcome, and the true life be attained instead? This question, which, according to a Talmudic legend (Tamid 32a), Alexander the Great put to the wise men of the South, was apparently the one uppermost also in the mind of Paul; and in the form of a vision of the crucified Christ the answer came to him to "die in order to live." This vision, seen in his ecstatic state, was to him more than a mere reality: it was the pledge ("'erabon" of the resurrection and the life of which he was in quest. Having seen "the first-born of the resurrection" (I Cor. xv. 20-24; the Messiah is called "the first-born" also in Midr. Teh. to Ps. lxxxix. 28, and in Ex. R. xix. 7), he felt certain of the new life which all "the sons of light" were to share. No sooner had the idea taken hold of him that the world of resurrection, or "the kingdom of God," had come, or would come with the speedy reappearance of the Messiah, than he would invest with higher powers "the elect ones" who were to participate in that life of the spirit. There can be no sin or sensual passion in a world in which the spirit rules. Nor is there need of any law in a realm where men live as angels (comp. "The dead is free from all obligations of the Law," Shab. 30a, 151b; Niddah 61b). To bring back the state of paradise and to undo the sin of Adam, the work of the serpent, which brought death into the world—this seems to have been the dream of Paul. The baptism of the Church, to which sinners and saints, women and men, Jews and Gentiles, were alike invited, suggested to him the putting off of the earthly Adam and the putting on of the heavenly Adam (Rom. vi.). He was certain that by the very power of their faith, which performed all the wonders of the spirit in the Church (I Cor. xii., xv.), would the believers in Christ at the time of his reappearance be also miraculously lifted to the clouds and transformed into spiritual bodies for the life of the resurrection (I Thess. iv.; I Cor. xv.; Rom. viii.). These are the elements of Paul's theology—a system of belief which endeavored to unite all men, but at the expense of sound reason and common sense.

His Missionary Travels.

According to Acts xiii., xiv., xvii-xviii, Paul began working along the traditional Jewish line of proselytizing in the various synagogues where the proselytes of the gate and the Jews met; and only because he failed to win the Jews to his views, encountering strong opposition and persecution from them, did he turn to the Gentile world after he had agreed at a convention with the apostles at Jerusalem to admit the Gentiles into the Church only as proselytes of the gate, that is, after their acceptance of the Noachian laws (Acts xv. 1-31). This presentation of Paul's work is, however, incompatible with the attitude toward the Jews and the Law taken by him in the Epistles. Nor can any historical value be attached to the statement in Gal. ii. 1-10 that, by an agreement with the seeming pillars of the Church, the work was divided between Peter and Paul, the "gospel of circumcision" being committed to the one, and the "gospel of uncircumcision" to the other; as the bitter and often ferocious attacks against both the Jews and the apostles of the Judæo-Christian Church (in Phil. iii. 2 he calls them "dogs") would then have been uncalled for and unpardonable.

In reality Paul had little more than the name of apostle in common with the actual disciples of Jesus. His field of work was chiefly, if not exclusively, among the Gentiles; he looked for a virgin soil wherein to sow the seeds of the gospel; and he succeeded in establishing throughout Greece, Macedonia, and Asia Minor churches in which there were "neither Jews nor Gentiles," but Christians who addressed each other as "brethren" or "saints." Regarding his great missionary journeys as described in the Acts after older documents. As to the chronology, much reliance can not be placed either on Gal. i. 17-ii. 3 or on the Acts with its contradictory statements.

From II Cor. xi. 24-32 (comp. ib. vi. 4; I Cor. iv. 11) it may be learned that his missionary work was beset with uncommon hardships. He labored hard day and night as a tent-maker for a livelihood (Acts xviii. 3; I Thess ii. 9; II Thess, iii. 8; I Cor. iv. 12, ix. 6-18). He says (II Cor. ix.) that more frequently than any other apostle he was imprisoned, punished with stripes, and in peril of death on land and sea; five times he received the thirtynine stripes in the synagogue, obviously for some public transgression of the Law (Deut. xxv. 3); three times was he beaten with rods, probably by the city magistrates (comp. Acts xvi. 22); once he was stoned by the people; and thrice he suffered shipwreck, being in the water a night and a day. In Damascus he was imprisoned by King Aretas at the instigation, not of the Jews, as is stated by modern historians, but of the Jerusalem authorities; and he escaped through being let down in a basket from a window (II Cor. xi. 24-32; comp. Acts xxvii. 41). He was besides this constantly troubled with his disease, which often made him "groan" for deliverance (I Thess. ii. 2, 19-iii. 1; II Cor. i. 8-10, iv. 7-v. 5, xii. 7; Gal. iv. 14).

Paul's Church versus the Synagogue.

In order to understand fully the organization and scope of the Church as mapped out by Paul in his Epistles, a comparison thereof with the organization and the work of the Synagogue, including the Essene community, seems quite proper. Each Jewish community when organized as a congregation possessed in, or together with, its synagogue an institution (1) for common worship, (2) for the instruction of young and old in the Torah, and (3) for systematic charity and benevolence. This threefold work was as a rule placed in charge of men of high social standing, prominent both in learning and in piety. The degree of knowledge and of scrupulousness in the observance of the Torah determined the rank of the members of the Synagogue. Among the members of the Essene brotherhood everyday life with its common meals came under special rules of sanctity, as did their prayers and their charities as well as their visits to the sick, the Holy Spirit being especially invoked by them as a divine factor, preparing them also for the Messianic kingdom of which they lived in expectation. The Christian Church, in adopting the name and form of the Essene Church (Εκκλησία), lent to both the bath and the communion meals a new character.

Influence of the Greek Mysteries.

Paul, the Hellenist, however, knowingly or unknowingly, seems to have taken the heathen cult associations as his pattern while introducing new features into the Church. To him baptism is no longer a symbolic rite suggestive of purification or regeneration, as in Jewish and Judæo-Christian circles, but a mystic rite by which the person that enters the water and emerges again undergoes an actual transformation, dying with Christ to the world of flesh and sin, and rising with him to the world of the spirit, the new life of the resurrection (Rom. vi. 1-10).

Still more is the partaking of the bread and the wine of the communion meal, the so-called "Lord's Supper," rendered the means of a mystic union with Christ, "a participation in his blood and body," exactly as was the Mithraic meal a real participation in the blood and body of Mithra. To Paul, the Holy Spirit itself is not an ethical but a magic power that works sanctification and salvation. It is a mystic substance permeating the Church as a dynamic force, rendering all the members saints, and pouring forth its graces in the various gifts, such as those of prophesying, speaking in tongues, and interpreting voices, and others displayed in teaching and in the administration of charity and similar Church functions (Rom. xii. 4-8; I Cor. xii., xiv).

The Church forms "the body of Christ" not in a figurative sense, but through the same mystic actuality as that by which the participants of heathen cults become, through their mysteries or sacraments, parts of their deities. Such is the expressed view of Paul when he contrasts the "table of Christ" with the "table of the demons" (I Cor. x. 20-21). While Paul borrows from the Jewish propaganda literature, especially the Sibyllines, the idea of the divine wrath striking especially those that commit the capital sins of idolatry and incest (fornication) and acts of violence or fraudulence (Rom. i. 18-32; I Thess. iv. 5), and while he accordingly wishes the heathen to turn from their idols to God, with desire of being saved by His son (I Thess. i. 9-10), his Church has by no means the moral perfection of the human race for its aim and end, as has Judaism. Salvation alone, that is, redemption from a world of perdition and sin, the attainment of a life of incorruption, is the object; yet this is the privilege only of those chosen and predestined "to be conformed to the image of His [God's] son" (Rom. viii. 28-30). It is accordingly not personal merit nor the greater moral effort that secures salvation, but some arbitrary act of divine grace which justifies one class of men and condemns the other (ib. ix.). It is not righteousness, nor even faith—in the Jewish sense of perfect trust in the all-loving and all-forgiving God and Father—which leads to salvation, but faith in the atoning power of Christ's death, which in some mystic or judicial manner justifies the undeserving (Rom. iii. 22, iv., v).

The Mystery of the Cross

Heathen as is the conception of a church securing a mystic union with the Deity by means of sacramental rites, equally pagan is Paul's conception of the crucifixion of Jesus. While he accepts the Judæo-Christian view of the atoning power of the death of Jesus as the suffering Messiah (Rom. iii. 25, viii. 3), the crucifixion of Jesus as the son of God assumes for him at the very beginning the character of a mystery revealed to him, "a stumbling-block to the Jews and folly to the Greeks" (I Cor. i. 23-ii. 2, ii. 7-10). It is to him a cosmic act by which God becomes reconciled to Himself. God sent "his own son in the likeness of sinful flesh" in order to have His wrath appeased by his death. "He spared not his own Son, but delivered him up," so that by his blood all men might be saved (Rom. v. 8; viii. 3, 32). To a Jewish mind trained by rabbinical acumen this is not pure monotheistic, but mythological, thinking. Paul's "Son of God" is, far more than the Logos of Philo, an infringement of the absolute unity of God. While the predicate "God" applied to him in Titus ii. 13 may be put to the account of Paul's school rather than to his own, throughout all the Epistles a share in the divinity is ascribed to Jesus in such a manner as to detract from the glory of God. He is, or is expected to be, called upon as "the Lord" (I Cor. i. 2; Rom. x. 13; Phil. ii. 10-11). Only the pagan idea of the "man-God" or "the second God," the world's artificer, and "son of God" (in Plato, in the Hermes-Tot literature), or the idea of a king of light descending to Hades, as in the Mandæan-Babylonian literature, could have suggested to Paul the conception of a God who surrenders the riches of divinity and descends to the poverty of earthly life in order to become a savior of the human race (I Cor. xv. 28, with ref. to Ps. viii. 6-7; Phil. ii. 6-10). Only from Alexandrian Gnosticism, only from pagan pantheism, could he have derived the idea of the "pleroma," "the fulness" of the Godhead dwelling in Christ as the head of all principality and power, as him who is before all things and in whom all things consist (Col. i. 15-19, ii. 9).

Conflict with Judaism and the Law.

Far then from making antagonism to the Law the starting-point of his apostolic activity, as under the influence of the Epistle to the Romans is assumed by almost all Christian theologians, except the so-called Dutch school of critics, there is intrinsic evidence that Paul's hostile attitude to both the Law and the Jews was the result of his conflicts with the latter and with the other apostles. There is no bitter hostility or antagonism to the Law noticeable in I Thessalonians (ii. 14b-16 is a late interpolation referring to the destruction of the Temple), Colossians, I Corinthians (xv. 56 is obviously interpolated), or II Corinthians (where iii. 6-iv. 4, on closer analysis, also proves to be a late addition disturbing the context); and so little opposition to the Law does Paul show in those epistles first addressed to the Gentiles, that in I Cor. xiv. 21 he quotes as the "law"—that is, Torah in the sense of Revelation—a passage from Isa. xxviii. 11; whereas he avoids the term "law" (νόμος) elsewhere, declaring all statutes to be worthless human teaching (Col. ii. 22).

Antinomianism and Jew-Hatred.

His antinomian theology is chiefly set forth in the Epistle to the Romans, many parts of which, however, are the product of the second-century Church with its fierce hatred of the Jew, e.g., such passages as ii. 21-24, charging the Jews with theft, adultery, sacrilege, and blasphemy, or ix. 22 and xi. 28 (comp. iii. 2). The underlying motive of Paul—the tearing down of the partition-wall between Jew and Gentile—is best expressed in Eph. ii. 14-22, where it is declared that the latter are no longer "gerim" and "toshabim" (A. V. "strangers" and "foreigners"), but "fellow citizens with the saints" of the Church and fully equal members "of the household of God." In order to accomplish his purpose, he argues that just as little as the heathen escapes the wrath of God, owing to the horrible sins he is urged to commit by his clinging to his idols, so little can the Jew escape by his Law, because "the law worketh sin and wrath" (Rom. iv. 15). Instead, indeed, of removing the germ of death brought into the world by Adam, the Law was given only to increase sin and to make all the greater the need of divine mercy which was to come through Christ, the new Adam (ib. v. 15-20).

By further twisting the Biblical words taken from Gen. xv. 6, which he interprets as signifying that Abraham's faith became a saving power to him, and from Gen. xvii. 5, which he takes as signifying that Abraham was to be the father of the Gentiles instead of nations, he argues that the saving grace of God lies in faith (that is, blind belief) and not in the works of the Law. And so he declares faith in Jesus' atoning death to be the means of justification and salvation, and not the Law, which demands servitude, whereas the spirit of Christ makes men children of God (Rom. iv.-viii.). The Pauline Jew-hatred was ever more intensified (see ib. ix.-xi., and comp. ix. 31)—which is clear evidence of a later origin—and culminates in Gal. iii., where, besides the repetition of the argument from Gen. xv. 6 and xvii. 5, the Law is declared, with reference to Deut. xxviii. 26 and Hab. ii. 4 (comp. Rom. i. 17), to be a curse from which the crucified Christ— himself "a curse" according to the Law (Deut. xxi. 23; probably an argument taken up from controversies with the Jews)—was to redeem the believer. Another sophistic argument against the Law, furnished in Gal. iii. 19-24, and often repeated in the second century (Heb. ii. 2; Acts vii. 38, 53; Aristides, "Apologia," xiv. 4), is that the Law was received by Moses as mediator from the angels—a quaint notion based upon Deut. xxxiii. 2, LXX.; comp. Josephus, "Ant." xv. 5, § 3—and that it is not the law of God, which is a life-giving law of righteousness. Furthermore the laws of the Jews and the idolatrous practises of the heathen are placed equally low as mere servitude of" the weak and beggarly elements" (="planets"; Gal. iv. 8-11), whereas those that have put on Christ by baptism have risen above alldistinctions of race, of class, and of sex, and have become children of God and heirs of Abraham (ib. iii. 26-29; what is meant by the words" There shall be neither male nor female" in verse 28 may be learned from Gal. v. 12, where eunuchism is advised; see B. Weiss's note ad loc.).

The Old Testament and the New One

The Pauline school writing under Paul's name, but scarcely Paul himself, worked out the theory, based upon Jer. xxxi. 30-31, that the Church of Christ represents the new covenant in place of the old (Rom. xi. 27; Gal. iv. 24; Heb. viii. 6-13, ix. 15-x. 17; and, following these passages, I Cor. xi. 23-28). Similarly the interpolator of II Cor. iii. 6-iv. 4, in connection with ib. iii. 3, contrasts the Old Testament with the New: the former by the letter of the Law offering but damnation and death because "the veil of Moses" is upon it, preventing God's glory from being seen; the latter being the life-giving spirit offering righteousness, that is, justification, and the light of the knowledge (gnosis) of the glory of God as reflected in the face of Jesus Christ. It is superfluous to state that this Gnostic conception of the spirit has nothing to do with the sound religious principle often quoted from I Cor. iii. 6: "The letter killeth, but the spirit giveth life." The privilege of seeing God's glory as Moses did face to face through a bright mirror held out in I Cor. xiii. 12 (comp. Suk. 45b; Lev. R. i. 14) to the saints in the future is claimed in II Cor. iii. 18 and iv. 4 as a power in the actual possession of the Christian believer. The highest hope of man is regarded as realized by the writer, who looks forward to the heavenly habitation as a release from the earthly tabernacle (II Cor. v. 1-8).

Spurious Writings Ascribed to Paul.

This unhealthy view of life maintained by Paul and his immediate followers was, however, changed by the Church the moment her organization extended over the world. Some epistles were written in the name of Paul with the view of establishing more friendly relations to society and government than Paul and the early Christians had maintained. While Paul warns his church-members not to bring matters of dispute before "the unjust," by which term he means the Gentiles (I Cor. vi. 1; comp. Jew. Encyc. iv. 590), these very heathen powers of Rome are elsewhere praised as the ministers of God and His avengers of wrong (Rom. xiii. 1-7); and while in I Cor. xi. 5 women are permitted to prophesy and to pray aloud in the church provided they have their heads covered, a later chapter, obviously interpolated, states, "Let your women keep silence in the churches" (ib. xiv. 34). So celibacy (ib. vii. 1-8) is declared to be the preferable state, and marriage is allowed only for the sake of preventing fornication (Eph. v. 21-33), while, on the other hand, elsewhere marriage is enjoined and declared to be a mystery or sacrament symbolizing the relation of the Church as the bride to Christ as the bridegroom.

A still greater change in the attitude toward the Law may be noticed in the so-called pastoral epistles. Here the Law is declared to be good as a preventive of wrong-doing (I Tim. i. 8-10), marriage is enjoined, and woman's salvation is declared to consist only in the performance of her maternal duty (ib. ii. 12, 15), while asceticism and celibacy are condemned (ib. iv. 3). So all social relations are regulated in a worldly spirit, and are no longer treated, as in Paul's genuine epistles, in the spirit of otherworldliness (ib. ii.-vi.; II Tim. ii. 4-6; Titus. ii.-iii.). Whether in collecting alms for the poor of the church on Sundays (I Cor. xvi. 2) Paul instituted a custom or simply followed one of the early Christians is not clear; from the "We" source in Acts xx. 7 it appears, however, that the church-members used to assemble for their communion meal in memory of the risen Christ, the Lord's Supper, on the first day of the week—probably because they held the light

created on that day to symbolize the light of the Savior that had risen for them. Little value can be attached to the story in Acts xviii. 18 that Paul brought a Nazarite sacrifice in the Temple, since for him the blood of Christ was the only sacrifice to be recognized. Only at a later time, when Pauline and Judean Christianity were merged, was account again taken, contrary to the Pauline system, of the Mosaic law regarding sacrifice and the priesthood; and so the Epistle to the Hebrews was written with the view of representing Jesus as "the high priest after the order of Melchizedek" who atoned for the sins of the world by his own blood (Heb. iv. 14-v. 10, vii.-xiii.). However, the name of Paul, connected with the epistle by Church tradition, was not attached to it in writing, as was the case with the other epistles.
Paul and Paulinism.

His System of Faith.

He construed a system of faithwhich was at the very outset most radically in conflict with the spirit of Judaism: (1) He substituted for the natural, childlike faith of man in God as the ever-present Helper in all trouble, such as the Old Testament represents it everywhere, a blind, artificial faith prescribed and imposed from without and which is accounted as a meritorious act. (2) He robbed human life of its healthy impulses, the human soul of its faith in its own regenerating powers, of its belief in its own self and in its inherent tendencies to goodness, by declaring Sin to be, from the days of Adam, the all-conquering power of evil ingrained in the flesh, working everlasting doom; the deadly exhalation of Satan, the prince of this world, from whose grasp only Jesus, the resurrected Christ, the prince of the other world, was able to save man. (3) In endeavoring to liberate man from the yoke of the Law, he was led to substitute for the views and hopes maintained by the apocalyptic writers the Christian dogma with its terrors of damnation and hell for the unbeliever, holding out no hope whatsoever for those who would not accept his Christ as savior, and finding the human race divided between the saved and the lost (Rom. ii. 12; I Cor. i. 18; II Cor. ii. 15, iv. 3; II Thess. ii. 10). (4) In declaring the Law to be the begetter of sin and damnation and in putting grace or faith in its place, he ignored the great truth that duty, the divine "command," alone renders life holy; that upon the law of rightcousness all ethics, individual or social, rest. (5) In condemning, furthermore, all human wisdom, reason, and common sense as "folly," and in appealing only to faith and vision, he opened wide the door to all kinds of mysticism and superstition. (6) Moreover, in place of the love greatly extolled in the panegyric in I Cor. xiii.—a chapter which strangely interrupts the connection between ch. xii. and xiv.—Paul instilled into the Church, by his words of condemnation of the Jews as "vessels of wrath fitted for destruction" (Rom. ix. 22; II Cor. iii. 9, iv. 3), the venom of hatred which rendered the earth unbearable for God's priest-people. Probably Paul is not responsible for these outbursts of fanaticism; but Paulinism is. It finally led to that systematic defamation and profanation of the Old Testament and its God by Marcion and his followers which ended in a Gnosticism so depraved and so shocking as to bring about a reaction in the Church in favor of the Old Testament against the Pauline antinomianism. Protestantism revived Pauline views and notions; and with these a biased opinion of Judaism and its Law took possession of Christian writers, and prevails even to the present.

2.2 Simon Cephas (Saint Peter)

The first of the Twelve Apostles; the chief disciple of Jesus and head of the early Church. His life became at an early stage the subject of popular legends, which extended even to his name. Besides the name of Simon, which had come into use in place of the Biblical "Simeon," he had, in accordance with the custom of the time, the second name of "Kaipha" (Aramaic equivalent for "rock"; whence the Latin "Petrus," from "petra" = "rock"). As legend would have it afterward, Jesus gave him this second name to signify that upon him, as upon a rock, his church should be built (Luke vi. 14; Matt. xvi. 18; John i. 42; Mark iii. 12 significantly omits the reason; comp. Midr. Yalk. i. 766 on Num. xxiii. 9: "Upon Abraham as top of the rocks God said I shall build my kingdom"). Simon, the son of Jonah (John i. 42; Matt. xvi. 17), was, like his brother Andrew, a fisherman of Capernaum, or of Bethsaida near by (John i. 44), on the Lake of Gennesaret in Galilee.

According to John i. 35-42, Jesus, at the time of his own baptism in the Jordan by John the Baptist, met the two brothers as disciples of John, and afterward bade them follow him to Galilee. According to the synoptic Gospels, which slightly differ from one another (Matt. iv. 18-22; Mark i. 16-20; Luke v. 1-11), Jesus met them on the Lake of Galilee at the beginning of his career, while they were casting nets from their boats, and told them to follow him and become "fishers of men." The house of Peter in Capernaum is represented by the synoptic Gospels as the starting-point and center of Jesus' activity. Peter's mother-in-law is the first person mentioned as having been cured by Jesus, and to Peter's house all the sick and demoniacs were brought in the evening of the Sabbath to be healed (Mark i. 29-34 and parallels). "Simon and they that were with him followed" Jesus thence throughout Galilee (Mark i. 36-39), and the latter, on his return, again stayed in Peter's house, and ever afterward did there his work of healing in Capernaum (Mark ii. 1, 15; iii. 20; ix. 33). Peter is the favorite disciple, who is always found at the side of Jesus (ib. v. 37; ix. 2; xiv. 33, 54), and who is foremost in addressing him or acting for him (ib. ix. 5, xiv 29-31; Luke viii. 45, xii. 41, xxii. 8).

He Pronounces Jesus the Messiah.

As the main reason, however, for the prominence (Matt. x. 2) and, afterward, the primateship accorded to Peter, the fact is stated that in answer to Jesus' question, "Whom say ye that I am," he, alone of all the disciples, declared him to be the Messiah, "the anointed of God" (Matt. xvi. 13-20; Luke ix. 18-21; Mark viii. 27-30); and, according to Matthew, the "keys of the kingdom of heaven," with the power of Binding and Loosing, were given to him by Jesus on that occasion. The real history underlying this legend is that Peter is mentioned by Paul (I Cor. xv. 5) and in older traditions (Mark xvi. 7; John xxi. 1-21; comp. Matt. xxviii. 16; Luke xxiv. 12, 34) as the first among the disciples who "saw" the departed Christ. On the other hand, while Jesus was alive Peter is represented as having encountered severe rebukes from his master for his lack of faith and his false zeal, as well as for his listlessness, for his antagonistic attitude at first, and for his cowardly fear at the critical hour (Mark viii. 32, xiv. 30-42, 54-72; Luke xxii. 31; John xviii. 10-11). As a matter of fact, Peter early became as much an object of popular legend as did Jesus his master. Thus, in Matt. xiv. 22-33 Peter walks on the water in the same manner as Jesus does (the original legend is found in John xxi. 1-24; comp. Luke v. 3-9); in the transfiguration story (Matt. xvii. 1-8) he stands out prominently; and he plays the chief rôle in the story of the coin found in the fish's mouth (Matt. xvii. 24-27). Both Matthew (xv. 15, xvii. 21) and Luke (viii. 25, xxii. 8), representing the older tradition, put him in the foreground, while the Pauline and Johannean traditions pushed him more and more into the background (John xiii. 24, xxi. 21, et al.).

Head of the Church.

While the acts recorded of Peter (in Acts i. 15, ii. 14 et seq., iii. 1-11, iv. 8 et seq., v. 29 et seq., viii. 14 et seq., ix. 32, x. 1-xi. 18, xv. 4 et seq.) can not claim historical character, the fact can not be questioned that he occupied the position of head of the Church of Jerusalem. As such, with his authority as the foremost disciple of Jesus, he exerted a determining influence upon thecharacter and organization of the Church; so much so that the Judæo-Christians in Corinth called themselves, in opposition to the church Paul had organized there, the church "of Cephas" (I Cor. i. 12). At the same time he was regarded only as one of the Twelve Apostles (Acts i. 14, ii. 14, v. 2, vi. 2), and in their name he speaks (Acts iv. 8, 19; v. 2, 29) in defense of the Church and hurls forth his anathemas against the transgressors (Acts viii. 20), the Holy Spirit always prompting his speeches and his acts. But he was also sent forth as a missionary through the land of Judea and Samaria (ib. viii. 14, ix. 32, x. 9), where many stories circulated among the people of the supernatural cures he performed, of his miraculous escapes from prison (ib. iii., ix., xii.), and of conversions of Gentiles: these could hardly have been inventions of the writer of the Acts. From I Cor. ix. 5 it may be learned that he, like other apostles, used to travel with his wife on his missionary journeys while he was supported by the Church.

Regarding the encounter of Peter with Simon Magus (Acts viii. 14-25). The story of the conversion of Cornelius, the Roman centurion in Cæsarea (Acts x. 1-45), in anticipation of which Peter was told in a vision to partake of the food of the heathen in order to win him to a belief in Christ, seems to indicate an early split in the Judæo-Christian Church rather than an intention on the part of the writer to identify Paulinism with that Church. It was probably independently of Paul that the question arose among the Judæo-Christians as to whether certain concessions to the proselytes of the gate were not advisable in the interest of the Church propaganda. Both the traditional and the progressive currents of thought in the Church find expression in the Cornelius story on the one hand, and, on the other, in the rather mythical account of the apostolic council presided over by James, the leader of the conservative side, in which Peter appears as the prime mover (Acts xv. 7 et seq.), and by which the observance of the Noachian laws is insisted upon as the condition of admitting proselytes.

Peter and Paul.

It is also of interest to note his declaration that the greatest commandment is "fear the Lord thy God . . . and serve Him" (Deut. x. 12), and to observe the harmony between his teaching and that of the Jewish Didache and Didascalia: "As you would not like to be murdered yourself, nor to have your wife commit adultery, nor to have your things stolen from you, so do not these things to others" ("Homilies," vii. 4, xvii. 7). In the original "Preaching of Peter," thirty, or sixty, or one hundred commandments for the Jewish converts are singled out (comp. Ḥul. 92a; Midr. Teh. to Ps. ii. 5; Gen. R. xcviii. 14). "Man is the true image of God" (not Christ only!); "The pure soul bears His likeness"; "therefore we must honor God's image by offering food to the hungry and clothing to the naked, caring for the sick, sheltering the stranger, visiting him who is in prison, and affording the "needy all the help we can" ("Homilies," xi. 4, xvii. 7). Accordingly, Peter acts in regard to food, prayers, fasts, and ablutions exactly as does a pious Jew or Essene ("Recognitiones," i. 19; ii. 19, 72; v. 36). Many similar passages show the close relation of this teaching, attributed to Peter, to that of the rabbinical schools.

Little value can, according to this, be attached to Gal. ii. 9 (a spurious epistle; see Saul of Tarsus), where Peter is charged by Paul with hypocrisy. That a disagreement in certain matters arose between the two disciples is certain; but whether it was Peter or Paul who was inconsistent and wavering still remains a matter of dispute.

According to the Clementines, Peter stayed at Cæsarea a long time, and then went, by way of Tripolis, to Rome. In John xxi. 19 his martyrdom is predicted to him by Jesus (comp. I Epistle of Clement of Rome, v.). Regarding his stay in Rome, reliance must be placed upon Eusebius ("Hist.Eccl." ii. 1; comp. iii. 39, 15); certainly the account of his meeting Philo (ib. ii. 17) and Paul in Rome is mythical.

His Supposed Writings.

According to the testimony of Papias (Eusebius, l.c.), Peter was not able to write expositions of his system of faith; the epistles that bear his name are products of the second century. The First Epistle, addressed to the (Pauline) churches of Asia, betrays the style and influence of the Pauline school; it was written during the persecutions of the Christians in the East in the second century, and, judging from iv. 3, the writer was a converted Gentile, not a born Jew. Possibly the whole epistle is based upon an older Judæo-Christian document (ii. 11-iii. 16, v. 1-12) that addressed its monitions to "the strangers and sojourners" (ii. 11; comp. i. 1). The epistle claims to have been written in Rome (v. 12). The Second Epistle, which shows in iii. 1 its dependence upon the First, and an acquaintance with apocalyptic literature, is a strong arraignment of the abuses of the Church due to Gnostic libertinism preached in some of the Pauline churches (i. 16, ii. 1-2, iii. 14-18); at the same time it endeavors to reconcile Paul's teachings with Peter's (iii. 15).

The so-called Gospel of Peter, of which fragments were found in Akhmym, Upper Egypt, in the year 1886-87 is of peculiar interest to the Jewish reader, inasmuch as, to judge from the fragments containing the story of the crucifixion, the whole is a product of fierce hatred toward the Jews, even to a greater extent than is the Fourth Gospel. Peter the Jew was made the mouthpiece of the Church at a time when hostility to his kinsmen had become the distinction of the orthodox Christian.

The Apocalypse of Peter.

The Apocalypse of Peter, a fragment of which was found at Akhmym together with the fragments of the Gospel of Peter, has been identified by Harnack (l.c.) with the one known to Clement of Alexandria

("Eclogi," 41, 48, 49) and other Church Fathers. It seems to have drawn its material from a similar Jewish apocalypse. It shows no traces of Jew-hatred. In it Peter speaks as having, with the other apostles, had intercourse with the departed Jesus on the mountain, and as having been shown by him the reward of the just in Paradise and the punishment of the wicked in Gehenna. Among those subjected to great torture by fire and by scourging are mentioned "those that made idols of wood for themselves and worshiped them instead of God"; also the usurers, the rich that fail to aid the needy, and those "who have forsaken the way of God." The excruciating pains which the wicked suffer wrest from them the confession: "O God, Thy judgment is righteous" (ed. Harnack, l.c. pp. 25, 33, 34). The whole work furnishes proof that its writer was still under Jewish influence, if he did not, indeed, simply take his material from a Jewish apocalypse and adapt it to the new creed.

2.3 Christians Beginnings. The Persecution of the Christians

TACITUS, The Annals of Imperial Rome Book XV, chapter 47 (A.D. 64) [during the Great Fire of Rome]

"...neither human resources, nor imperial generosity, nor appeasement of the gods, eliminated the sinister suspicion that the fire had been deliberately started. To stop the rumor, NERO, made scapegoats--and punished with every refinement the notoriously depraved CHRISTIANS (as they were popularly called). Their originator, CHRIST, had been executed in Tiberius' reign by the Procurator of Judaea, PONTIUS PILATUS (governor from 26 to 36 A.D.). But in spite of this temporary setback, the deadly superstition had broken out again, not just in Judaea (where the mischief had started) but even in Rome. All degraded and shameful practices collect and flourish in the capital. First, NERO had the self-admitted Christians arrested. Then, on their information, large numbers of others were condemned--not so much for starting fires as because of their hatred for the human race. Their deaths were made amusing. Dressed in wild animals' skins, they were torn to pieces by dogs, or crucified, or made into torches to be seton fire after dark as illumination.... Despite their guilt as Christians, and the ruthless punishment it deserved, the victims were pitied. For it was felt that they were being sacrificed to one man's brutality rather than to the national interest."

SUETONIUS, Life of the Emperor Claudius, chapter 25:
"Since the Jews were constantly causing disturbances at the instigation of CHRESTUS, he expelled them from the city..."

SUETONIUS, Life of the Emperor Nero, chapter 16:
"[After the Great Fire]...punishments were also inflicted on the CHRISTIANS, a sect professing a new and mischievous religious belief...."

PLINY (Governor of the Province of Bithynia-Pontus) Epistles Book 10 #96 addressed to the Emperor Trajan (ca. 112 A.D.)
"...I have never been present at an examination of Christians. So, I do not know the nature or the extent of the punishments usually dealt out to them, nor the grounds for starting an investigation and how far it should be carried...For the moment this is the line I have taken with all persons brought before me on the charge of being Christians. I have asked them in person if they are Christians; if they admit it, I repeat the question a second and athird time, with a warning of the punishment awaiting them. If they persist, I order them to be led away for punishment; for whatever the nature of their admission, I am convinced that their stubbornness (contumacia) and unshakeable obstinacy ought to be punished. There have been others similarly fanatical who are Roman citizens; I have entered them on the list of persons to be sent to Rome for punishment.... I considered that I should dismiss any who denied that they were or ever had been Christians, once they had repeated after me a formula of invocation to the gods and had made offerings of wine and incense to your statue (which I had ordered to be brought into court for this purpose along with images of the gods), and furthermore had ursed the name of Christ. Real Christians (I understand) can never be induced to do these things....They declared that the sum total of their guilt or error amounted to no more than this: they had met regularly before dawn on a fixed day to chant verses alternately among themselves in honor of Christ as if to a god, and also to bind themselves by oath, not for any criminal purpose, but to abstain from theft, robbery and adultery, to commit no breach of trust and not to refuse toreturn a deposit upon

demand. After this ceremony it had been their custom to disperse and later to take food of an ordinary harmless kind. But they had in fact given this up since my edict, issued on your instructions which banned all political societies. This made me decide it was all the more necessary to extract the truth from two slave women (whom they call `deaconesses' bytorture. I found nothing but a degenerate sort of cult carried to xtravagant lengths... I have therefore postponed any further examination and hastened toconsult you..."

THE EMPEROR TRAJAN TO PLINY:
"You have followed the right course of procedure, my dear Pliny, in your examination of the cases of persons charged with being Christians. For it is impossible to lay down a general rule to a fixed formula. These people must not be hunted out. But if they are brought before you and the charge against them is proved true, they must be punished. But in the case of anyone who denies that he is a Christian, and makes it clear that he is not, by offering prayers to our gods, he is to be pardoned as a result of his repentance--however suspect his conduct may have been in the past. But pamphlets circulated anonymously must play NO part in any accusation. They create the worst precedent, and are quite out of keeping with the spirit of our age."

2.4 The Teaching of the Lord to the Gentiles by the Twelve Apostles (The Didache, 2nd Century CE)

Didache 1:1
There are two ways, one of life and one of death, and there is a great difference between the two ways.
Didache 1:2
The way of life is this. First of all, thou shalt love the God that made thee; secondly, Thy neighbor as thyself. And all things whatsoever thou wouldst not have befall thyself, neither do thou unto another.
Didache 1:3
Now of these words the doctrine is this. Bless them that curse you, and pray for your enemies and fast for them that persecute you; for

what thank is it, if ye love them that love you? Do not even the Gentiles the same? But do ye love them that hate you that hate you, and ye shall not have an enemy.
Didache 1:4
Abstain thou from fleshly and bodily lusts. If any man give thee a blow on thy right cheek, turn to him the other also, and thou shalt be perfect; If a man impress thee to go with him one mile, go with him twain; if a man take away thy cloak, give him thy coat also; if a man take away from thee that which is thy own, ask it not back, for neither art thou able.
Didache 1:5
To every man that asketh of thee give, and ask not back for the Father desireth that gifts be given to all from His own bounties. Blessed is he that giveth according to the commandment; for he is guiltless. Woe to him that receiveth; for, if a man receiveth having need, he is guiltless; but he that hath no need shall give satisfaction why and wherefore he received and being put in confinement he shall be examined concerning the deeds that he hath done, and he shall not come out thence until he hath given back the last farthing.
Didache 1:6
Yea, as touching this also it is said; Let thine alms sweat into thine hands, until thou have learnt to whom to give.
Didache 2:1
And this is the second commandment of the teaching.
Didache 2:2
Thou shalt do no murder, thou shalt not commit adultery, thou shalt not corrupt boys, thou shalt not commit fornication, thou shalt not steal, thou shalt not deal in magic, thou shalt do no sorcery, thou shalt not murder a child by abortion nor kill them when born, thou shalt not covet thy neighbors goods,
Didache 2:3
thou shalt not perjure thyself, thou shalt not bear false witness, thou shalt not speak evil, thou shalt not cherish a grudge,
Didache 2:4
thou shalt not be double-minded nor double-tongued; for the double tongue is a snare of death.
Didache 2:5
Thy word shall not be false or empty, but fulfilled by action.

Didache 2:6
Thou shalt not be avaricious nor a plunderer nor a hypocrite nor ill-tempered nor proud. Thou shalt not entertain an evil design against thy neighbor.
Didache 2:7
Thou shalt not hate any man but some thou shalt reprove, and for others thou shalt pray, and others thou shalt love more than thy life.
Didache 3:1
My child, flee from every evil and everything that resembleth it.
Didache 3:2
Be not angry, for anger leadeth to murder, nor jealous nor contentious nor wrathful; for of all these things murders are engendered.
Didache 3:3
My child, be not lustful, for lust leadeth to fornication, neither foul-speaking neither with uplifted eyes; for of all these things adulteries are engendered.
Didache 3:4
My child, be no dealer in omens, since it leads to idolatry, nor an enchanter nor an astrologer nor a magician, neither be willing to look at them; for from all these things idolatry is engendered.
Didache 3:5
My child, be not a liar, since lying leads to theft, neither avaricious neither vainglorious; for from all these things thefts are engendered.
Didache 3:6
My child, be not a murmurer, since it leadeth to blasphemy, neither self-willed neither a thinker of evil thoughts; for from all these things blasphemies are engendered.
Didache 3:7
But be meek, since the meek shall inherit the earth.
Didache 3:8
Be long-suffering and pitiful and guileless and quiet and kindly and always fearing the words which thou hast heard.
Didache 3:9
Thou shalt not exalt thyself, neither shalt thou admit boldness into thy soul. Thy soul shall not cleave together with the lofty, but with the righteous and humble shalt thou walk.
Didache 3:10
The accidents that befall thee thou shalt receive as good, knowing that nothing is done without God.

Didache 4:1
My child, thou shalt remember him that speaketh unto thee the word of God night and day, and shalt honor him as the Lord; for whencesoever the Lordship speaketh, there is the Lord.
Didache 4:2
Moreover thou shalt seek out day by day the persons of the saints, that thou mayest find rest in their words.
Didache 4:3
Thou shalt not make a schism, but thou shalt pacify them that contend; thou shalt judge righteously, thou shalt not make a difference in a person to reprove him for transgressions.
Didache 4:4
Thou shalt not doubt whether a thing shall be or not be.
Didache 4:5
Be not thou found holding out thy hands to receive, but drawing them in as to giving.
Didache 4:6
If thou hast ought passing through thy hands, thou shalt give a ransom for thy sins.
Didache 4:7
Thou shalt not hesitate to give, neither shalt thou murmur when giving; for thou shalt know who is the good paymaster of thy reward.
Didache 4:8
Thou shalt not turn away from him that is in want, but shalt make thy brother partaker in all things, and shalt not say that anything is thy own. For if ye are fellow-partakers in that which is imperishable, how much rather in the things which are perishable?
Didache 4:9
Thou shalt not withhold thy hand from thy son or from thy daughter, but from their youth thou shalt teach them the fear of God.
Didache 4:10
Thou shalt not command thy bondservant or thine handmaid in thy bitterness who trust in the same God as thyself, lest haply they should cease to fear the God who is over both of you; for He cometh, not to call men with respect of persons, but He cometh to those whom the Spirit hath prepared.
Didache 4:11
But ye, servants, shall be subject unto your masters, as to a type of God, in shame and fear.

Didache 4:12
Thou shalt hate all hypocrisy, and everything that is not pleasing to the Lord.
Didache 4:13
Thou shalt never forsake the commandments of the Lord but shalt keep those things which thou hast received, neither adding to them nor taking away from them.
Didache 4:14
In church thou shalt confess thy transgressions, and shalt not betake thyself to prayer with an evil conscience. This is the way of life.
Didache 5:1
But the way of death is this. First of all, it is evil and full of a curse; murders, adulteries, lusts, fornications, thefts, idolatries, magical arts, witchcrafts, plunderings, false witnessings, hypocrisies, doubleness of heart, treachery, pride, malice, stubbornness, covetousness, foul—speaking, jealousy, boldness, exaltation, boastfulness;
Didache 5:2
persecutors of good men, hating truth, loving a lie, not perceiving the reward of righteousness, not cleaving to the good nor to righteous judgment, wakeful not for that which is good but for that which is evil-from whom gentleness and forbearance stand aloof; loving vain things, pursuing a recompense, not pitying the poor man, not toiling for him that is oppressed with toil, not recognizing Him that made them, murderers of children, corrupters of the creatures of God, turning away from him that is in want, oppressing him that is afflicted, advocates of the wealthy, unjust judges of the poor, altogether sinful. May ye be delivered, my children, from all these things.
Didache 6:1
See lest any man lead you astray from this way of righteousness, for he teacheth thee apart from God.
Didache 6:2
For if thou art able to bear the whole yoke of the Lord, thou shalt be perfect; but if thou art not able, do that which thou art able.
Didache 6:3
But concerning eating, bear that which thou art able; yet abstain by all means from meat sacrificed to idols; for it is the worship of dead gods.

Didache 7:1
But concerning baptism, thus shall ye baptize. Having first recited all these things, baptize in the name of the Father and of the Son and of the Holy Spirit in living (running) water.
Didache 7:2
But if thou hast not living water, then baptize in other water; and if thou art not able in cold, then in warm.
Didache 7:3
But if thou hast neither, then pour water on the head thrice in the name of the Father and of the Son and of the Holy Spirit.
Didache 7:4
But before the baptism let him that baptizeth and him that is baptized fast, and any others also who are able; and thou shalt order him that is baptized to fast a day or two before.
Didache 8:1
And let not your fastings be with the hypocrites, for they fast on the second and the fifth day of the week; but do ye keep your fast on the fourth and on the preparation (the sixth) day.
Didache 8:2
Neither pray ye as the hypocrites, but as the Lord commanded in His Gospel, thus pray ye:
Our Father, which art in heaven,
hallowed be Thy name;
Thy kingdom come;
Thy will be done,
as in heaven, so also on earth;
give us this day our daily bread;
and forgive us our debt,
as we forgive our debtors;
and lead us not into temptation,
but deliver us from the evil one;
for Thine is the power and the glory for ever and ever.
Didache 8:3
Three times in the day pray ye so.
Didache 9:1
But as touching the eucharistic thanksgiving give ye thanks thus.
Didache 9:2
First, as regards the cup:
We give Thee thanks, O our Father,

for the holy vine of Thy son David,
which Thou madest known unto us
through Thy Son Jesus;
Thine is the glory for ever and ever.
Didache 9:3
Then as regarding the broken bread:
We give Thee thanks, O our Father,
for the life and knowledge
which Thou didst make known unto us
through Thy Son Jesus;
Thine is the glory for ever and ever.
Didache 9:4
As this broken bread was scattered upon the mountains
and being gathered together became one,
so may Thy Church be gathered together
from the ends of the earth into Thy kingdom;
for Thine is the glory and the power
through Jesus Christ for ever and ever.
Didache 9:5
But let no one eat or drink of this eucharistic thanksgiving, but they that have been baptized into the name of the Lord; for concerning this also the Lord hath said: Give not that which is holy to the dogs.
Didache 10:1
And after ye are satisfied thus give ye thanks:
Didache 10:2
We give Thee thanks, Holy Father,
for Thy holy name,
which Thou hast made to tabernacle in our hearts, and for the knowledge and faith and immortality,
which Thou hast made known unto us
through Thy Son Jesus;
Thine is the glory for ever and ever.
Didache 10:3
Thou, Almighty Master,
didst create all things for Thy name's sake,
and didst give food and drink unto men for enjoyment, that they might render thanks to Thee;
but didst bestow upon us spiritual food and drink and eternal life through Thy Son.

Didache 10:4
Before all things we give Thee thanks
that Thou art powerful;
Thine is the glory for ever and ever.
Didache 10:5
Remember, Lord, Thy Church
to deliver it from all evil
and to perfect it in Thy love;
and gather it together from the four winds- even the Church which has been sanctified-
into Thy kingdom which Thou hast prepared for it; for Thine is the power and the glory for ever and ever.
Didache 10:6
May grace come and may this world pass away.
Hosanna to the God of David.
If any man is holy, let him come;
if any man is not, let him repent.
Maran Atha. Amen.
Didache 10:7
But permit the prophets to offer thanksgiving as much as they desire.
Didache 11:1
Whosoever therefore shall come and teach you all these things that have been said before, receive him;
Didache 11:2
but if the teacher himself be perverted and teach a different doctrine to the destruction thereof, hear him not; but if to the increase of righteousness and the knowledge of the Lord, receive him as the Lord.
Didache 11:3
But concerning the apostles and prophets, so do ye according to the ordinance of the Gospel.
Didache 11:4
Let every apostle, when he cometh to you, be received as the Lord;
Didache 11:5
but he shall not abide more than a single day, or if there be need, a second likewise; but if he abide three days, he is a false prophet.
Didache 11:6
And when he departeth let the apostle receive nothing save bread, until he findeth shelter; but if he ask money, he is a false prophet.

Didache 11:7
And any prophet speaking in the Spirit ye shall not try neither discern; for every sin shall be forgiven, but this sin shall not be forgiven.
Didache 11:8
Yet not every one that speaketh in the Spirit is a prophet, but only if he have the ways of the Lord. From his ways therefore the false prophet and the prophet shall be recognized.
Didache 11:9
And no prophet when he ordereth a table in the Spirit shall eat of it; otherwise he is a false prophet.
Didache 11:10
And every prophet teaching the truth, if he doeth not what he teacheth, is a false prophet.
Didache 11:11
And every prophet approved and found true, if he doeth ought as an outward mystery typical of the Church, and yet teacheth you not to do all that he himself doeth, shall not be judged before you; he hath his judgment in the presence of God; for in like manner also did the prophets of old time.
Didache 11:12
And whosoever shall say in the Spirit, Give me silver or anything else, ye shall not listen to him; but if he tell you to give on behalf of others that are in want, let no man judge him.
Didache 12:1
But let every one that cometh in the name of the Lord be received; and then when ye have tested him ye shall know him, for ye shall have understanding on the right hand and on the left.
Didache 12:2
If the comer is a traveler, assist him, so far as ye are able; but he shall not stay with you more than two or three days, if it be necessary.
Didache 12:3
But if he wishes to settle with you, being a craftsman, let him work for and eat his bread.
Didache 12:4
But if he has no craft, according to your wisdom provide how he shall live as a Christian among you, but not in idleness.
Didache 12:5
If he will not do this, he is trafficking upon Christ. Beware of such men.

Didache 13:1
But every time prophet desiring to settle among you is worthy of his food.
Didache 13:2
In like manner a true teacher is also worthy, like the workman, of his food.
Didache 13:3
Every firstfruit then of the produce of the wine-vat and of the threshing- floor, of thy oxen and of thy sheep, thou shalt take and give as the firstfruit to the prophets; for they are your chief-priests.
Didache 13:4
But if ye have not a prophet, give them to the poor.
Didache 13:5
If thou makest bread, take the firstfruit and give according to the commandment.
Didache 13:6
In like manner, when thou openest a jar of wine or of oil, take the firstfruit and give to the prophets;
Didache 13:7
yea and of money and raiment and every possession take the firstfruit, as shall seem good to thee, and give according to the commandment.
Didache 14:1
And on the Lord's own day gather yourselves together and break bread and give thanks, first confessing your transgressions, that your sacrifice may be pure.
Didache 14:2
And let no man, having his dispute with his fellow, join your assembly until they have been reconciled, that your sacrifice may not be defiled;
Didache 14:3
for this sacrifice it is that was spoken of by the Lord; In every place and at every time offer me a pure sacrifice; for I ama a great king, saith the Lord, and My name is wonderful among the nations.
Didache 15:1
Appoint for yourselves therefore bishops and deacons worthy of the Lord, men who are meek and not lovers of money, and true and approved; for unto you they also perform the service of the prophets and teachers.

Didache 15:2
Therefore despise them not; for they are your honorable men along with the prophets and teachers.
Didache 15:3
And reprove one another, not in anger but in peace, as ye find in the Gospel; and let no one speak to any that has gone wrong towards his neighbor, neither let him hear a word from you, until he repent.
Didache 15:4
But your prayers and your almsgiving and all your deeds so do ye as ye find it in the Gospel of our Lord.
Didache 16:1
Be watchful for your life; let your lamps not be quenched and your loins not ungirdled, but be ye ready; for ye know not the hour the hour in which our Lord cometh.
Didache 16:2
And ye shall gather yourselves together frequently, seeking what is fitting for your souls; for the whole time of your faith shall not profit you, if ye be not perfected at the last season.
Didache 16:3
For in the last days the false prophets and corrupters shall be multiplied, and the sheep shall be turned into wolves, and love shall be turned into hate.
Didache 16:4
For as lawlessness increaseth, they shall hate one another and shall persecute and betray. And then the world-deceiver shall appear as a son of God; and shall work signs and wonders, and the earth shall be delivered into his hands; and he shall do unholy things, which have never been since the world began.
Didache 16:5
Then all created mankind shall come to the fire of testing, and many shall be offended and perish; but they that endure in their faith shall be saved by the Curse Himself.
Didache 16:6
And then shall the signs of the truth appear; first a sign of a rift in the heaven, then a sign of a voice of a trumpet, and thirdly a resurrection of the dead;
Didache 16:7
yet not of all, but as it was said The Lord shall come and all His saints with Him.

Didache 16:8
Then shall the world see the Lord coming upon the clouds of heaven.

2.5 Oxyrhynchus hymn

Oxyrhynchus was among Egypt's most prominent cities under its Hellenistic and Roman rulers. It was a prosperous regional capital, third city of Egypt, and home town of Athenaeus. Today its name is el-Bahnasa. The town lies roughly 300 km south of the coastal metropolis of Alexandria, or 160 km south-west of Cairo (ancient Memphis).

They have yielded the largest collection of ancient papyrus ever discovered. Among these papyrus fragments is the earliest known Christian hymn, dating from the second or third century AD. Here are the words of the hymn in the original Greek, together with the English translation:

neo sigato, d' astra phasesphora lampesthon amon rhothion pasai nnounton d'hemon patera k'hyion agion pneuma ai dynameis epiphounounton Amen tos, ainos aei kai doxa theoi Empire, eri monoi panton agathon.	...Let it be si Let the Luminous stars not s Let the winds and all the noisy rivers down; And as we hymn the Father, the Son and Holy S Amen Let all the powers add "Amen Ar praise always, and glory to Amen Amen The sole giver of good th Amen Amen.

2.6 Eusebius and the Early Church

The History of the Church, (to A.D. 324) was written ca. 325 A.D., by the bishop of Caesarea Maritima in Palestine, who was a friend and (ca. 337-339) the biographer of the Emperor Constantine.

Book 1.1: Then there was JAMES who was known as the brother of the Lord. For he too was called Joseph's son, and Joseph Christ's father, though in fact the Virgin was his betrothed, and before they came together she was found to be with child by the Holy Spirit, as the inspired Gospel narrative tells us. This James, as the, whom the early Christians surnamed the Righteous' because of his outstanding virtue, was the first (as the records tell us) to be elected to the episcopal throne of the Jerusalem church.... Clement, in Outlines Book VI, puts it thus, 'Peter, James and John, after the Ascension of the Saviour, did not claim pre-eminence because the Saviour had especially honored them, but chose James the Righteous as Bishop of Jerusalem.... James the Righteous, John, and Peter were entrusted by the Lord after his resurrection with the higher knowledge. They imparted it to the other apostles, and the other apostles to the seventy...'

II.23: Such is the story of JAMES, to whom is attributed the first of the 'general' epistles. Admittedly its authenticity is doubted, since few early writers refer to it, any more than to 'Jude's', which is also one of the seven called general. But the fact remains that these two, like the others, have been regularly used in very many churches.

III.11: After the martyrdom of JAMES and the capture of Jerusalem which instantly followed, there is a firm tradition that those of the apostles and disciples of the Lord who were still alive assembled from all parts together with those who, humanly speaking, were kinsmen of the Lord--for most of them were still living. Then they all discussed together whom they should choose as a fit person to succeed James, and voted unanimously that SIMEON, son of the Cleophas mentioned in the gospel narrative (John 19:25) was a fit person to occupy the throne of the Jerusalem church. He was, so it is said, a cousin of the Saviour, for Hegesippus tells us that Cleophas was Joseph's brother.

III.19: The [Emperor Domitian] ordered the execution of all who were of David's line, and there is an old and firm tradition that a group of heretics accused the descendants of Jude--the brother, humanly speaking, of the Saviour--on the ground that they were of David's line and related to Christ himself. HEGESIPPUS states:

And there still survived of the Lord's family the grandsons of JUDE, who was said to be his brother, humanly speaking. These were informed against as being of David's line, and brought by the evocatus before Domitian Caesar, who was as afraid of the advent of Christ as Herod had been. Domitian asked them if they were descended from David, and they admitted it. Then he asked them what property they owned and what funds they had at their disposal. They replied that they had only 9,000 denarii between them, half belonging to each. This they said was not available in cash, but was the estimated value of only 25 acres of land, from which they raised the money to pay their taxes and the funds to support themselves by their own toil... On hearing this, Domitian found no fault with them, but despising them as beneath his notice let them go free and issued orders terminating the persecution of the church. On their release they became leaders of the churches, both because they had borne testimony and because they were of the Lord's family. And thanks to the establishment of peace they lived on into Trajan's time (98-117).

2.7 Pagan Influences in Early Christianity

Like Osiris, Dionysus, Attis, Mithras and many others, Jesus was a God shaped like a man, walking, talking, eating, but still having magic God powers. Like the other Pagan godmen Jesus was a subordinate God, son of the great universal God, miraculously conceived in a mortal woman, living for a while on Earth rather than in Heaven, helping people. Studing the early Christendom we have to analysis all the influences of the pagan religions, and how they were mixed with ascetics Judaism, and Gnosticism, in order to produce early Christianity.

We can review some examples:

a. Mithras; he was the head deity of Mithraism. Trying to piece together the actual legends relating to Mithras is difficult as the earliest evidence relating to him is only found in artistic reliefs- the original texts regarding Mithraism have long since been lost, leaving behind only fragments. For this discussion, we will focus on Roman Mithraism as this is the Mithras the critics claim as being the inspiration for Jesus. As stated previously, there is no mention of Jesus being born in a cave anywhere in the canonical Scriptures. As for Mithras, he also was not born in a cave but from solid rock. Many religious festivals were consolidated into one holiday to coincide with the winter solstice. Christmas is only celebrated on December 25th due to this tradition. This argument already proves to be insignificant as there is nothing in the Scriptures which mentions this date.

The earliest existing account of Mithras' birth is found in a relief depicting him emerging from a rock with the assistance of men who certainly appear to be shepherds. There is no mention of a virgin birth in Mithraism. The earliest reliefs depict a fully-mature Mithras emerging from a rock (as shown in three illustrations to the left). Mithras did not have twelve disciples, but I can relate a far-fetched similarity to this allegation. In two of the reliefs to the left, Mithras is surrounded by the twelve signs of the zodiac. Claiming Mithras had twelve disciples because there are twelve signs of the zodiac is the connection critics try to make. The critics simply see twelve beings and claim the figures are disciples. Some go as far to defend their position by mimicking Franz Cumont's theory, claiming the figures were actually Mithras' twelve disciples dressed up in zodiac costumes! How they can make this connection is unknown as no inscriptions accompany the original reliefs.

There are two reliefs which show Mithras celebrating a banquet. The first relief shows Mithras and Helios dining together after the sacrifice of the bull. The other depicts Mithras dining with the sun before ascending into paradise with the other gods. But for some reason the tale becomes distorted with Mithras saying to his (imaginary) disciples, "He who shall not eat of my body nor drink of my blood so that he may be one with me and I with him, shall not be saved." SUNDAY was A HOLY DAY, at least for Roman Mithraism

Mithraism had a strong sense of community among its members (only men were allowed to be members, by the way); it taught the immortality of the human soul (so did Judaism which preceded Mithraism). Mithraism placed emphasis on living an ethical and moral life (so did Judaism which preceded Mithraism). Mithraism believed in the concept of good verses evil Mithraism taught all life sprouted from god(s) (so did Judaism which preceded Mithraism), it performed miraculous deeds and taught the eventual destruction of the earth

b. Attis; he was worshipped as a deity in what is known today as modern Turkey, with his cult later spreading throughout the Roman Empire. According to the legend, Agdistis, a hermaphroditic monster, arises from the earth as a descendant of Zeus. Agdistis gives birth to the Sangarius river which brings forth the nymph, Nana, who either holds an almond to her breast and becomes impregnated by the almond or sits beneath a tree where an almond falls into her lap and impregnates her. Nana later abandons the child who is raised by a goat. We are left to assume Attis was conceived from an almond seed which fell from a tree as a result of Zeus' spilled semen.

Attis castrates himself beneath a pine tree after he is made to go insane before his wedding by Agdistis when the he-she becomes enamoured with him. His blood flows onto the ground from his severed organ and brings forth a patch of violets. Critics try to associate Attis' death beneath a tree with Jesus' death on a "tree." In one version, Agdistis is overcome with remorse for her actions and requests Zeus to preserve the beautiful corpse of Attis so it never decomposes. In another account, Agdistis and The Great Mother (or Cybele) carry the pine tree back to a cave where they both mourn the death of Attis. Again, no resurrection. The resurrection story doesn't surface until much later when Attis is transformed into a pine tree.

Critics claim the followers of Attis celebrated the god with a wine-bread communion. The only mention of such an activity is when they would eat a sanctified meal out of sacred tambourines and cymbals, though it is never mentioned what they eat. Critics speculate it was bread and wine but this is unlikely considering wine was restricted during the Attis festivals.

Hymn to Demeter

This Homeric Hymn, composed in approximately the seventh century BCE, served for centuries thereafter as the canonical hymn of the Eleusinian Mysteries.

"I begin to sing of rich-haired Demeter, awful goddess -- of her and her trim-ankled daughter whom Aidoneus [Hades] rapt away, given to him by all-seeing Zeus the loud-thunderer. Apart from Demeter, lady of the golden sword and glorious fruits, she was playing with the deep-bosomed daughters of Oceanus and gathering flowers over a soft meadow, roses and crocuses and beautiful violets, irises also and hyacinths and the narcissus which Earth made to grow at the will of Zeus and to please the Host of Many, to be a snare for the bloom-like girl -- a marvellous, radiant flower. It was a thing of awe whether for deathless gods or mortal men to see: from its root grew a hundred blooms and it smelled most sweetly, so that all wide heaven above and the whole earth and the sea's salt swell laughed for joy. And the girl was amazed and reached out with both hands to take the lovely toy; but the wide-pathed earth yawned there in the plain of Nysa, and the lord, Host of Many, with his immortal horses sprang out upon her -- the Son of Cronos, He who has many names. He caught her up reluctant on his golden car and bare her away lamenting. Then she cried out shrilly with her voice, calling upon her father, the Son of Cronos, who is most high and excellent. But no one, either of the deathless gods or of mortal men, heard her voice, nor yet the olive-trees bearing rich fruit: only tenderhearted Hecate, bright-coiffed, the daughter of Persaeus, heard the girl from her cave, and the lord Helios, Hyperion's bright son, as she cried to her father, the Son of Cronos. But he was sitting aloof, apart from the gods, in his temple where many pray, and receiving sweet offerings from mortal men. So he, that Son of Cronos, of many names, who is Ruler of Many and Host of Many, was bearing her away by leave of Zeus on his immortal chariot -- his own brother's child and all unwilling.

[Line 33] And so long as she, the goddess, yet beheld earth and starry heaven and the strong-flowing sea where fishes shoal, and the rays of the sun, and still hoped to see her dear mother and the tribes of the eternal gods, so long hope calmed her great heart for all her trouble... . and the heights of the mountains and the depths of the sea rang with her immortal voice: and her queenly mother heard her. Bitter pain seized her heart, and she rent the covering upon her divine hair with her dear hands: her dark cloak she cast down from both her shoulders and sped, like a wild-bird, over the firm land and yielding sea, seeking her child. But no one would tell her the truth, neither god nor mortal man; and of the birds of omen none came with true news for her. Then for nine days queenly Deo wandered over the earth with flaming torches in her hands, so grieved that she never tasted ambrosia and the sweet draught of nectar, nor sprinkled her body with water. But when the tenth enlightening dawn had come, Hecate, with a torch in her hands, met her, and spoke to her and told her news:

"Queenly Demeter, bringer of seasons and giver of good gifts, what god of heaven or what mortal man has rapt away Persephone and pierced with sorrow your dear heart? For I heard her voice, yet saw not with my eyes who it was. But I tell you truly and shortly all I know..."

The Eleusinian Mysteries

"Happy is he among men upon earth who has seen these mysteries; but he who is uninitiate and who has no part in them never has lot of like good things once he is dead, down in the darkness and gloom." Hymn to Demeter, 480-2

Thrice happy are those of mortals, who having seen those rites depart for Hades; for to them alone is it granted to have true life there; to the rest all there is evil. Sophocles, Frag. 719

Happy is he who, having seen these rites, goes below the hollow earth; for he knows the end of life and he knows its god-sent beginning. Pindar, Frag. 102

"Beautiful indeed is the Mystery given us by the blessed gods: death is for mortals no longer an evil, but a blessing." Inscription found at Eleusis

"Pausanias avoided explanations regarding the Mysteries and refrained
from describing the buildings to be seen in the sacred precincts of Demeter both at Eleusis and Athens:

I purposed to pursue the subject, and describe all the objects that admit of description in the sanctuary at Athens called the Eleusinion, but I was prevented from so doing by a vision in a dream. I will, therefore, turn to what may be lawfully told to everybody.
Pausanias, I, 14, 3

"And the synthema (pass-word) of the Eleusinian mysteries is as follows: 'I fasted; I drank the kykeon; I took out of the chest; having done my task, I put again into the basket, and from the basket again into the chest.' Clement of Alexandria, Protreptikos, II, 21. [For the interpretations of this sacred formula]

"The Phrygians, the Naassene says, assert that God is a fresh ear of cutwheat, and following the Phrygians the Athenians, when they initiate in the Eleusinia exhibit in silence to the epoptai the mighty and marvellous and most complete epoptic mystery, an ear of cut-wheat." Hippolytus, Philosophoumena, V, 8

Death and Initiation in the Mysteries

"The soul [at the point of death] has the same experience are being initiated into great mysteries. . . . At first one wearily hurries to and fro, and journeys with suspicion dark as one uninitiated: then come all the terrors be initiation, shuddering, trembling, sweating, amazement: then one is struck with a marvellous light, one is received into pure regions and meadows, with voices and dances and the majesty of holy sounds and shapes: among these he who has fulfilled initiation wanders free, and released and bearing his crown joins in the divine communion, and consorts with pure and holy men, beholding those who live here uninitiated, an uncleansed horde, trodden under foot of him and huddled together in mud and fog, abiding in their miseries through fear of death and mistrust of the blessings there." (Plutarch, 'On the Soul')

The Worship of Cybele (Lucretius (98-c.55 BCE)

The cult Cybele, the "Magna Mater, the Mother Goddess of Phrygia, was braought to Rome in 205/4 BCE. The Goddess was served by self-emasculated priests known as galli. Until the emperor Claudius, Roman citizens could not become priests of Cybele, but after that worship of her and her lover Attis took their place in the state cult. One aspect of the cult was the use of baptism in the blood of a bull, a practice later taken over by Mithraism.

"Wherefore great mother of gods, and mother of beasts,
And parent of man hath she alone been named.
Her hymned the old and learned bards of Greece.
Seated in chariot o'er the realms of air
To drive her team of lions, teaching thus
That the great earth hangs poised and cannot lie
Resting on other earth. Unto her car
They've yoked the wild beasts, since a progeny,
However savage, must be tamed and chid
By care of parents. They have girt about
With turret-crown the summit of her head,
Since, fortressed in her goodly strongholds high,
'Tis she sustains the cities; now, adorned
With that same token, to-day is carried forth,
With solemn awe through many a mighty land,
The image of that mother, the divine.
Her the wide nations, after antique rite,
Do name Idaean Mother, giving her
Escort of Phrygian bands, since first, they say,
From out those regions 'twas that grain began
Through all the world. To her do they assign
The Galli, the emasculate, since thus
They wish to show that men who violate
The majesty of the mother and have proved
Ingrate to parents are to be adjudged
Unfit to give unto the shores of light

A living progeny. The Galli come:
And hollow cymbals, tight-skinned tambourines
Resound around to bangings of their hands;
The fierce horns threaten with a raucous bray;
The tubed pipe excites their maddened minds
In Phrygian measures; they bear before them knives,
Wild emblems of their frenzy, which have power
The rabble's ingrate heads and impious hearts
To panic with terror of the goddess' might.
And so, when through the mighty cities borne,
She blesses man with salutations mute,
They strew the highway of her journeyings
With coin of brass and silver, gifting her
With alms and largesse, and shower her and shade
With flowers of roses falling like the snow
Upon the Mother and her companion-bands.
Here is an armed troop, the which by Greeks
Are called the Phrygian Curetes. Since
Haply among themselves they use to play
In games of arms and leap in measure round
With bloody mirth and by their nodding shake
The terrorizing crests upon their heads,
This is the armed troop that represents
The arm'd Dictaean Curetes, who, in Crete,
As runs the story, whilom did out-drown
That infant cry of Zeus, what time their band,
Young boys, in a swift dance around the boy,
To measured step beat with the brass on brass,
That Saturn might not get him for his jaws,
And give its mother an eternal wound
Along her heart. And it is on this account
That armed they escort the mighty Mother,
Or else because they signify by this
That she, the goddess, teaches men to be
Eager with armed valour to defend
Their motherland, and ready to stand forth,
The guard and glory of their parents' years."

Initiation into the Mysteries of Cybele. The Taurobolium (Prudentius, 'Peristephanon,' X, 101 1-50)

"The high priest who is to be consecrated is brought down under ground in a pit dug deep, marvellously adorned with a fillet, binding his festive temples with chaplets, his hair combed back under a golden crown, and wearing a silken toga caught up with Gabine girding. Over this they make a wooden floor with wide spaces, woven of planks with an open mesh; they then divide or bore the area and repeatedly pierce the wood with a pointed tool that it may appear full of small holes.
Hither a huge bull, fierce and shaggy in appearance, is led, bound with flowery garlands about its flanks, and with its horns sheathed; Yea, the forehead of the victim sparkles with gold, and the flash of metal plates colours its hair.

Here, as is ordained, the beast is to be slain, and they pierce its breast with a sacred spear; the gaping wound emits a wave of hot blood, and the smoking river flows into the woven structure beneath it and surges wide. Then by the many paths of the thousand openings in the lattice the falling shower rains down a foul dew, which the priest buried within catches, putting his shameful head under all the drops, defiled both in his clothing and in all his body. Yea, he throws back his face, he puts his cheeks in the way of the blood, he puts under it his ears and lips, he interposes his nostrils, he washes his very eyes with the fluid, nor does he even spare his throat but moistens his tongue, until he actually drinks the dark gore. Afterwards, the flamens draw the corpse, stiffening now that the blood has gone forth, off the lattice, and the pontiff, horrible in appearance, comes forth, and shows his wet head, his beard heavy with blood, his dripping fillets and sodden garments. This man, defiled with such contagions and foul with the gore of the recent sacrifice, all hail and worship1 at a distance, because profane blood 2 and a dead ox have washed him while concealed in a filthy cave".

Isis, Queen of Heaven (Lucius Apuleius, c.155 CE)

The cult of Isis was one of the most important of the empire wide cults in the later empire, and perhaps its greatest monument is in

Lucius Apuleius very strange novel, The Golden Ass. Here Isis appears to Lucius, and claims to be all goddesses. We see here the workings of an intense religious syncretism. Isis is here the Queen of Heaven, and principal of all the gods and goddesses.

"When I had ended this prayer, and made known my needs to the Goddess, I fell asleep, and by and by appeared unto me a divine and venerable face, worshipped even by the Gods themselves. Then by little and little I seemed to see the whole figure of her body, mounting out of the sea and standing before me, and so I shall describe her divine appearance, if the poverty of my human speech will allow me, or her divine power give me eloquence to do so. First she had a great abundance of hair, dispersed and scattered about her neck, on the crown of her head she wore many garlands interlaced with flowers, just above her brow was a disk in the form of a mirror, or resembling the light of the Moon, in one of her hands she bore serpents, in the other, blades of corn, her robe was of fine silk shimmering in divers colors, sometime yellow, sometime rose, sometime flamy, and sometimes (which sore troubled my spirit) dark and obscure, covered with a black robe in manner of a shield, and pleated in most subtle fashion at the skirts of her garments, the welts appeared comely, whereas here and there the stars peaked out, and in the middle of them was placed the Moon, which shone like a flame of fire, round about the robe was a coronet or garland made with flowers and fruits. In her right hand she had a timbrel of brass, which gave a pleasant sound, in her left hand she bore a cup of gold, out of the mouth whereof the serpent Aspis lifted up his head, with a swelling throat, her sweet feet were covered with shoes interlaced and wrought with victorious palm. Thus the divine shape breathing out the pleasant spice of fertile Arabia, disdained not with her divine voice to utter these words unto me:

"Behold Lucius I am come, thy weeping and prayers has moved me to succor thee. I am she that is the natural mother of all things, mistress and governess of all the elements, the initial progeny of worlds, chief of powers divine, Queen of heaven, the principal of the Gods celestial, the light of the goddesses: at my will the planets of the air, the wholesome winds of the Seas, and the silences of hell be disposed; my name, my divinity is adored throughout all the world in divers manners, in variable customs and in many names, for the Phrygians call me Pessinuntica, the mother of the Gods: the Athenians call me Cecropian Artemis: the Cyprians, Paphian Aphrodite: the Candians, Dictyanna: the Sicilians, Stygian Proserpine: and the Eleusians call me Mother of the Corn. Some call me Juno, others Bellona of the Battles, and still others Hecate. Principally the Ethiopians which dwell in the Orient, and the Egyptians which are excellent in all kind of ancient doctrine, and by their proper ceremonies accustomed to worship me, do call me Queen Isis. Behold I am come to take pity of thy fortune and tribulation, behold I am present to favor and aid thee. Leave off thy weeping and lamentation, put away thy sorrow, for behold the healthful day which is ordained by my providence, therefore be ready to attend to my commandment." Lucius Apuleius: Metamophoses or The Golden Ass. Book 11, Chap 47.

ns: 2nd-3rd Centuries
3. Early Church: 2nd-3rd Centuries

a. Persecution and Survival

Letters of Pliny the Younger and the Emperor Trajan

These letters concern an episode which marks the first time the Roman government recognized Christianity as a religion separate from Judaism, and sets a precedent for the massive persecution of Christians that takes place in the second and third centuries. In the year 112, Pliny the Younger was faced with a dilemma. He was the governor in the Roman province of Bithynia (modern day Turkey) when a number of Christians were brought into his court. It is unclear what the initial charges are, but he ultimately decided, despite the fact that the Christians seemed generally harmless to him, that he should execute them if they refused to recant their faith. Because he is unsure as to whether he can kill them legally for no other crime than their faith, he writes to his friend the Emperor for advice. The Emperor replies that he did the right thing in excecuting them, but advises him not to seek out Christians for prosecution.

Pliny's Epistle To Trajan About 112 CE

Sir,
It is my constant method to apply myself to you for the resolution of all my doubts; for who can better govern my dilatory way of proceeding or instruct my ignorance? I have never been present at the examination of the Christians [by others], on which account I am unacquainted with what uses to be inquired into, and what, and how far they used to be punished; nor are my doubts small, whether there be not a distinction to be made between the ages [of the accused]? and whether tender youth ought to have the same punishment with strong men? Whether there be not room for pardon upon repentance?" or whether it may not be an advantage to one that had been a Christian, that he has forsaken Christianity? Whether the bare name, without any crimes besides, or the crimes adhering to that name, be to be punished? In the meantime, I have taken this course about those who have been brought before me as Christians. I asked them whether they were Christians or not? If they confessed that they were Christians, I

asked them again, and a third time, intermixing threatenings with the questions. If they persevered in their confession, I ordered them to be executed; for I did not doubt but, let their confession be of any sort whatsoever, this positiveness and inflexible obstinacy deserved to be punished. There have been some of this mad sect whom I took notice of in particular as Roman citizens, that they might be sent to that city. After some time, as is usual in such examinations, the crime spread itself and many more cases came before me. A libel was sent to me, though without an author, containing many names [of persons accused]. These denied that they were Christians now, or ever had been. They called upon the gods, and supplicated to your image, which I caused to be brought to me for that purpose, with frankincense and wine; they also cursed Christ; none of which things, it is said, can any of those that are ready Christians be compelled to do; so I thought fit to let them go. Others of them that were named in the libel, said they were Christians, but presently denied it again; that indeed they had been Christians, but had ceased to be so, some three years, some many more; and one there was that said he had not been so these twenty years. All these worshipped your image, and the images of our gods; these also cursed Christ. However, they assured me that the main of their fault, or of their mistake was this:-That they were wont, on a stated day, to meet together before it was light, and to sing a hymn to Christ, as to a god, alternately; and to oblige themselves by a sacrament [or oath], not to do anything that was ill: but that they would commit no theft, or pilfering, or adultery; that they would not break their promises, or deny what was deposited with them, when it was required back again; after which it was their custom to depart, and to meet again at a common but innocent meal, which they had left off upon that edict which I published at your command, and wherein I had forbidden any such conventiclers. These examinations made me think it necessary to inquire by torments what the truth was; which I did of two servant maids, who were called Deaconesses: but still I discovered no more than that they were addicted to a bad and to an extravagant superstition. Hereupon I have put off any further examinations, and have recourse to you, for the affair seems to be well worth consultation, especially on account of the number of those that are in danger; for there are many of every age, of every rank, and of both sexes, who are now and hereafter likely to be called to account, and to be in danger; for this superstition is spread like a contagion, not only into cities and towns, but into country villages also, which yet there is reason to hope may be stopped and corrected. To be sure, the temples, which were almost forsaken, begin already to be frequented; and the holy solemnities, which were long intermitted, begin to be revived. The sacrifices begin to sell well everywhere, of which very few purchasers had of late appeared; whereby it is easy to suppose how great a multitude of men may be amended, if place for repentance be admitted.

TRAJAN'S EPISTLE TO PLINY

My Pliny,
You have taken the method which you ought in examining the causes of those that had been accused as Christians, for indeed no certain and general form of judging can be ordained in this case. These people are not to be sought for; but if they be accused and convicted, they are to be punished; but with this caution, that he who denies himself to be a Christian, and makes it plain that he is not so by supplicating to our gods, although he had been so formerly, may be allowed pardon, upon his repentance. As for libels sent without an author, they ought to have no place in any accusation whatsoever, for that would be a thing of very ill example, and not agreeable to my reign.

The Martyrdom of Saints Perpetua and Felicitas

This is the prison diary of a young woman martyered in Carthage in 202 or 203 CE. The beginning and ending are related by an editor/narrator; the central text contains the words of Perpetua herself.

"A number of young catechumens were arrested, Revocatus and his fellow slave Felicitas, Saturninus and Secundulus, and with them Vibia Perpetua, a newly married woman of good family and upbringing. Her mother and father were still alive and one of her two brothers was a catechumen like herself. She was about twenty-two years old and had an infant son at the breast. (Now from this point on the entire account of her ordeal is her own, according to her own ideas and in the way that she herself wrote it down.) While we were still under arrest (she said) my father out of love for me was trying to

persuade me and shake my resolution. 'Father,' said I, 'do you see this vase here, for example, or waterpot or whatever?'
'Yes, I do', said he.
And I told him: 'Could it be called by any other name than what it is?'
And he said: 'No.'
'Well, so too I cannot be called anything other than what I am, a Christian.'
At this my father was so angered by the word 'Christian' that he moved towards me as though he would pluck my eyes out. But he left it at that and departed, vanquished along with his diabolical arguments.
For a few days afterwards I gave thanks to the Lord that I was separated from my father, and I was comforted by his absence. During these few days I was baptized, and I was inspired by the Spirit not to ask for any other favour after the water but simply the perseverance of the flesh. A few days later we were lodged in the prison; and I was terrified, as I had never before been in such a dark hole. What a difficult time it was! With the crowd the heat was stifling; then there was the extortion of the soldiers; and to crown all, I was tortured with worry for my baby there.
Then Tertius and Pomponius, those blessed deacons who tried to take care of us, bribed the soldiers to allow us to go to a better part of the prison to refresh ourselves for a few hours. Everyone then left that dungeon and shifted for himself. I nursed my baby, who was faint from hunger. In my anxiety I spoke to my mother about the child, I tried to comfort my brother, and I gave the child in their charge. I was in pain because I saw them suffering out of pity for me. These were the trials I had to endure for many days. Then I got permission for my baby to stay with me in prison. At once I recovered my health, relieved as I was of my worry and anxiety over the child. My prison had suddenly become a palace, so that I wanted to be there rather than anywhere else.
Then my brother said to me: 'Dear sister, you are greatly privileged; surely you might ask for a vision to discover whether you are to be condemned or freed.'
Faithfully I promised that I would, for I knew that I could speak with the Lord, whose great blessings I had come to experience. And so I said: 'I shall tell you tomorrow.' Then I made my request and this was the vision I had.

I saw a ladder of tremendous height made of bronze, reaching all the way to the heavens, but it was so narrow that only one person could climb up at a time. To the sides of the ladder were attached all sorts of metal weapons: there were swords, spears, hooks, daggers, and spikes; so that if anyone tried to climb up carelessly or without paying attention, he would be mangled and his flesh would adhere to the weapons.

At the foot of the ladder lay a dragon of enormous size, and it would attack those who tried to climb up and try to terrify them from doing so. And Saturus was the first to go up, he who was later to give himself up of his own accord. He had been the builder of our strength, although he was not present when we were arrested. And he arrived at the top of the staircase and he looked back and said to me: 'Perpetua, I am waiting for you. But take care; do not let the dragon bite you.'

'He will not harm me,' I said, 'in the name of Christ Jesus.'

Slowly, as though he were afraid of me, the dragon stuck his head out from underneath the ladder. Then, using it as my first step, I trod on his head and went up.

Then I saw an immense garden, and in it a gray-haired man sat in shepherd's garb; tall he was, and milking sheep. And standing around him were many thousands of people clad in white garments. He raised his head, looked at me, and said: 'I am glad you have come, my child.' He called me over to him and gave me, as it were, a mouthful Of the milk he was drawing; and I took it into my cupped hands and consumed it. And all those who stood around said: 'Amen!' At the sound of this word I came to, with the taste of something sweet still in my mouth. I at once told this to my brother, and we realized that we would have to suffer, and that from now on we would no longer have any hope in this life.

A few days later there was a rumour that we were going to be given a hearing. My father also arrived from the city, worn with worry, and he came to see me with the idea of persuading me.

'Daughter,' he said, 'have pity on my grey head--have pity on me your father, if I deserve to be called your father, if I have favoured you above all your brothers, if I have raised you to reach this prime of your life. Do not abandon me to be the reproach of men. Think of your brothers, think of your mother and your aunt, think of your child, who will not be able to live once you are gone. Give up your pride!

You will destroy all of us! None of us will ever be able to speak freely again if anything happens to you.'
This was the way my father spoke out of love for me, kissing my hands and throwing himself down before me. With tears in his eyes he no longer addressed me as his daughter but as a woman. I was sorry for my father's sake, because he alone of all my kin would be unhappy to see me suffer.
I tried to comfort him saying: 'It will all happen in the prisoner's dock as God wills; for you may be sure that we are not left to ourselves but are all in his power.'
And he left me in great sorrow.
One day while we were eating breakfast we were suddenly hurried off for a hearing. We arrived at the forum, and straight away the story went about the neighbourhood near the forum and a huge crowd gathered. We walked up to the prisoner's dock. All the others when questioned admitted their guilt. Then, when it came my turn, my father appeared with my son, dragged me from the step, and said: 'Perform the sacrifice--have pity on your baby!'
Hilarianus the governor, who had received his judicial powers as the successor of the late proconsul Minucius Timinianus, said to me: 'Have pity on your father's grey head; have pity on your infant son. Offer the sacrifice for the welfare of the emperors.'
'I will not', I retorted.
'Are you a Christian?' said Hilarianus.
And I said: 'Yes, I am.'
When my father persisted in trying to dissuade me, Hilarianus ordered him to be thrown to the ground and beaten with a rod. I felt sorry for father, just as if I myself had been beaten. I felt sorry for his pathetic old age.
Then Hilarianus passed sentence on all of us: we were condemned to the beasts, and we returned to prison in high spirits. But my baby had got used to being nursed at the breast and to staying with me in prison. So I sent the deacon Pomponius straight away to my father to ask for the baby. But father refused to give him over. But as God willed, the baby had no further desire for the breast, nor did I suffer any inflammation; and so I was relieved of any anxiety for my child and of any discomfort in my breasts....
Some days later, an adjutant named Pudens, who was in charge of the prison, began to show us great honour, realizing that we possessed

some great power within us. And he began to allow many visitors to see us for our mutual comfort.

Now the day of the contest was approaching, and my father came to see me overwhelmed with sorrow. He started tearing the hairs from his beard and threw them on the ground; he then threw himself on the ground and began to curse his old age and to say such words as would move all creation. I felt sorry for his unhappy old age.

The day before we were to fight with the beasts I saw the following vision. Pomponius the deacon came to the prison gates and began to knock violently. I went out and opened the gate for him. He was dressed in an unbelted white tunic, wearing elaborate sandals. And he said to me: 'Perpetua, come; we are waiting for you.'

Then he took my hand and we began to walk through rough and broken country. At last we came to the amphitheatre out of breath, and he led me into the centre of the arena.

Then he told me: 'Do not be afraid. I am here, struggling with you.' Then he left.

I looked at the enormous crowd who watched in astonishment. I was surprised that no beasts were let loose on me; for I knew that I was condemned to die by the beasts. Then out came an Egyptian against me, of vicious appearance, together with his seconds, to fight with me. There also came up to me some handsome young men to be my seconds and assistants.

My clothes were stripped off, and suddenly I was a man. My seconds began to rub me down with oil (as they are wont to do before a contest). Then I saw the Egyptian on the other side rolling in the dust. Next there came forth a man of marvelous stature, such that he rose above the top of the amphitheatre. He was clad in a beltless purple tunic with two stripes (one on either side) running down the middle of his chest. He wore sandals that were wondrously made of gold and silver, and he carried a wand like an athletic trainer and a green branch on which there were golden apples.

And he asked for silence and said: 'If this Egyptian defeats her he will slay her with the sword. But if she defeats him, she will receive this branch.' Then he withdrew.

We drew close to one another and began to let our fists fly. My opponent tried to get hold of my feet, but I kept striking him in the face with the heels of my feet. Then I was raised up into the air and I began to pummel him without as it were touching the ground. Then when I noticed there was a lull, I put my two hands together linking the fingers of one hand with those of the other and thus I got hold of his head. He fell flat on his face and I stepped on his head.

The crowd began to shout and my assistants started to sing psalms. Then I walked up to the trainer and took the branch. He kissed me and said to me: 'Peace be with you, my daughter!' I began to walk in triumph towards the Gate of Life. Then I awoke. I realized that it was not with wild animals that I would fight but with the Devil, but I knew that I would win the victory. So much for what I did up until the eve of the contest. About what happened at the contest itself, let him write of it who will.

[Here Saturus tells the story of a vision he had of Perpetua and himself, after they were killed, being carried by four angels into heaven where they were reunited with other martyrs killed in the same persecution.]

[Here the editor/narrator begins to relate the story]:

Such were the remarkable visions of these martyrs, Saturus and Perpetua, written by themselves. As for Secundulus, God called him from this world earlier than the others while he was still in prison, by a special grace that he might not have to face the animals. Yet his flesh, if not his spirit, knew the sword.

As for Felicitas, she too enjoyed the Lord's favour in this wise. She had been pregnant when she was arrested, and was now in her eighth month. As the day of the spectacle drew near she was very distressed that her martyrdom would be postponed because of her pregnancy; for it is against the law for women with child to be executed. Thus she might have to shed her holy, innocent blood afterwards along with others who were common criminals. Her comrades in martyrdom were also saddened; for they were afraid that they would have to leave behind so fine a companion to travel alone on the same road to hope. And so, two days before the contest, they poured forth a prayer to the Lord in one torrent of common grief. And immediately after their prayer the birth pains came upon her. She suffered a good deal in her labour because of the natural difficulty of an eight months' delivery.

Hence one of the assistants of the prison guards said to her: 'You suffer so much now--what will you do when you are tossed to the beasts? Little did you think of them when you refused to sacrifice.'

'What I am suffering now', she replied, 'I suffer by myself. But then another will be inside me who will suffer for me, just as I shall be suffering for him.'

And she gave birth to a girl; and one of the sisters brought her up as her own daughter.

Therefore, since the Holy Spirit has permitted the story of this contest to be written down and by so permitting has willed it, we shall carry out the command or, indeed, the commission of the most saintly Perpetua, however unworthy I might be to add anything to this glorious story. At the same time I shall add one example of her perseverance and nobility of soul.

The military tribune had treated them with extraordinary severity because on the information of certain very foolish people he became afraid that they would be spirited out of the prison by magical spells.

Perpetua spoke to him directly. 'Why can you not even allow us to refresh ourselves properly? For we are the most distinguished of the condemned prisoners, seeing that we belong to the emperor; we are to fight on his very birthday. Would it not be to your credit if we were brought forth on the day in a healthier condition?'

The officer became disturbed and grew red. So it was that he gave the order that they were to be more humanely treated; and he allowed her brothers and other persons to visit, so that the prisoners could dine in their company. By this time the adjutant who was head of the gaol was himself a Christian.

On the day before, when they had their last meal, which is called the free banquet, they celebrated not a banquet but rather a love feast. They spoke to the mob with the same steadfastness, warned them of God's judgement, stressing the joy they would have in their suffering, and ridiculing the curiosity of those that came to see them. Saturus said: 'Will not tomorrow be enough for you? Why are you so eager to see something that you dislike? Our friends today will be our enemies on the morrow. But take careful note of what we look like so that you will recognize us on the day.' Thus everyone would depart from the prison in amazement, and many of them began to believe.

The day of their victory dawned, and they marched from the prison to the amphitheatre joyfully as though they were going to heaven, with calm faces, trembling, if at all, with joy rather than fear. Perpetua went along with shining countenance and calm step, as the beloved of God, as a wife of Christ, putting down everyone's stare by her own intense gaze. With them also was Felicitas, glad that she had safely given birth so that now she could fight the beasts, going from one blood bath to another, from the midwife to the gladiator, ready to wash after childbirth in a second baptism.

They were then led up to the gates and the men were forced to put on the robes of priests of Saturn, the women the dress of the priestesses of Ceres. But the noble Perpetua strenuously resisted this to the end.

'We came to this of our own free will, that our freedom should not be violated. We agreed to pledge our lives provided that we would do no such thing. You agreed with us to do this.'

Even injustice recognized justice. The military tribune agreed. They were to be brought into the arena just as they were. Perpetua then began to sing a psalm: she was already treading on the head of the Egyptian. Revocatus, Saturninus, and Saturus began to warn the on looking mob. Then when they came within sight of Hilarianus, they suggested by their motions and gestures: 'You have condemned us, but God will condemn you' was what they were saying.

At this the crowds became enraged and demanded that they be scourged before a line of gladiators. And they rejoiced at this that they had obtained a share in the Lord's sufferings.

But he who said, Ask and you shall receive, answered their prayer by giving each one the death he had asked for. For whenever they would discuss among themselves their desire for martyrdom, Saturninus indeed insisted that he wanted to be exposed to all the different beasts, that his crown might be all the more glorious. And so at the outset of the contest he and Revocatus were matched with a leopard, and then while in the stocks they were attacked by a bear. As for Saturus, he dreaded nothing more than a bear, and he counted on being killed by one bite of a leopard. Then he was matched with a wild boar; but the gladiator who had tied him to the animal was gored by the boar and died a few days after the contest, whereas Saturus was only dragged along. Then when he was bound in the stocks awaiting the bear, the animal refused to come out of the cages, so that Saturus was called back once more unhurt.

For the young women, however, the Devil had prepared a mad heifer. This was an unusual animal, but it was chosen that their sex might be matched with that of the beast. So they were stripped naked, placed in nets and thus brought out into the arena. Even the crowd was horrified when they saw that one was a delicate young girl and the other was a woman fresh from childbirth with the milk still dripping from her breasts. And so they were brought back again and dressed in unbelted tunics.

First the heifer tossed Perpetua and she fell on her back. Then sitting up she pulled down the tunic that was ripped along the side so that it covered her thighs, thinking more of her modesty than of her pain. Next she asked for a pin to fasten her untidy hair: for it was not right that a martyr should die with her hair in disorder, lest she might seem to be mourning in her hour of triumph.

Then she got up. And seeing that Felicitas had been crushed to the ground, she went over to her, gave her hand, and lifted her up. Then the two stood side by side. But the cruelty of the mob was by now appeased, and so they were called back through the Gate of Life.

There Perpetua was held up by a man named Rusticus who was at the time a catechumen and kept close to her. She awoke from a kind of sleep (so absorbed had she been in ecstasy in the Spirit) and she began to look about her. Then to the amazement of all she said: 'When are we going to be thrown to that heifer or whatever it is?'

When told that this had already happened, she refused to believe it until she noticed the marks of her rough experience on her person and her dress. Then she called for her brother and spoke to him together with the catechumens and said: 'You must all stand fast in the faith and love one another, and do not be weakened by what we have gone through.'

At another gate Saturus was earnestly addressing the soldier Pudens. 'It is exactly', he said, 'as I foretold and predicted. So far not one animal has touched me. So now you may believe me with all your heart: I am going in there and I shall be finished off with one bite of the leopard.' And immediately as the contest was coming to a close a leopard was let loose, and after one bite Saturus was so drenched with blood that as he came away the mob roared in witness to his second baptism: 'Well washed! Well washed!' For well washed indeed was one who had been bathed in this manner.

Then he said to the soldier Pudens: 'Good-bye. Remember me, and remember the faith. These things should not disturb you but rather strengthen you.'

And with this he asked Pudens for a ring from his finger, and dipping it into his wound he gave it back to him again as a pledge and as a record of his bloodshed.

Shortly after he was thrown unconscious with the rest in the usual spot to have his throat cut. But the mob asked that their bodies be brought out into the open that their eyes might be the guilty witnesses of the sword that pierced their flesh. And so the martyrs got up and went to the spot of their own accord as the people wanted them to, and kissing one another they sealed their martyrdom with the ritual kiss of peace. The others took the sword in silence and without moving, especially Saturus, who being the first to climb the stairway was the first to die. For once again he was waiting for Perpetual Perpetua, however, had yet to taste more pain. She screamed as she was struck on the bone; then she took the trembling hand of the young gladiator and guided it to her throat. It was as though so great a woman, feared as she was by the unclean spirit, could not be dispatched unless she herself were willing.

Ah, most valiant and blessed martyrs! Truly are you called and chosen for the glory of Christ Jesus our Lord! And any man who exalts, honours, and worships his glory should read for the consolation of the Church these new deeds of heroism which are no less significant than the tales of old. For these new manifestations of virtue will bear witness to one and the same Spirit who still operates, and to God the Father almighty, to his Son Jesus Christ our Lord, to whom is splendour and immeasurable power for all the ages. Amen."

Tertullian (Apology)

Chapter 1
Rulers of the Roman Empire, if, seated for the administration of justice on your lofty tribunal, under the gaze of every eye, and occupying there all but the highest position in the state, you may not openly inquire into and sift before the world the real truth in regard to the charges made against the Christians; if in this case alone you are afraid or ashamed to exercise your authority in making public inquiry with the carefulness which becomes justice; if, finally, the extreme severities inflicted on our people in recently private judgments, stand in the way of our being permitted to defend ourselves before you, you cannot surely forbid the Truth to reach your ears by the secret pathway of a noiseless book. She has no appeals to make to you in regard of her condition, for that does not excite her wonder. She

knows that she is but a sojourner on the earth, and that among strangers she naturally finds foes; and more than this, that her origin, her dwelling-place, her hope, her recompense, her honours, are above. One thing, meanwhile, she anxiously desires of earthly rulers— not to be condemned unknown. What harm can it do to the laws, supreme in their domain, to give her a hearing? Nay, for that part of it, will not their absolute supremacy be more conspicuous in their condemning her, even after she has made her plea? But if, unheard, sentence is pronounced against her, besides the odium of an unjust deed, you will incur the merited suspicion of doing it with some idea that it is unjust, as not wishing to hear what you may not be able to hear and condemn. We lay this before you as the first ground on which we urge that your hatred to the name of Christian is unjust. And the very reason which seems to excuse this injustice (I mean ignorance) at once aggravates and convicts it. For what is there more unfair than to hate a thing of which you know nothing, even though it deserve to be hated? Hatred is only merited when it is known to be merited. But without that knowledge, whence is its justice to be vindicated? For that is to be proved, not from the mere fact that an aversion exists, but from acquaintance with the subject. When men, then, give way to a dislike simply because they are entirely ignorant of the nature of the thing disliked, why may it not be precisely the very sort of thing they should not dislike? So we maintain that they are both ignorant while they hate us, and hate us unrighteously while they continue in ignorance, the one thing being the result of the other either way of it. The proof of their ignorance, at once condemning and excusing their injustice, is this, that those who once hated Christianity because they knew nothing about it, no sooner come to know it than they all lay down at once their enmity. From being its haters they become its disciples. By simply getting acquainted with it, they begin now to hate what they had formerly been, and to profess what they had formerly hated; and their numbers are as great as are laid to our charge. The outcry is that the State is filled with Christians— that they are in the fields, in the citadels, in the islands: they make lamentation, as for some calamity, that both sexes, every age and condition, even high rank, are passing over to the profession of the Christian faith; and yet for all, their minds are not awakened to the thought of some good they have failed to notice in it. They must not allow any truer suspicions to cross their minds; they have no desire to make closer trial. Here alone the curiosity of human nature slumbers. They like to be ignorant, though to others the knowledge has been bliss. Anacharsis reproved the rude venturing to criticise the cultured; how much more this judging of those who know, by men who are entirely ignorant, might he have denounced! Because they already dislike, they want to know no more. Thus they prejudge that of which they are ignorant to be such, that, if they came to know it, it could no longer be the object of their aversion; since, if inquiry finds nothing worthy of dislike, it is certainly proper to cease from an unjust dislike, while if its bad character comes plainly out, instead of the detestation entertained for it being thus diminished, a stronger reason for perseverance in that detestation is obtained, even under the authority of justice itself. But, says one, a thing is not good merely because multitudes go over to it; for how many have the bent of their nature towards whatever is bad! How many go astray into ways of error! It is undoubted. Yet a thing that is thoroughly evil, not even those whom it carries away venture to defend as good. Nature throws a veil either of fear or shame over all evil. For instance, you find that criminals are eager to conceal themselves, avoid appearing in public, are in trepidation when they are caught, deny their guilt, when they are accused; even when they are put to the rack, they do not easily or always confess; when there is no doubt about their condemnation, they grieve for what they have done. In their self-communings they admit their being impelled by sinful dispositions, but they lay the blame either on fate or on the stars. They are unwilling to acknowledge that the thing is theirs, because they own that it is wicked. But what is there like this in the Christian's case? The only shame or regret he feels, is at not having been a Christian earlier. If he is pointed out, he glories in it; if he is accused, he offers no defence; interrogated, he makes voluntary confession; condemned he renders thanks. What sort of evil thing is this, which wants all the ordinary peculiarities of evil— fear, shame, subterfuge, penitence, lamenting? What! Is that a crime in which the criminal rejoices? To be accused of which is his ardent wish, to be punished for which is his felicity? You cannot call it madness, you who stand convicted of knowing nothing of the matter.

The Ritual Cannabilism Charge Against Christians (Minucius Felix. Octavius)

And now, as wickeder things advance more fruitfully, and abandoned manners creep on day by day, those abominable shrines of an impious assembly are maturing themselves throughout the whole world. Assuredly this confederacy ought to be rooted out and execrated. They know one another by secret marks and insignia, and they love one another almost before they know one another; everywhere also there is mingled among them a certain religion of lust, and they call one another promiscuously brothers and sisters, that even a not unusual debauchery may by the intervention of that sacred name become incestuous: it is thus that their vain and senseless superstition glories in crimes.

Nor, concerning these things, would intelligent report speak of things so great and various, and requiring to be prefaced by an apology, unless truth were at the bottom of it. I hear that they adore the head of an ass, that basest of creatures, consecrated by I know not what silly persuasion, a worthy and appropriate religion for such manners. Some say that they worship the genitals of their pontiff and priest, and adore the nature, as it were, of their common parent. I know not whether these things are false; certainly suspicion is applicable to secret and nocturnal rites; and he who explains their ceremonies by reference to a man punished by extreme suffering for his wickedness, and to the deadly wood of the cross, appropriates fitting altars for reprobate and wicked men, that they may worship what they deserve.

Now the story about the initiation of young novices is as much to be detested as it is well known. An infant covered over with meal, that it may deceive the unwary, is placed before him who is to be stained with their rites: this infant is slain by the young pupil, who has been urged on as if to harmless blows on the surface of the meal, with dark and secret wounds. Thirstily - O horror! they lick up its blood; eagerly they divide its limbs. By this victim they are pledged together; with this consciousness of wickedness they are covenanted to mutual silence.

Hippolytus. Apostolic Tradition

When one has been consecrated bishop all give him the kiss of peace . . . and the deacons bring him the offering . . . he lays hands upon it with all the priests and gives thanks, saying, "The Lord be with you." And all answer, "And with your spirit." "Lift up your hearts." "We have lifted them up to the Lord." "Let us give thanks to the Lord." "It is right and just." And he thus continues, "We give thanks to you O God through your beloved son Jesus Christ whom in these last times you have sent to us as the redeemer and saviour and messenger of your will. He is your inseparable Word, through whom you created all things and who was acceptable to you. You sent him from heaven into the Virgin's womb and in her womb he was made man and was manifested your son, born of the Holy Spirit and of the Virgin. Fulfilling your will and buying for you a holy people, he stretched forth his hands when he suffered, that by his Passion he might deliver those who believed in you. When he was delivered over to his Passion of his own will, to destroy death, to break the bonds of the devil, to trample upon Hell, to enlighten the just, and to manifest his resurrection, taking bread and giving thanks to you, he said: Take and eat, this is my body which shall be broken for you. And taking likewise the cup, he said: This is my blood which shall be shed for you; when you do this, do it in memory of me. "Mindful therefore of his death and resurrection, we offer you this bread and cup, giving thanks to you because you have found us worthy to stand before you and serve you. And we beg you to send the Holy Spirit upon the offering of the holy church and gather into one all who have received it . . . that we may praise and glorify you through your son Jesus Christ, through whom is glory and honor to the Father and the Son and the Holy Spirit, in your holy church both now and forever. Amen."

Deeds of Zenophilus. How the Romans Tried to Seize Christian Books, c. 395 CE

In the great persecution started by Diocletian, a special effort was made to seize all copies of the Christian scriptures, in the hope of depriving the persecuted sect of the means of preserving and propagating its doctrines. The following tells how the search for the books was conducted in Cirta, an important city of Numidia.

"When the magistrates and a policeman, guided by the apostatizing secretaries of the bishop, came to the house of Felix the tailor, he brought out five books, and when they came to the house of Proiectus he brought out five big and two little books. Victor the schoolmaster brought out two books, and four books of five volumes each. Felix the "Perpetual Flamen" said to him: "Bring your scriptures out: you have more." Victor the schoolmaster said, "If I had had more I should have brought them out." When they came to the house of Eutychia who was a Caesarian [i.e., in the government service], the flamen said, "Bring out your books that you may obey the law." "I have none," he replied. "Your answer," said Felix the flamen, "is taken down." At the house of Coddeo, Coddeo's wife brought out six books. Felix said "Look and see if you have not got some more." The woman said, "I have no more." Felix said to Bos, the policeman, "Go in and see if she has any more." The policeman reported "I have looked and found none."

Celsus' view of Christians and Christianity (Contra Celsus, Origen)

Celsus was a Greek writer in the second century who criticized Christianity as a threat to the stable communities and worldview that the "pagan" religious and social system sought to uphold. His work as a whole has been lost, but when the third century theologian Origen sought to answer Celsus' charges in a work appropriately called Against Celsus, he preserved most of Celsus' criticisms. Origen's replies are certainly worth reading in their own right, but the following excerpts are chosen in order to show how a thoughtful "pagan" viewed Christianity. In the excerpts that follow, Celsus' words are highlighted for easy of reading.

BOOK 1
Chap. 28
...[Celsus] accuses [Jesus] of having "invented his birth from a virgin," and upbraids Him with being "born in a certain Jewish village, of a poor woman of the country, who gained her subsistence by spinning, and who was turned out of doors by her husband, a carpenter by trade, because she was convicted of adultery; that after

being driven away by her husband, and wandering about for a time, she disgracefully gave birth to Jesus, an illegitimate child, who having hired himself out as a servant in Egypt on account of his poverty, and having there acquired some miraculous powers, on which the Egyptians greatly pride themselves, returned to his own country, highly elated on account of them, and by means of these proclaimed himself a God."...

BOOK 3

Chap. 44

After these points Celsus quotes some objections against the doctrine of Jesus, made by a very few individuals who are considered Christians, not of the more intelligent, as he supposes, but of the more ignorant class, and asserts that "the following are the rules laid down by them. Let no one come to us who has been instructed, or who is wise or prudent (for such qualifications are deemed evil by us); but if there be any ignorant, or unintelligent, or uninstructed, or foolish persons, let them come with confidence. By which words, acknowledging that such individuals are worthy of their God, they manifestly show that they desire and are able to gain over only the silly, and the mean, and the stupid, with women and children."...

Chap. 55

But as Celsus delights to heap up calumnies against us, and, in addition to those which he has already uttered, has added others, let us examine these also, and see whether it be the Christians or Celsus who have reason to be ashamed of what is said. He asserts, "We see, indeed, in private houses workers in wool and leather, and fullers, and persons of the most uninstructed and rustic character, not venturing to utter a word in the presence of their elders and wiser masters; but when they get hold of the children privately, and certain women as ignorant as themselves, they pour forth wonderful statements, to the effect that they ought not to give heed to their father and to their teachers, but should obey them; that the former are foolish and stupid, and neither know nor can perform anything that is really good, being preoccupied with empty trifles; that they alone know how men ought to live, and that, if the children obey them, they will both be happy themselves, and will make their home happy also. And while thus speaking, if they see one of the instructors of youth approaching, or one of the more intelligent class, or even the father himself, the more timid among them become afraid, while the more forward incite the children to throw off the yoke, whispering that in the presence of father and teachers they neither will nor can explain to them any good thing, seeing they turn away with aversion from the silliness and stupidity of such persons as being altogether corrupt, and far advanced in wickedness, and such as would inflict punishment upon them; but that if they wish (to avail themselves of their aid,) they must leave their father and their instructors, and go with the women and their playfellows to the women's apartments, or to the leather shop, or to the fuller's shop, that they may attain to perfection;--and by words like these they gain them over."

Chap. 59

This statement also is untrue, that it is "only foolish and low individuals, and persons devoid of perception, and slaves, and women, and children, of whom the teachers of the divine word wish to make converts."... After this it is superfluous for us to wish to offer a reply to such statements of Celsus as the following: "For why is it an evil to have been educated, and to have studied the best opinions, and to have both the reality and appearance of wisdom? What hindrance does this offer to the knowledge of God? Why should it not rather be an assistance, and a means by which one might be better able to arrive at the truth?"...

Chap. 64

But since he says, in addition to this, "What is this preference of sinners over others?" and makes other remarks of a similar nature, we have to reply....

BOOK 4

Chap. 14

But let us look at what Celsus next with great ostentation announces in the following fashion: "And again," he says, "let us resume the subject from the beginning, with a larger array of proofs. And I make no new statement, but say what has been long settled. God is good, and beautiful, and blessed, and that in the best and most beautiful degree. But if he come down among men, he must undergo a change, and a change from good to evil, from virtue to vice, from happiness to misery, and from best to worst. Who, then, would make choice of such a change? It is the nature of a mortal, indeed, to undergo change and remoulding, but of an immortal to remain the same and unaltered. God, then, could not admit of such a change."...

b. Church Organization

St. Jerome. Letter to a Soldier

St. Jerome is best known for his translation of the Bible into Latin. This letter to a friend was written in 374.

"Pampered soldier, why are you wasting time in your father's house? Where is the rampart, the ditch, the winter campaign under canvas? Behold the trumpet sounds from heaven! Our General, fully armed, comes amid the clouds to overcome the world. From our King's mouth comes the double-edged sword that cuts down all in its path. Are you going to remain in your chamber and not come out to join in the battle? . . . Listen to your King's proclamation: "He who is not with me is against me, and he who does not gather with me scatters."
Remember when you joined up as a recruit, when buried with Christ in baptism, you took the oath of allegiance to him, declaring that you would spare neither your father nor your mother? But now the adversary in your own heart is trying to kill Christ! Now the enemy's camp has its sights on your loyalty! Though your little nephew twine his arms around your neck; though your mother, with disheveled hair and tearing her robe asunder, point to the breast with which she nourished you; though your father fall down on the threshold before you--trample on his body and go your way! Fly with tearless eyes to the standard of the Cross. In this matter cruelty is your duty . . .
I know well the chains which you will say hinder you. Indeed, my breast is not made of iron, nor my heart of stone. I was not born from a rock or raised by Hyrcanian tigers. I have been through this experience too. Your widowed sister may throw her gentle arms around you. The household slaves, in whose company you grew up, will cry, "To what master are you abandoning us?" Your old nurse and her husband, who, after your own natural father, have the next claim to your devotion, say, "Wait awhile until we die so you can bury us!" Perhaps your foster mother, with sagging breasts and wrinkled face, will sing you your old childhood lullaby! . . . But the love of Christ and the fear of Gehenna will easily break such bonds.
You will claim that the Scriptures command us to obey our parents. On the contrary, whoever loves his parents more than Christ, loses his

own soul. If my enemy takes up a sword to kill me, will I be held back by my mother's tears? Should I desert from the army because of my father, to whom in the cause of Christ I owe no burial because in his cause I owe burial to everyone? . . . You may claim that all your fellow citizens are Christians, but your case is not the same as everyone else. Hear what the Lord has to say: "If you would be perfect, go and sell what you have and follow me." You promised to be perfect.

When you resigned from the army and "made yourself an eunuch for the kingdom of Christ," what else had you in mind besides a perfect life? A perfect servant of Christ has nothing besides Christ. Indeed, if he has anything besides Christ, he is not perfect . . . If you are perfect, why do you pine for your father's property? But if you are not perfect, you have failed the Lord. The Gospel thunders the divine words: "You cannot serve two masters." Does anyone dare to make Christ a liar by serving Mammon and the Lord at the same time? Does he not say often, "If anyone will come after me, let him deny himself, take up his cross and follow me"? If I load myself with gold, do I imagine I am following Christ? . . .

0 desert, green with the flowers of Christ! 0 solitude in which the stones of the Great City of the King mentioned in the Apocalypse are found! 0 wilderness rejoicing in the presence of God! Brother, what are you doing in the world when you are so much more important than the world? How long are the shadows of a roof going to hold you back? How long will the smoky dungeon of these cities imprison you? . . . How refreshing to fling off the burdens of the flesh and fly to the sparkling aether? . . . You are spoiled indeed, dear friend, if you wish to rejoice here on earth--and afterwards reign with Christ!"

Gregory Nazianzus. On divorce

"Verianus, a citizen of Nazianzus, had been offended by his son-in-law, and on this account wished his daughter to sue for a divorce. Olympius, prefect of Cappadocia Secunda, referred the matter to the Episcopal arbitration of S. Gregory, who refused to countenance the proceeding, and writes the two following letters, the first to the Prefect, the second to Verianus himself. [Note that Gregory refers to a difference of view between Christian regulations and Roman law;

also, he refers to the fact that Christians were entitled to seek judgement or legal redress from a bishop, bypassing the regular judicial system.]"

Codex Justinianus. Book IX, Title IX. On the Lex Julia Relating to Adultery and Fornication

33. The Emperors Theodosius, Arcadius, and Honorius to Rufinus, Praetorian Prefect.
When a charge of adultery has been made, We order that all civil exceptions by means of which a dowry may be claimed, or any other debt demanded, and which are ordinarily pleaded and examined, to be set aside, and that the progress of the case shall not be delayed through their inter-position. But when the accusation has been formulated, that is to say, when it has been regularly instituted, whether it was filed under the right of a husband, or under that of a stranger, the crime shall be investigated, the evidence produced, the more important matters in dispute settled, and all civil actions be subordinated to the criminal prosecution. The woman will afterwards have the right to begin any civil proceedings to which he is entitled, provided they do not interfere with the conduct of the criminal case.... [392CE]

Extract from Justinian, Novel 134, Chapter X. Latin Text.
At present, however, a woman convicted of adultery is placed in a monastery, from which her husband is permitted to remove her within the term of two years. After the two years have expired, without her husband having taken her back, or, before that, if he should have died, the adulteress, having had her head shaved, and assumed a religious habit, shall remain there during lifetime, and her property, if she has any, shall be divided into three parts, two of which should be given to her children, and the third to the monastery. When she has no children, and her parents are living and did not consent to her crime, they shall receive a third part of her property, and the monastery two-thirds of the same. If her aforesaid relatives are not livin , all of her property shall be acquired by her monastery, and, in every instance, all rights under dotal agreements are reserved for the benefit of the husband.... [556CE]

Ambrose (c.339-4 April 397), Bishop of Milan. On the characteristics suitable for a bishop

EPISTLE LXIII

To the Church at Vercellae
Limenius, Bishop of Vercellae, having died, the see remained long vacant owing to domestic factions. St. Ambrose, therefore, as Exarch, writes to the Christians at Vercellae, and commences by reference to the speedy and unanimous election of Eusebius, a former Bishop, and reminds them of the presence of Christ as a reason for concord, He refers next to two apostate monks, Sarmatio and Barbatianus, and inveighs against sensuality, which degrades men below the beasts. Thence he passes to the virtues required in a bishop, referring again to Eusebius, and to Dionysius, Bishop of Milan, comparing the clerical and monastic lives, and ends with exhortations to Christian virtue. The letter seems to have been written A.D. 396.
AMBROSE, a servant of Christ, called to be a Bishop, to the Church of Vercellae, and to those who call on the Name of our Lord Jesus Christ, Grace be fulfilled unto you in the Holy Spirit from God the Father and His only-begotten Son.
1. I am spent with grief that the Church of God which is among you is still without a bishop, and now alone of all the regions of Liguria and AEmilia, and of the Venetiae all the and other neighbouring parts of Italy needs that care which other churches were wont to ask for themselves from it; and what is a greater source of shame to myself, the tension amongst you which causes the obstacle is laid to my charge. Now since there are dissensions among you, how can we decree anything, or you elect, or anyone agree to undertake this office amongst those who are at variance which he could hardly sustain amongst those who are at unity.
2. Is this the training of a confessor, are these the offspring of those righteous fathers who, as soon as they saw, approved of holy Eusebius, whom they had never known before, preferring him to their fellow-citizens, and he was no sooner amongst them than he was approved, and much more when they had observed him. Justly did he turn out so great a man, whom the whole Church elected, justly was it

believed that he whom all had demanded was elected by the judgment of God. It is fitting then that you follow the example of your parents, especially since you who have been instructed by a holy confessor ought to be so much better than your fathers, as a better teacher has taught and instructed you, and to manifest a sign of your moderation and concord by agreeing in your request for a Bishop.

3. For if according to the Lord's saying, that which two shall have agreed upon on earth concerning anything which they shall ask, shall be done for them, as He says, by My Father, Who is in heaven, for: "Where two or three are gathered together in My Name, there am I in the midst of them, how much less, where the full congregation is gathered in the Name of the Lord. Where the demand of all is unanimous, ought we to doubt that the Lord Jesus is there as the Author of that desire, and the Hearer of the petition, the Presider over the ordination, and the Giver of the grace?

4. Make yourselves then to appear worthy that Christ should be in your midst. For where peace is, there is Christ, for Christ is Peace; and where righteousness is, there is Christ, for Christ is Righteousness. Let Him be in the midst of you, that you may see Him, lest it be said to you also: "There standeth One in the midst of you, Whom ye see not." The Jews saw not Him in Whom they believed not; we look upon Him by devotion, and behold Him by faith.

5. Let Him therefore stand in your midst, that the heavens, which declare the glory of God, may be opened to you, that you may do His will, and work His works. He who sees Jesus, to him are the heavens opened as they were opened to Stephen, when he said: "Behold I see the heavens opened and Jesus standing at the right hand of God." Jesus was standing as his advocate, He was standing as though anxious, that He might help His athlete Stephen in his conflict, He was standing as though ready to crown His martyr.

6. Let Him then be standing for you, that you may not be afraid of Him sitting; for when sitting He judges, as Daniel says: "The thrones were placed, and the books were opened, and the Ancient of days did sit." But in the eighty-first[second] Psalm it is written: "God stood in the congregation of gods, and decideth among the gods." So then when He sits He judges, when He stands He decides, and He judges concerning the imperfect, but decides among the gods. Let Him stand for you as a defender, as a good shepherd, lest the fierce wolves assault you.

7. And not in vain is my warning turned to this point; for I hear that Sarmatio and Barbatianus are come to you, foolish talkers, who say that there is no merit in abstinence no grace in a frugal life, none in virginity, that all are valued at one price, that they are mad who chasten their flesh with fastings, that they may bring it into subjection to the spirit. But if he had thought it madness, Paul the Apostle would never himself have acted thus, nor written to instruct others. For he glories in it, saying: "But I chasten my body, and bring it into bondage, lest, after preaching to others, I myself should be found reprobate." So they who do not chasten their body, and desire to preach to others, are themselves esteemed reprobates.

8. For is there anything so reprobate as that which excites to luxury, to corruption, to wantonness, as the incentive to lust, the enticer to pleasure, the fuel of incontinence, the firebrand of desire? What new school has sent out these Epicureans? Not a school of philosophers, as they themselves say, but of unlearned men who preach pleasure, persuade to luxury, esteem chastity to be of no use. They were with us, but they were not of us, for we are not ashamed to say what the Evangelist John said. But when settled here they used to fast at first, they were enclosed within the monastery, there was no place for luxury, the opportunity of mocking and disputing was cut off.

9. This these dainty men could not endure. They went abroad, then when they desired to return they were not received; for I had heard many thinks which necessitated my being cautious; I admonished them, but effected nothing. And so boiling over they began to disseminate such things as made them the miserable enticers to all vices. They utterly lost the benefit of having fasted; they lost the fruits of their temporary continence. And so now they with Satanic eagerness envy the good works of others, the fruit of which themselves have failed to keep.

10. What virgin can hear that there is no reward for her chastity and not groan? Far be it from her to believe this easily, and still more to lay aside her zeal, or change the intention of her mind. What widow, when she learnt that there was no profit in her widowhood, would choose to preserve her marriage faith and live in sorrow, rather than give herself up to a happier condition? Who, bound by the marriage-bond, if she hear that there is no honour in chastity, might not be tempted by careless levity of body or mind? And for this reason the

Church in the holy lessons, and in the addresses of her priests, proclaims the praise of chastity and the glory of virginity.

11. In vain, then, does the Apostle say: "I wrote to you, in an Epistle, not to mingle with fornicators;" and lest perchance they should say, We are not speaking of all the fornicators of the world, but we say that he who has been baptized in Christ ought not now to be esteemed a fornicator, but his life, whatever it is, is accepted of God, the Apostle has added "Not at all[meaning] with the fornicators of this world," and farther on, "If any that is named a brother be a fornicator, or covetous, or an idolator, or a reviler, or a drunkard, or an extortioner, with such an one not even to eat. For what have I to do with judging them that are without?" And to the Ephesians: "But fornication, and all uncleanness, and covetousness let it not even be named among you, as becometh saints." And immediately he adds: "For this ye know, that no immodest person, nor unclean, nor covetous, which is an idolator, hath any inheritance in the kingdom of Christ and of God." It is clear that this is said of the baptized, for they receive the inheritance, who are baptized into the death of Christ and are buried together with Him, that they may rise again with Him. Therefore they are heirs of God, and joint heirs with Christ: heirs of God, because the grace of Christ is conveyed to them; joint-heirs with Christ, because they are renewed into His life; heirs also of Christ; because to them is given by His death as it were the inheritance of the testator.

12. These then ought to take heed to themselves who have that which they may lose, rather than they who have it not. These ought to act with greater care, these ought to guard against the allurements of vice, or incentives to error, which arise chiefly from food and drink. For "the people sat down to eat and drink, and rose up to play."

13. Epicurus himself also, whom these persons think they should follow rather than the apostles, the advocate of pleasure, although he denies that pleasure brings in evil, does not deny that certain things result from it from which evils are generated; and asserts in fine that the life of the luxurious which is filled with pleasures does not seem to be reprehensible, unless it be disturbed by the fear either of pain or of death. But how far he is from the truth is perceived even from this, that he asserts that pleasure was originally created in man by God its author, as Philomarus his follower argues in his Epitomae, asserting that the Stoics are the authors of this opinion.

14. But Holy Scripture refutes this, for it teaches us that pleasure was suggested to Adam and Eve by the craft and enticements of the serpent. Since, indeed, the serpent itself is pleasure, and therefore the passions of pleasure are various and slippery, and as it were infected with the poison of corruptions, it is certain then that Adam, being deceived by the desire of pleasure, fell away from the commandment of God and from the enjoyment of grace. How then can pleasure recall us to paradise, seeing that it alone deprived us of it?

15. Wherefore also the Lord Jesus, wishing to make us more strong against the temptations of the devil, fasted when about to contend with him, that we might know that we can in no other way overcome the enticements of evil. Further, the devil himself hurled the first dart of his temptations from the quiver of pleasure, saying: "If Thou be the Son of God, command that these stones become bread." After which the Lord said: "Man doth not live by bread alone, but by every word of God;" and would not do it, although He could, in order to teach us by a salutary precept to attend rather to the pursuit of reading than to pleasure. And since they say that we ought not to fast, let them prove for what cause Christ fasted, unless it were that His fast might be an example to us. Lastly, in His later words He taught us that evil cannot be easily overcome except by our fasting, saying: "This kind of devils is not cast out but by prayer and fasting."

16. And what is the intention of the Scripture which teaches us that Peter fasted, and that the revelation concerning the baptism of Gentiles was made to him when fasting and praying, except to show that the Saints themselves advance when they fast. Finally, Moses received the Law when he was fasting; and so Peter when fasting was taught the grace of the New Testament. Daniel too by virtue of his fast stopped the mouths of the lions and saw the events of future times. And what safety can there be for us unless we wash away our sins by fasting, since ScriptUre says that fasting and alms do away sin?

17. Who then are these new teachers who reject the merit of fasting? Is it not the voice of heathen who say, "Let us eat and drink?" whom the Apostle well ridicules, when he says: "If after the manner of men I have fought with beasts at Ephesus, what advantageth it me if the dead rise not? Let us eat and drink, for to-morrow we die." That is to say, What profited me my contention even unto death, except that I might redeem my body? And it is redeemed in vain if there is no hope

of the resurrection. And, consequently, if all hope of the resurrection is lost, let us eat and drink, let us not lose the enjoyment of things present, who have none of things to come. It is then for them to indulge in meats and drinks who hope for nothing after death.

18. Rightly then does the Apostle, arguing against these men, warn us that we be not shaken by such opinions, saying: "Be not deceived, evil communications corrupt good manners. Be ye righteously sober and sin not, for some have no knowledge of God." Sobriety, then, is good, for drunkenness is sin.

19. But as to that Epicurus himself, the defender of pleasure, of whom, therefore, we have made frequent mention in order to prove that these men are either disciples of the heathen and followers of the Epicurean sect or himself, whom the very philosophers exclude from their company as the patron of luxury, what if we prove him to be more tolerable than these men? He declares, as Demarchus asserts, that neither drinking, nor banquets, nor offspring, nor embraces of women, nor abundance of fish, and other such like things which are prepared for the service of a sumptuous banquet, make life sweet, but sober discussion. Lastly, he added that those who do not use the banquets of society in excess, use them with moderation. He who willingly makes use of the juices of plants alone together with bread and water, despises feasts on delicacies, for many inconveniences arise from them. In another place they also say: It is not excessive banquets, nor drinking which give rise to the enjoyment of pleasure, but a life of temperance.

20. Since, then, philosophy has disowned those men, is the Church not to exclude them? Seeing, too, that they, because they have a bad cause, frequently fall foul of themselves by their own assertions. For, although their chief opinion is that there is no enjoyment of pleasure except such as is derived from eating and drinking, yet understanding that they cannot, without the greatest shame, cling to so disgraceful a definition, and that they are forsaken by all, they have tried to colour it with a sort of stain of specious arguments; so that one of them has said: Whilst we are aiming at pleasure by means of banquets and songs, we have lost that which is infused into us by the reception of the Word, whereby alone we can be saved.

21. Do not they by these various arguments show themselves to us as differing and disagreeing one with the other? And Scripture too condemns them, not passing over those whom the Apostle refuted, as

Luke, who wrote the book as a history, tells us in the Acts of the Apostles, "And certain also of the Epicurean and Stoic philosophers disputed with him. And some said, What does this babbler mean? And others said, He seemeth to be a setter forth of new gods."

22. Yet from this hand too the Apostle did not go forth without success, since even Dionysius the Areopagite together with his wife Damaris and many others believed. And so that company of most learned and eloquent men showed themselves overcome in a simple discussion by the example of those who believed. What then do those men mean, who endeavour to prevent those whom the Apostle has gained, and whom Christ has redeemed with His own blood? asserting that the baptized ought not to give themselves to the discipline of the virtues, that revellings injure them not, nor abundance of pleasures; that they are foolish who go without them, that virgins ought to marry, bear children, and likewise widows to repeat that converse with man which they have once experienced with ill results; and that even if they can contain, they are in error who will not again enter the marriage bond.

23. What then? Would you have us put off the man in order to put on the beast, and stripping ourselves of Christ, clothe ourselves or be superclothed with the garments of the devil? But since the very teachers of the heathen did not think that honour and pleasure could be joined together, because they would seem thus to class beasts with men, shall we as it were infuse the habits of beasts into the human breast, and inscribe on the reasonable mind the unreasoning ways of wild beasts?

24. And yet there are many kinds of animals, which, when they have lost their fellow, will not mate again, and spend their time as it were in solitary life; many too live on simple herbs, and will not quench their thirst except at a pure stream; one can also often see dogs refrain from food forbidden them, so that they close their famishing mouths if restraint is bidden them. Must men then be warned against that wherein brutes have learned not to transgress?

26. But what is more admirable than abstinence, which makes even the years of youth to ripen, so that there is an old age of character? For as by excess of food and by drunkenness even mature age is excited, so the wildness of youth is lessened by scanty feasts and by the running stream. An external fire is extinguished by pouring on water, it is then no wonder if the inward heat of the body is cooled by

draughts from the stream, for the flame is fed or fails according to the fuel. As hay, straw, wood, oil, and such like things are the nourishment which feeds fire, if you take them away, or do not supply them, the fire is extinguished. In like manner then the heat of the body is supported or lessened by food, it is excited by food and lessened by food. Luxury then is the mother of lust.

27. And is not temperance agreeable to nature, and to that divine law, which in the very beginning of all created things gave the springs for drink and the fruits of the trees for food? After the Flood the just man found wine a source of temptation to him. Let us then use the natural drink of temperance, and would that we all were able to do so. But because all are not strong the Apostle said: "Use a little wine because of thy frequent infirmities." We must drink it then not for the sake of pleasure, but because of infirmity, and therefore sparingly as a remedy, not in excess as a gratification.

28. Lastly, Elijah, whom the Lord was training to the perfection of virtue, found at his head a cake and a cruse of water; and then fasted in the strength of that food forty days and forty nights. Our fathers, when they passed across the sea on foot, drank water not wine. Daniel and the Hebrew children, fed with their peculiar food, and with water to drink, overcame, the former the fury of the lions; the latter saw the burning fire play around their limbs with harmless touch.

26. And why should I speak of men? Judith, in no way moved by the luxurious banquet of Holophernes, carried off the triumph of which men's arms despaired, solely in right of her temperance; delivered her country from occupation and slew the leader of the expedition with her own hands. A clear proof both that his luxury had enervated that warrior, terrible to the nations, and that temperance made this woman stronger than men. In this case it was not in her sex that nature was surpassed, but she overcame by her diet. Esther by her fasts moved a proud king. Anna, who for eighty-four years in her widowhood had served God with fasts and prayers day and night in the temple, recognized Christ, Whom John, the master of abstinence, and as it were a new angel on earth, announced.

30. O foolish Elisha, for feeding the prophets with wild and bitter gourds! O Ezra forgetful of Scripture, though he did restore the Scriptures from memory! foolish Paul, who glories in fastings, if fastings profit nothing.

31. But how should that not be profitable by which our sins are purged? And if you offer this with humility and with mercy, your bones, as Isaiah said, shall be fat, and you shall be like a well-watered garden. So, then, your soul shall grow fat and its virtues also by the spiritual richness of fasting, and your fruits shall be multiplied by the fertility of your mind, so that there may be in you the inebriation of soberness, like that cup of which the Prophet says: "Thy cup which inebriates, how excellent it is!"

32. But not only is that temperance worthy of praise which moderates food, but also that which moderates lust. Since it is written: "Go not after thy lusts, and deny thy appetite. If thou givest her desires to thy soul, thou wilt be a joy to thine enemies;" and farther on; "Wine and women make even wise men to fall away; " So that Paul teaches temperance even in marriage itself; for he who is incontinent in marriage is a kind of adulterer, and violates the law of the Apostle.

33. And why should I tell how great is the grace of virginity, which was found worthy to be chosen by Christ, that it might be even the bodily temple of God, in which as we read the fulness of the Godhead dwelt bodily. A Virgin conceived the Salvation of the world, a Virgin brought forth the life of all. Virginity then ought not to be left to itself, seeing that it benefited all in Christ. A Virgin bore Him Whom this world cannot contain or support. And when He was born from His mother's womb, He yet preserved the fence of her chastity and the inviolate seal of her virginity. And so Christ found in the Virgin that which He willed to make His own, that which the Lord of all might take to Himself Further, our flesh was cast out of Paradise by a man and woman and was joined to God through a Virgin.

34. What shall I say concerning the other Mary, the sister of Moses, who as leader of the women passed on foot the straits of the sea? By the same gift Thecla also was reverenced by the lions, so that the unfed beasts stretched at the feet of their prey prolonged a holy fast, and harmed the virgin neither with wanton look nor claw, since virginity is injured even by a look.

35. Again, with what reverence for virginity has the holy Apostle spoken: "Concerning virgins I have no commandment of the Lord, but I give my counsel, as having obtained mercy of the Lord." He has received no commandment, but a counsel, for that which beyond the law is not commanded, but is rather advised by way of counsel. Authority is not assumed but grace is shown, and this is not shown by

anyone, but by him who obtained mercy from the Lord. Are then the counsels of these men better than those of the apostles? The Apostle says, "I give my counsel," but they think it right to dissuade any from cultivating virginity."

4. The Emergence of Theologies

Heresy in Early Chruch. Early Christendom Sects

Heresy is the rejection of one or more established beliefs of a religious body, or adherence to "other beliefs." Christian heresy refers to non-orthodox practices and beliefs that were deemed to be heretical by one or more of the Christian churches. In the West, the term "heresy" most commonly refers to those beliefs which were declared to be anathema by the Catholic Church prior to the schism of 1054. In the East, the term "heresy" most commonly refers to those beliefs declared to be "heretical" by the First Seven Ecumenical Councils. However, since the Great Schism and the Protestant Reformation, various Christian churches have also used the concept in proceedings against individuals and groups deemed to be heretical by those churches. The Catholic Church considers the Protestant denominations to be heretical and considers the Eastern Orthodox schismatics.

One of the roles of bishops, and the purpose of many Christian writings, was to refute heresies. During those first three centuries, Christianity was effectively outlawed by requirements to venerate the Roman emperor and Roman gods. Consequently, when the Church labeled its enemies as heretics and cast them out of its congregations or severed ties with dissident churches, it remained without the power to persecute them. Before 313 AD, the "heretical" nature of some beliefs was a matter of much debate within the churches, and there was no true mechanism in place to resolve the various differences of beliefs. Heresy was to be approached by the leader of the church according to Eusebius, author of The Church History. It was only after the legalisation of Christianity, which began under Constantine I in 313 AD that the various beliefs of the Church began to be made uniform and formulated as dogma through the canons promulgated by the General Councils. Each phrase in the Nicene Creed, which was hammered out at the Council of Nicaea, addresses some aspect that had been under passionate discussion prior to Constantine I, and closes the books on the argument, with the weight of the agreement of the over 300 bishops, as well as Constantine I in attendance. [Constantine had invited all 1800 bishops of the Christian church (about 1000 in the east and 800 in the west).

Irenaeus (c. 130–202) was the first to argue that his "orthodox" position was the same faith that Jesus gave to the apostles, and that the identity of the apostles, their successors, and the teachings of the same were all well-known public knowledge. This was therefore an early argument supported by apostolic succession. Irenaeus first established the doctrine of four gospels and no more, with the synoptic gospels interpreted in the light of John. Irenaeus' opponents, however, claimed to have received secret teachings from Jesus via other apostles which were not publicly known. Gnosticism is predicated on the existence of such hidden knowledge, but brief references to private teachings of Jesus have also survived in the canonic Scripture as did warning by the Christ that there would be false prophets or false teachers. Irenaeus' opponents also claimed that the wellsprings of divine inspiration were not dried up, which is the doctrine of continuing revelation. The first known usage of the term 'heresy' in a civil legal context was in 380 AD by the "Edict of Thessalonica" of Theodosius I. Prior to the issuance of this edict, the Church had no state sponsored support for any particular legal mechanism to counter what it perceived as 'heresy'. By this edict, in some senses, the line between the Catholic Church's spiritual authority and the Roman State's jurisdiction was blurred. One of the outcomes of this blurring of Church and State was a sharing of State powers of legal enforcement between Church and State authorities. At its most extreme reach, this new legal backing of the Church gave its leaders the power to, in effect, pronounce the death sentence upon those whom they might perceive to be 'heretics'. Within 5 years of the official 'criminalization' of heresy by the emperor, the first Christian heretic, Priscillian was executed in 385 by Roman officials

Against Heresies (St. Irenaeus)

Book I, Chapter 22
Deviations of heretics from the truth.
1. The rule of truth which we hold, is, that there is one God Almighty, who made all things by His Word, and fashioned and formed, out of that which had no existence, all things which exist. Thus says the Scripture, to that effect By the Word of the Lord were the heavens

established, and all the might of them, by the spirit of His mouth. And again, All things were made by Him, and without Him was nothing made. John 1:3 There is no exception or deduction stated; but the Father made all things by Him, whether visible or invisible, objects of sense or of intelligence, temporal, on account of a certain character given them, or eternal; and these eternal things He did not make by angels, or by any powers separated from His Ennœa. For God needs none of all these things, but is He who, by His Word and Spirit, makes, and disposes, and governs all things, and commands all things into existence—He who formed the world (for the world is of all)—He who fashioned man—He [who] is the God of Abraham, and the God of Isaac, and the God of Jacob, above whom there is no other God, nor initial principle, nor power, nor pleroma,— He is the Father of our Lord Jesus Christ, as we shall prove. Holding, therefore, this rule, we shall easily show, notwithstanding the great variety and multitude of their opinions, that these men have deviated from the truth; for almost all the different sects of heretics admit that there is one God; but then, by their pernicious doctrines, they change [this truth into error], even as the Gentiles do through idolatry—thus proving themselves ungrateful to Him that created them. Moreover, they despise the workmanship of God, speaking against their own salvation, becoming their own bitterest accusers, and being false witnesses [against themselves]. Yet, reluctant as they may be, these men shall one day rise again in the flesh, to confess the power of Him who raises them from the dead; but they shall not be numbered among the righteous on account of their unbelief.

2. Since, therefore, it is a complex and multiform task to detect and convict all the heretics, and since our design is to reply to them all according to their special characters, we have judged it necessary, first of all, to give an account of their source and root, in order that, by getting a knowledge of their most exalted Bythus, you may understand the nature of the tree which has produced such fruits.

Doctrines and practices of Simon Magus and Menander.

1. Simon the Samaritan was that magician of whom Luke, the disciple and follower of the apostles, says, But there was a certain man, Simon by name, who beforetime used magical arts in that city, and led astray the people of Samaria, declaring that he himself was some great one, to whom they all gave heed, from the least to the greatest, saying, This is the power of God, which is called great. And to him they had

regard, because that of long time he had driven them mad by his sorceries. Acts 8:9-11 This Simon, then— who feigned faith, supposing that the apostles themselves performed their cures by the art of magic, and not by the power of God; and with respect to their filling with the Holy Ghost, through the imposition of hands, those that believed in God through Him who was preached by them, namely, Christ Jesus— suspecting that even this was done through a kind of greater knowledge of magic, and offering money to the apostles, thought he, too, might receive this power of bestowing the Holy Spirit on whomsoever he would—was addressed in these words by Peter: Your money perish with you, because you have thought that the gift of God can be purchased with money: you have neither part nor lot in this matter, for your heart is not right in the sight of God; for I perceive that you are in the gall of bitterness, and in the bond of iniquity. He, then, not putting faith in God a whit the more, set himself eagerly to contend against the apostles, in order that he himself might seem to be a wonderful being, and applied himself with still greater zeal to the study of the whole magic art, that he might the better bewilder and overpower multitudes of men. Such was his procedure in the reign of Claudius Cæsar, by whom also he is said to have been honoured with a statue, on account of his magical power. This man, then, was glorified by many as if he were a god; and he taught that it was himself who appeared among the Jews as the Son, but descended in Samaria as the Father while he came to other nations in the character of the Holy Spirit. He represented himself, in a word, as being the loftiest of all powers, that is, the Being who is the Father over all, and he allowed himself to be called by whatsoever title men were pleased to address him.

2. Now this Simon of Samaria, from whom all sorts of heresies derive their origin, formed his sect out of the following materials:— Having redeemed from slavery at Tyre, a city of Phœnicia, a certain woman named Helena, he was in the habit of carrying her about with him, declaring that this woman was the first conception of his mind, the mother of all, by whom, in the beginning, he conceived in his mind [the thought] of forming angels and archangels. For this Ennœa leaping forth from him, and comprehending the will of her father, descended to the lower regions [of space], and generated angels and powers, by whom also he declared this world was formed. But after she had produced them, she was detained by them through motives of

jealousy, because they were unwilling to be looked upon as the progeny of any other being. As to himself, they had no knowledge of him whatever; but his Ennœa was detained by those powers and angels who had been produced by her. She suffered all kinds of contumely from them, so that she could not return upwards to her father, but was even shut up in a human body, and for ages passed in succession from one female body to another, as from vessel to vessel. She was, for example, in that Helen on whose account the Trojan war was undertaken; for whose sake also Stesichorus was struck blind, because he had cursed her in his verses, but afterwards, repenting and writing what are called palinodes, in which he sang her praise, he was restored to sight. Thus she, passing from body to body, and suffering insults in every one of them, at last became a common prostitute; and she it was that was meant by the lost sheep. Matthew 18:12

3. For this purpose, then, he had come that he might win her first, and free her from slavery, while he conferred salvation upon men, by making himself known to them. For since the angels ruled the world ill because each one of them coveted the principal power for himself, he had come to amend matters, and had descended, transfigured and assimilated to powers and principalities and angels, so that he might appear among men to be a man, while yet he was not a man; and that thus he was thought to have suffered in Judæa, when he had not suffered. Moreover, the prophets uttered their predictions under the inspiration of those angels who formed the world; for which reason those who place their trust in him and Helena no longer regarded them, but, as being free, live as they please; for men are saved through his grace, and not on account of their own righteous actions. For such deeds are not righteous in the nature of things, but by mere accident, just as those angels who made the world, have thought fit to constitute them, seeking, by means of such precepts, to bring men into bondage. On this account, he pledged himself that the world should be dissolved, and that those who are his should be freed from the rule of them who made the world.

4. Thus, then, the mystic priests belonging to this sect both lead profligate lives and practise magical arts, each one to the extent of his ability. They use exorcisms and incantations. Love-potions, too, and charms, as well as those beings who are called Paredri (familiars) and Oniropompi (dream-senders), and whatever other curious arts can be had recourse to, are eagerly pressed into their service. They also have

an image of Simon fashioned after the likeness of Jupiter, and another of Helena in the shape of Minerva; and these they worship. In fine, they have a name derived from Simon, the author of these most impious doctrines, being called Simonians; and from them knowledge, falsely so called, 1 Timothy 6:20 received its beginning, as one may learn even from their own assertions.

5. The successor of this man was Menander, also a Samaritan by birth, and he, too, was a perfect adept in the practice of magic. He affirms that the primary Power continues unknown to all, but that he himself is the person who has been sent forth from the presence of the invisible beings as a saviour, for the deliverance of men. The world was made by angels, whom, like Simon, he maintains to have been produced by Ennœa. He gives, too, as he affirms, by means of that magic which he teaches, knowledge to this effect, that one may overcome those very angels that made the world; for his disciples obtain the resurrection by being baptized into him, and can die no more, but remain in the possession of immortal youth.

(See Chapter 24 for Doctrines of Saturninus and Basilides, Chapter 25 Doctrines of Carpocrates, Chapter 26 Doctrines of Cerinthus, the Ebionites, and Nicolaitanes, Chapter 27 Doctrines of Cerdo and Marcion, Chapter 28 Doctrines of Tatian, the Encratites, and others, Chapter 29 Doctrines of various other Gnostic sects, and especially of the Barbeliotes, or Borborians, Chapter 30 Doctrines of the Ophites and Sethians, Chapter 31 Doctrines of the Cainites).

The Muratorian Canon (170 CE)

I. ...those things at which he was present he placed thus.23 The third book of the Gospel, that according to Luke, the well-known physician Luke wrote in his own name in order after the ascension of Christ, and when Paul had associated him with himself as one studious of right. Nor did he himself see the Lord in the flesh; and he, according as he was able to accomplish it, began his narrative with the nativity of John. The fourth Gospel is that of John, one of the disciples. When his fellow-disciples and bishops entreated him, he said, "Fast ye now with me for the space of three days, and let us recount to each other whatever may be revealed to each of us." On the same night it was revealed to Andrew, one of the apostles, that John should narrate all things in his own name as they called them to mind. And hence, although different points are taught us in the several books of the Gospels, there is no difference as regards the faith of believers, inasmuch as in all of them all things are related under one imperial Spirit, which concern the Lord's nativity, His passion, His resurrection, His conversation with His disciples, and His twofold advent,-the first in the humiliation of rejection, which is now past, and the second in the glory of royal power, which is yet in the future. What marvel is it, then, that John brings forward these several things so constantly in his epistles also, saying in his own person, "What we have seen with our eyes, and heard with our ears, and our hands have handled, that have we written." For thus he professes himself to be not only the eye-witness, but also the hearer; and besides that, the historian of all the wondrous facts concerning the Lord in their order.

2. Moreover, the Acts of all the Apostles are comprised by Luke in one book, and addressed to the most excellent Theophilus, because these different events took place when he was present himself; and he shows this clearly-i.e., that the principle on which he wrote was, to give only what fell under his own notice-by the omission of the passion of Peter, and also of the journey of Paul, when he went from the city-Rome-to Spain.

3. As to the epistles of Paul, again, to those who will understand the matter, they indicate of themselves what they are, and from what place or with what object they were directed. He wrote first of all, and at considerable length, to the Corinthians, to check the schism of heresy; and then to the Galatians, to forbid circumcision; and then to the Romans on the rule of the Oid Testament Scriptures, and also to show them that Christ is the first object35 in these;-which it is needful for us to discuss severally,36 as the blessed Apostle Paul, following the rule of his predecessor John, writes to no more than seven churches by name, in this order: the first to the Corinthians, the second to the Ephesians, the third to the Philippians, the fourth to the Colossians, the fifth to the Galatians, the sixth to the Thessalonians, the seventh to the Romans. Moreover, though he writes twice to the Corinthians and Thessalonians for their correction, it is yet shown-i.e., by this sevenfold writing-that there is one Church spread abroad through the whole world. And John too, indeed, in the Apocalypse, although he writes only to seven churches, yet addresses all. He

wrote, besides these, one to Philemon, and one to Titus, and two to Timothy, in simple personal affection and love indeed; but yet these are hallowed in the esteem of the Catholic Church, and in the regulation of ecclesiastical discipline. There are also in circulation one to the Laodiceans, and another to the Alexandrians, forged under the name of Paul, and addressed against the heresy of Marcion; and there are also several others which cannot be received into the Catholic Church, for it is not suitable for gall to be mingled with honey.

4. The Epistle of Jude, indeed, and two belonging to the above-named John-or bearing the name of John-are reckoned among the Catholic epistles. And the book of Wisdom, written by the friends of Solomon in his honour. We receive also the Apocalypse of John and that of Peter, though some amongst us will not have this latter read in the Church. The Pastor, moreover, did Hermas write very recently in our times in the city of Rome, while his brother bishop Plus sat in the chair of the Church of Rome. And therefore it also ought to be read; but it cannot be made public38 in the Church to the people, nor placed among the prophets, as their number is complete, nor among the apostles to the end of time. Of the writings of Arsinous, called also Valentinus, or of Miltiades, we receive nothing at all. Those are rejected too who wrote the new Book of Psalms for Marcion, together with Basilides and the founder of the Asian Cataphrygians.

Origen of Alexandria (185—254 CE)

He was one of the greatest Christian theologians, is famous for composing the seminal work of Christian Neoplatonism, his treatise On First Principles. Origen lived through a turbulent period of the Christian Church, when persecution was wide-spread and little or no doctrinal consensus existed among the various regional churches. In this environment, Gnosticism flourished, and Origen was the first truly philosophical thinker to turn his hand not only to a refutation of Gnosticism, but to offer an alternative Christian system that was more rigorous and philosophically respectable than the mythological speculations of the various Gnostic sects. Origen was also an astute critic of the pagan philosophy of his era, yet he also learned much from it, and adapted its most useful and edifying teachings to a grand elucidation of the Christian faith. Porphyry (the illustrious student of Plotinus), though a tenacious adversary of Christianity, nevertheless grudgingly admitted Origen's mastery of the Greek philosophical tradition. Although Origen did go on to compose numerous biblical commentaries and sermons, his importance for the history of philosophy rests mainly on two works, the systematic treatise On First Principles, and his response to the pagan philosopher Celsus' attack on Christianity, the treatise Against Celsus. Since the purpose of this article is to introduce students and interested laypersons to the philosophy of Origen, it will be necessary to focus mainly on the treatise On First Principles, which is the most systematic and philosophical of Origen's numerous writings. In this work Origen establishes his main doctrines, including that of the Holy Trinity (based upon standard Middle Platonic triadic emanation schemas); the pre-existence and fall of souls; multiple ages and transmigration of souls; and the eventual restoration of all souls to a state of dynamic perfection in proximity to the godhead.

Origen, De Principiis.

Book I.

Chapter I.—On God.
1. I know that some will attempt to say that, even according to the declarations of our own Scriptures, God is a body, because in the writings of Moses they find it said, that "our God is a consuming fire;". and in the Gospel according to John, that "God is a Spirit, and they who worship Him must worship Him in spirit and in truth." Fire and spirit, according to them, are to be regarded as nothing else than a body. Now, I should like to ask these persons what they have to say respecting that passage where it is declared that God is light; as John writes in his Epistle, "God is light, and in Him there is no darkness at all.". Truly He is that light which illuminates the whole understanding of those who are capable of receiving truth, as is said in the thirty-sixth Psalm, "In Thy light we shall see Light". For what other light of God can be named, "in which any one sees light," save an influence of God, by which a man, being enlightened, either thoroughly sees the truth of all things, or comes to know God Himself, who is called the truth? Such is the meaning of the

expression, "In Thy light we shall see light;" i.e., in Thy word and wisdom which is Thy Son, in Himself we shall see Thee the Father. Because He is called light, shall He be supposed to have any resemblance to the light of the sun? Or how should there be the slightest ground for imagining, that from that corporeal light any one could derive the cause of knowledge, and come to the understanding of the truth?

2. If, then, they acquiesce in our assertion, which reason itself has demonstrated, regarding the nature of light, and acknowledge that God cannot be understood to be a body in the sense that light is, similar reasoning will hold true of the expression "a consuming fire." For what will God consume in respect of His being fire? Shall He be thought to consume material substance, as wood, or hay, or stubble? And what in this view can be called worthy of the glory of God, if He be a fire, consuming materials of that kind? But let us reflect that God does indeed consume and utterly destroy; that He consumes evil thoughts, wicked actions, and sinful desires, when they find their way into the minds of believers; and that, inhabiting along with His Son those souls which are rendered capable of receiving His word and wisdom, according to His own declaration, "I and the Father shall come, and We shall make our abode with him?". He makes them, after all their vices and passions have been consumed, a holy temple, worthy of Himself. Those, moreover, who, on account of the expression "God is a Spirit," think that He is a body, are to be answered, I think, in the following manner. It is the custom of sacred Scripture, when it wishes to designate anything opposed to this gross and solid body, to call it spirit, as in the expression, "The letter killeth, but the spirit giveth life,". where there can be no doubt that by "letter" are meant bodily things, and by "spirit" intellectual things, which we also term "spiritual." The apostle, moreover, says, "Even unto this day, when Moses is read, the veil is upon their heart: nevertheless, when it shall turn to the Lord, the veil shall be taken away: and where the Spirit of the Lord is, there is liberty." For so long as any one is not converted to a spiritual understanding, a veil is placed over his heart, with which veil, i.e., a gross understanding, Scripture itself is said or thought to be covered: and this is the meaning of the statement that a veil was placed over the countenance of Moses when he spoke to the people, i.e., when the law was publicly read aloud. But if we turn to the Lord, where also is the word of God, and where the Holy Spirit

reveals spiritual knowledge, then the veil is taken away, and with unveiled face we shall behold the glory of the Lord in the holy Scriptures.

3. And since many saints participate in the Holy Spirit, He cannot therefore be understood to be a body, which being divided into corporeal parts, is partaken of by each one of the saints; but He is manifestly a sanctifying power, in which all are said to have a share who have deserved to be sanctified by His grace. And in order that what we say may be more easily understood, let us take an illustration from things very dissimilar. There are many persons who take a part in the science Disciplina. or art of medicine: are we therefore to suppose that those who do so take to themselves the particles of some body called medicine, which is placed before them, and in this way participate in the same? Or must we not rather understand that all who with quick and trained minds come to understand the art and discipline itself, may be said to be par243takers of the art of healing? But these are not to be deemed altogether parallel instances in a comparison of medicine to the Holy Spirit, as they have been adduced only to establish that that is not necessarily to be considered a body, a share in which is possessed by many individuals. For the Holy Spirit differs widely from the method or science of medicine, in respect that the Holy Spirit is an intellectual existence Subsistentia. and subsists and exists in a peculiar manner, whereas medicine is not at all of that nature.

4. But we must pass on to the language of the Gospel itself, in which it is declared that "God is a Spirit," and where we have to show how that is to be understood agreeably to what we have stated. For let us inquire on what occasion these words were spoken by the Saviour, before whom He uttered them, and what was the subject of investigation. We find, without any doubt, that He spoke these words to the Samaritan woman, saying to her, who thought, agreeably to the Samaritan view, that God ought to be worshipped on Mount Gerizim, that "God is a Spirit." For the Samaritan woman, believing Him to be a Jew, was inquiring of Him whether God ought to be worshipped in Jerusalem or on this mountain; and her words were, "All our fathers worshipped on this mountain, and ye say that in Jerusalem is the place where we ought to worship." To this opinion of the Samaritan woman, therefore, who imagined that God was less rightly or duly worshipped, according to the privileges of the different localities,

either by the Jews in Jerusalem or by the Samaritans on Mount Gerizim, the Saviour answered that he who would follow the Lord must lay aside all preference for particular places, and thus expressed Himself: "The hour is coming when neither in Jerusalem nor on this mountain shall the true worshippers worship the Father. God is a Spirit, and they who worship Him must worship Him in spirit and in truth." And observe how logically He has joined together the spirit and the truth: He called God a Spirit, that He might distinguish Him from bodies; and He named Him the truth, to distinguish Him from a shadow or an image. For they who worshipped in Jerusalem worshipped God neither in truth nor in spirit, being in subjection to the shadow or image of heavenly things; and such also was the case with those who worshipped on Mount Gerizim.

5. Having refuted, then, as well as we could, every notion which might suggest that we were to think of God as in any degree corporeal, we go on to say that, according to strict truth, God is incomprehensible, and incapable of being measured. "Inæstimabilem." For whatever be the knowledge which we are able to obtain of God, either by perception or reflection, we must of necessity believe that He is by many degrees far better than what we perceive Him to be. For, as if we were to see any one unable to bear a spark of light, or the flame of a very small lamp, and were desirous to acquaint such a one, whose vision could not admit a greater degree of light than what we have stated, with the brightness and splendour of the sun, would it not be necessary to tell him that the splendour of the sun was unspeakably and incalculably better and more glorious than all this light which he saw? So our understanding, when shut in by the fetters of flesh and blood, and rendered, on account of its participation in such material substances, duller and more obtuse, although, in comparison with our bodily nature, it is esteemed to be far superior, yet, in its efforts to examine and behold incorporeal things, scarcely holds the place of a spark or lamp. But among all intelligent, that is, incorporeal beings, what is so superior to all others—so unspeakably and incalculably superior—as God, whose nature cannot be grasped or seen by the power of any human understanding, even the purest and brightest?

6. But it will not appear absurd if we employ another similitude to make the matter clearer. Our eyes frequently cannot look upon the nature of the light itself—that is, upon the substance of the sun; but

when we behold his splendour or his rays pouring in, perhaps, through windows or some small openings to admit the light, we can reflect how great is the supply and source of the light of the body. So, in like manner. the works of Divine Providence and the plan of this whole world are a sort of rays, as it were, of the nature of God, in comparison with His real substance and being. As, therefore, our understanding is unable of itself to behold God Himself as He is, it knows the Father of the world from the beauty of His works and the comeliness of His creatures. God, therefore, is not to be thought of as being either a body or as existing in a body, but as an uncompounded intellectual nature, "Simplex intellectualis natura." admitting within Himself no addition of any kind; so that He cannot be believed to have within him a greater and a less, but is such that He is in all parts Μονάς, and, so to speak, Ἑνάς, and is the mind and source from which all intellectual nature or mind takes its beginning. But mind, for its movements or operations, needs no physical space, nor sensible magnitude, nor bodily shape, nor colour, nor any other of those adjuncts which are the properties of body or matter. Wherefore that simple and wholly intellectual nature "Natura illa simplex et tota mens." can admit of no delay or hesitation in its movements or operations, lest the simplicity of the divine nature should appear to be circumscribed or in some degree hampered by such adjuncts, and lest that which is the beginning of all things should be found composite and differing, and that which ought to be free from all bodily intermixture, in virtue of being the one sole species of Deity, so to speak, should prove, instead of being one, to consist of many things. That mind, moreover, does not require space in order to carry on its movements agreeably to its nature, is certain from observation of our own mind. For if the mind abide within its own limits, and sustain no injury from any cause, it will never, from diversity of situation, be retarded in the discharge of its functions; nor, on the other hand, does it gain any addition or increase of mobility from the nature of particular places. And here, if any one were to object, for example, that among those who are at sea, and tossed by its waves the mind is considerably less vigorous than it is wont to be on land, we are to believe that it is in this state, not from diversity of situation, but from the commotion or disturbance of the body to which the mind is joined or attached. For it seems to be contrary to nature, as it were, for a human body to live at sea; and for that reason it appears, by a sort of inequality of its own, to enter upon its mental operations in a slovenly and irregular manner, and to perform the acts of the intellect with a duller sense, in as great degree as those who on land are prostrated with fever; with respect to whom it is certain, that if the mind do not discharge its functions as well as before, in consequence of the attack of disease, the blame is to be laid not upon the place, but upon the bodily malady, by which the body, being disturbed and disordered, renders to the mind its customary services under by no means the well-known and natural conditions: for we human beings are animals composed of a union of body and soul, and in this way (only) was it possible for us to live upon the earth. But God, who is the beginning of all things, is not to be regarded as a composite being, lest perchance there should be found to exist elements prior to the beginning itself, out of which everything is composed, whatever that be which is called composite. Neither does the mind require bodily magnitude in order to perform any act or movement; as when the eye by gazing upon bodies of larger size is dilated, but is compressed and contracted in order to see smaller objects. The mind, indeed, requires magnitude of an intellectual kind, because it grows, not after the fashion of a body, but after that of intelligence. For the mind is not enlarged, together with the body, by means of corporal additions, up to the twentieth or thirtieth year of life; but the intellect is sharpened by exercises of learning, and the powers implanted within it for intelligent purposes are called forth; and it is rendered capable of greater intellectual efforts, not being increased by bodily additions, but carefully polished by learned exercises. But these it cannot receive immediately from boyhood, or from birth, because the framework of limbs which the mind employs as organs for exercising itself is weak and feeble; and it is unable to bear the weight of its own operations, or to exhibit a capacity for receiving training.

7. If there are any now who think that the mind itself and the soul is a body, I wish they would tell me by way of answer how it receives reasons and assertions on subjects of such importance—of such difficulty and such subtlety? Whence does it derive the power of memory? and whence comes the contemplation of invisible. Some read "visible." things? How does the body possess the faculty of understanding incorporeal existences? How does a bodily nature investigate the processes of the various arts, and contemplate the reasons of things? How, also, is it able to perceive and understand

divine truths, which are manifestly incorporeal? Unless, indeed, some should happen to be of opinion, that as the very bodily shape and form of the ears or eyes contributes something to hearing and to sight, and as the individual members, formed by God, have some adaptation, even from the very quality of their form, to the end for which they were naturally appointed; so also he may think that the shape of the soul or mind is to be understood as if created purposely and designedly for perceiving and understanding individual things, and for being set in motion by vital movements. I do not perceive, however, who shall be able to describe or state what is the colour of the mind, in respect of its being mind, and acting as an intelligent existence. Moreover, in confirmation and explanation of what we have already advanced regarding the mind or soul—to the effect that it is better than the whole bodily nature—the following remarks may be added. There underlies every bodily sense a certain peculiar sensible substance, "Substantia quædam sensibilis propria," on which the bodily sense exerts itself. For example, colours, form, size, underlie vision; voices and sound, the sense of hearing; odours, good or bad, that of smell; savours, that of taste; heat or cold, hardness or softness, roughness or smoothness, that of touch. Now, of those senses enumerated above, it is manifest to all that the sense of mind is much the best. How, then, should it not appear absurd, that under those senses which are inferior, substances should have been placed on which to exert their powers, but that under this power, which is far better than any other, i.e., the sense of mind, nothing at all of the nature of a substance should be placed, but that a power of an intellectual nature should be an accident, or consequent upon bodies? Those who assert this, doubtless do so to the disparagement of that better substance which is within them; nay, by so doing, they even do wrong to God Himself, when they imagine He may be understood by means of a bodily nature, so that according to their view He is a body, and that which may be understood or perceived by means of a body; and they are unwilling to have it understood that the mind bears a certain relationship to God, of whom the mind itself is an intellectual image, and that by means of this it may come to some knowledge of the nature of divinity, especially if it be purified and separated from bodily matter.

8. But perhaps these declarations may seem to have less weight with those who wish to be instructed in divine things out of the holy

Scriptures, and who seek to have it proved to them from that source how the nature of God surpasses the nature of bodies. See, therefore, if the apostle does not say the same thing, when, speaking of Christ, he declares, that "He is the image of the invisible God, the first-born of every creature." Not, as some suppose, that the nature of God is visible to some and invisible to others: for the apostle does not say "the image of God invisible" to men or "invisible" to sinners, but with unvarying constancy pronounces on the nature of God in these words: "the image of the invisible God." Moreover, John, in his Gospel, when asserting that "no one hath seen God at any time," manifestly declares to all who are capable of understanding, that there is no nature to which God is visible: not as if, He were a being who was visible by nature, and merely escaped or baffled the view of a frailer creature, but because by the nature of His being it is impossible for Him to be seen. And if you should ask of me what is my opinion regarding the Only-begotten Himself, whether the nature of God, which is naturally invisible, be not visible even to Him, let not such a question appear to you at once to be either absurd or impious, because we shall give you a logical reason. It is one thing to see, and another to know: to see and to be seen is a property of bodies; to know and to be known, an attribute of intellectual being. Whatever, therefore, is a property of bodies, cannot be predicated either of the Father or of the Son; but what belongs to the nature of deity is common to the Father and the Son. "Constat inter Patrem et Filium." Finally, even He Himself, in the Gospel, did not say that no one has seen the Father, save the Son, nor any one the Son, save the Father; but His words are: "No one knoweth the Son, save the Father; nor any one the Father, save the Son.". By which it is clearly shown, that whatever among bodily natures is called seeing and being seen, is termed, between the Father and the Son, a knowing and being known, by means of the power of knowledge, not by the frailness of the sense of sight. Because, then, neither seeing nor being seen can be properly applied to an incorporeal and invisible nature, neither is the Father, in the Gospel, said to be seen by the Son, nor the Son by the Father, but the one is said to be known by the other.

9. Here, if any one lay before us the passage where it is said, "Blessed are the pure in heart, for they shall see God,". from that very passage, in my opinion, will our position derive additional strength; for what else is seeing God in heart, but, according to our exposition

as above, understanding and knowing Him with the mind? For the names of the organs of sense are frequently applied to the soul, so that it may be said to see with the eyes of the heart, i.e., to perform an intellectual act by means of the power of intelligence. So also it is said to hear with the ears when it perceives the deeper meaning of a statement. So also we say that it makes use of teeth, when it chews and eats the bread of life which cometh down from heaven. In like manner, also, it is said to employ the services of other members, which are transferred from their bodily appellations, and applied to the powers of the soul, according to the words of Solomon, "You will find a divine sense." For he knew that there were within us two kinds of senses: the one mortal, corruptible, human; the other immortal and intellectual, which he now termed divine. By this divine sense, therefore, not of the eyes, but of a pure heart, which is the mind, God may be seen by those who are worthy. For you will certainly find in all the Scriptures, both old and new, the term "heart" repeatedly used instead of "mind," i.e., intellectual power. In this manner, therefore, although far below the dignity of the subject, have we spoken of the nature of God, as those who understand it under the limitation of the human understanding. In the next place, let us see what is meant by the name of Christ.

Gnostic, Marcion (2nd Cent CE): Gospel of the Lord c. 220 CE

Marcion was a rich shipowner of Sinope, the chief port of Pontus, on the southern shore of the Black Sea; he was also a bishop and the son of a bishop. His chief activity at Rome may be placed somewhere between the years 150 and 160. At first he was in communion with the church at Rome, and contributed handsomely to its funds; as, however, the presbyters could not explain his difficulties and refused to face the important questions he set before them, he is said to have threatened to make a schism in the church; and apparently was finally excommunicated.

But as a matter of fact the origin of Marcionism is entirely wrapped in obscurity, and we know nothing of a reliable nature of the lives of either Cerdo or Marcion. The Church writers at the end of the second century, who are our best authorities, cannot tell the story of the beginning of the movement with any certainty. For all we know, Marcion may have developed his theories long before he came to Rome, and may have based them on information he gleaned and opinions he heard on his long voyages.

This much we know, that the views of Marcion spread rapidly over the "whole world," to use the usual Patristic phrase for the Graeco-Roman dominions; and as late as the fifth century we hear of Theodoret converting more than a thousand Marcionites. In Italy, Egypt, Palestine, Arabia, Syria, Asia Minor and Persia, Marcionite churches sprang up, splendidly organized, with their own bishops and the rest of the ecclesiastical discipline, with a cult and service of the same nature as those of what subsequently became the Catholic Church. Orthodoxy had not declared for any party as yet, and the Marcionite view had then as good a chance as any other of becoming the universal one. What then was the secret of Marcion's success? As already pointed out, it was the same as that of the success of modern criticism as applied to the problem of the Old Testament.

Marcion's view was in some respects even more moderate than the judgment of some of our modern thinkers; he was willing to admit that the Yahweh of the Old Testament was just. With great acumen he arranged the sayings and doings ascribed to Yahweh by the writers, and compilers, and editors of the heterogeneous books of the Old Testament collection, in parallel columns, so to say, with the sayings and teachings of the Christ-in a series of antitheses which brought out in startling fashion the fact, that though the best of the former might be ascribed to the idea of a Just God, they were foreign to the ideal of the Good God preached by the Christ. We know how in these latter days the best minds in the Church have rejected the horrible sayings and doings ascribed to God in some of the Old Testament documents, and we thus see how Marcion formulated a protest which must have already declared itself in the hearts of thousands of the more enlightened of the Christian name.

As to actual history, then, Marcion started with Paul; he was the first who had really understood the mission of the Christ, and had rescued the teaching from the obscurantism of Jewish sectarianism. Of the manifold versions of the Gospel, he would have the Pauline alone. He rejected every other recension, including those now ascribed to Matthew, Mark, and John. The Gospel according to Luke, the "follower of Paul," he also rejected, regarding it as a recension to suit the views of the Judaising party. His Gospel was presumably the collection of Sayings in use among the Pauline churches of his day. Of course the Patristic writers say that Marcion mutilated Luke's version; but it is almost impossible to believe that, if he did this, so keen a critic as Marcion should have retained certain verses which made against his strong anti-Judaistic views. The Marcionites, on the contrary, contended that their Gospel was written by Paul from the direct tradition, and that Luke had nothing to do with it. But this is also a difficulty, for it is highly improbable that Paul wrote any Gospel.

The Marcionites were the most rigid of ascetics, abstaining from marriage, flesh and wine, the latter being excluded from their Eucharist. They also rejoiced beyond all other sects in the number of their martyrs. The Marcionites have also given us the most ancient dated Christian inscription. It was discovered over the doorway of a house in a Syrian village, and formerly marked the site of a Marcionite meeting-house or church, which curiously enough was called a synagogue. The date is October 1, A.D. 318 and the most remarkable point about it is that the church was dedicated to "The Lord and Saviour Jesus, the Good - "Chrestos", not Christos.

The Arrival of Jesus at Capernaum

Adv.Marc.iv.7 ; Panarion 42
3:1/4:31 In the fifteenth year of Tiberius Caesar,
Pontius Pilate being governor of Judea,
Jesus descended [out of heaven] into Capernaum, a city in Galilee,
and was teaching [in the synagogue] on the Sabbath days;
And they were astonished at his doctrine,
Adv.Marc.iv.7
for his word was in authority.
33 And in the synagogue there was a man,which had a spirit of an unclean devil,
and cried out with a loud voice, saying,

34 Let us alone; what have we to do with thee, thou Jesus ?
art thou come to destroy us? I know thee who thou art; the Holy One of God.
Adv.Marc.iv.7
35 And Jesus rebuked him, saying,
Hold thy peace, and come out of him.
And when the devil had thrown him in the midst,
he came out of him, and hurt him not.
36 And they were all amazed, and spake among themselves, saying,
What a word is this!
for with authority and power he commandeth the unclean spirits,
and they come out.
37 And the fame of him went out into every place of the country
round about.

[4:38-39 unattested]

The Synagogue in Nazareth

Adv.Marc.iv.8
4: 16 And he came to Nazareth,
and went into the synagogue on the sabbath day,
and sat down.
21 And he began to speak to them,
and all wondered at the words which proceeded out of his mouth.
23 And he said unto them,
Ye will surely say unto me this proverb,
Physician, heal thyself: whatsoever we have heard done in Capernaum,
do also here in thy country.

Zahn omits - relocated to 17:19:

[25 But I tell you of a truth, many widows were in Israel in the days of Elijah,
when the heaven was shut up three years and six months,
when great famine was throughout all the land;
26 But unto none of them was Elias sent, save unto Sarepta, a city of Sidon,

unto a woman that was a widow.
27 And many lepers were in Israel in the time of Elisha the prophet; and none of them was cleansed, saving Naaman the Syrian.]

28 And they were all filled with wrath in the synagogue,
29 And rose up, and thrust him out of the city,
and led him unto the brow of the hill whereon their city was built,
that they might cast him down headlong.
30 But he passing through the midst of them went his way.

At the Setting of the Sun

40 Now when the sun was setting,
all they that had any sick with divers diseases brought them unto him;
and he laid his hands on every one of them, and healed them.
41 And devils also came out of many, crying out, and saying,
Thou art the Son of God.
Adv.Marc.iv.8
[-41c] And he rebuking them suffered them not to speak.
42 And when it was day, he departed and went into a desert place:
Adv.Marc.iv.8
and the people sought him,
and came unto him, and stayed him, that he should not depart from them.
43 And he said unto them,
I must preach the kingdom of God to other cities also:
for therefore am I sent.
44 And he preached in the synagogues of Galilee.

The Lake of Gennesaret

5: 1 And it came to pass, he stood by the lake of Gennesaret,
2 And saw two ships standing by the lake:
but the fishermen were gone out of them,
and were washing their nets.
3 And he entered into one of the ships, which was Simon's,
and prayed him that he would thrust out a little from the land.
And he sat down, and taught the people out of the ship.
4 Now when he had left speaking, he said unto Simon,

Launch out into the deep,
and let down your nets for a draught.
5 And Simon answering said unto him,
Teacher, we have toiled all the night,
and have taken nothing:
nevertheless at thy word I will let down the net.
6 And when they had this done, they inclosed a great multitude of fishes:
and their net brake.
7 And they beckoned unto their partners, which were in the other ship,
that they should come and help them.
And they came, and filled both the ships, so that they began to sink.
8 When Simon Peter saw it, he fell down at Jesus' knees, saying,
Depart from me; for I am a sinful man, O Lord.
9 For he was astonished, and all that were with him,
at the draught of the fishes which they had taken:
10 And so was also James, and John, the sons of Zebedee,
which were partners with Simon.
And Jesus said unto Simon,
Fear not; from henceforth thou shalt catch men alive.
Adv.Marc.iv.9
11 And when they had brought their ships to land,
they forsook all, and followed him.

Orthodoxy, Tertullian, On Pagan Learning, c. 220 CE (On the Proscription of Heretics)

For philosophy it is which is the material of the world's wisdom, the rash interpreter of the nature and the dispensation of God. Indeed heresies are themselves instigated by philosophy. From this source came the Aeons, and I known not what infinite forms, and the Trinity of Man in the system of Valentinus, who was of Plato's school. From the same source came Marcion's better god, with all his tranquillity; he came of the Stoics. Then, again, the opinion that the soul dies is held by the Epicureans; while the denial of the restoration of the body is taken from the aggregate school of all the philosophers; also, when matter is made equal to God, then you have the teaching of Zeno; and when any doctrine is alleged touching a god of fire, then Heraclitus comes in. The same matter is discussed over and over again by the heretics and the philosophers; the same arguments are involved. Whence comes evil? Why is it permitted? What is the origin of Man? And in what way does he come? Besides the question which Valentinus has very lately proposed--Whence comes God? Which he settles with the answer: From enthymesis and ectroma. Unhappy Aristotle! who invented for these men dialectics, the art of building up and pulling down; an art so evasive in its propositions, so far-fetched in its conjectures, so harsh, in its arguments, so productive of contentions, embarrassing even to itself, retracting everything, and really treating of nothing! Whence spring those "fables and endless genealogies," and "unprofitable questions," and "words which spread like a cancer?" From all these, when the apostle would restrain us, he expressly names philosophy as that which he would have us be on our guard against. Writing to The Colossians, he says, "See that no one beguile you through philosophy and vain deceit, after the tradition of men, and contrary to the wisdom of the Holy Ghost." He had been at Athens, and had in his interviews (with its philosophers) become acquainted with that human wisdom which pretends to know the truth, while it only corrupts it, and is itself divided into its own manifold heresies, by the variety of its mutually repugnant sects.

What indeed has Athens to do with Jerusalem? What concord is there between the Academy and the Church? What between heretics and Christians? Our instruction comes from "the porch of Solomon," who had himself taught that "the Lord should be sought in simplicity of heart." Away with all attempts to produce a mottled Christianity of Stoic, Platonic, and dialectic composition! We want no curious disputation after possessing Christ Jesus, no inquisition after enjoying the gospel! With our faith, we desire no further belief. For this is our primary faith, that there is nothing which we ought to believe besides!

5. The "Triumph" of the Church

The List of Popes.

The historical lists of the popes, from those drawn up in the second century to those of the present day, form in themselves a considerable body of literature. It is desirable to indicate very briefly what are our authorities for the names and the durations in office of the popes for the first two centuries of the Church's existence. St. Irenaeus, writing between 175 and 190, not many years after his Roman sojourn, enumerates the series from Peter to Eleutherius (Against Heresies III.3.3; Eusebius, Church History V.6). His object was to establish the orthodoxy of the traditional doctrine, as opposed to heretical novelties, by showing that the bishop was the natural inheritor of the Apostolic teaching. He gives us the names alone, not the length of the various episcopates. This need is supplied by other witnesses.

Most important evidence is furnished by the document entitled the "Liberian Catalogue" — so called from the Pope whose name ends the list. The collection of tracts of which this forms a part was edited (apparently by one Furius Dionysius Philocalus) in 354. The catalogue consists of a list of the Roman bishops from Peter to Liberius, with the length of their respective episcopates, the consular dates, the name of the reigning emperor, and in many cases other details. There is the strongest ground for believing that the earlier part of the catalogue, as far as Pontian (230-35), is the work of Hippolytus of Portus. It is manifest that up to this point the fourth century compiler was making use of a different authority from that which he employs for the subsequent popes: and there is evidence rendering it almost certain that Hippolytus's work "Chronica" contained such a list. The reign of Pontian, moreover, would be the point at which that list would have stopped: for Hippolytus and he were condemned to servitude in the Sardinian mines — a fact which the chronographer makes mention when speaking of Pontian's episcopate. Lightfoot has argued that this list originally contained nothing but the names of the bishops and the duration of their episcopates, the remaining notes being additions by a later hand. The list of popes is identical with that of Irenaeus, save that Anacletus is doubled into Cletus and Anacletus, while Clement appears before, instead of after, these two names. The order of Popes Pius and Anicetus has also been interchanged. There is every reason to regard these differences as due to the errors of copyists.

Another witness is Eusebius. The names and episcopal years of the bishops can be gathered alike from his "History" and his "Chronicle". The notices in the two works; can be shown to be in agreement, notwithstanding certain corruptions in many texts of the "Chronicle". This Eastern list in the hands of Eusebius is seen to have been identical with the Western list of Hippolytus, except that in the East the name of Linus's successor seems to have been given as Anencletus, in the original Western list as Cletus.

The two authorities presuppose the following list: (1) Peter, xxv; (2) Linus, xii; (3) Anencletus [Cletus], xii; (4) Clement, ix; (5) Evarestus, viii; (6) Alexander, x; (7) Sixtus, x; (8) Telesophorus, xi; (9) Hyginus, iv; (10) Pius, xv; (11) Anicetus, xi;, (12) Soter, viii; (13) Eleutherius, xv; (14) Victor, x; (15) Zephyrinus, xviii; (16) Callistus, v; (17) Urban, viii; (18) Pontian, v (Harnack, "Chronologie", I, 152).

We learn from Eusebius (Church History IV.22) that in the middle of the second century Hegesippus, the Hebrew Christian, visited Rome and that he drew up a list of bishops as far as Anicetus, the then pope. Eusebius does not quote his catalogue, but Lightfoot sees ground for holding that we possess it in a passage of Epiphanius (Haer. 27:6), in which the bishops as far as Anicetus are enumerated. This list of Hegesippus, drawn up less than a century after the martyrdom of St. Peter, was he believes, the foundation alike of the Eusebian and Hippolytan catalogues (Clement of Rome I, 325 so.). His view has been accepted by many scholars. Even those who, like Harnack (Chronologie, I, 184 sq.), do not admit that this list is really that of Hegesippus, recognize it as a catalogue of Roman origin and of very early date, furnishing testimony independent alike of the Eusebian and Liberian lists.
The "Liber Pontificalis", long accepted as an authority of the highest value, is now acknowledged to have been originally composed at the beginning of the fifth century, and, as regards the early popes, to be dependent on the "Liberian Catalogue".

Eusebius: The Conversion of Constantine

CHAPTER XXVII.
Being convinced, however, that he needed some more powerful aid than his military forces could afford him, on account of the wicked and magical enchantments which were so diligently practiced by the tyrant, he sought Divine assistance, deeming the possession of arms and a numerous soldiery of secondary importance, but believing the co-operating power of Deity invincible and not to be shaken. He considered, therefore, on what God he might rely for protection and assistance. While engaged in this enquiry, the thought occurred to him, that, of the many emperors who had preceded him, those who had rested their hopes in a multitude of gods, and served them with sacrifices and offerings, had in the first place been deceived by flattering predictions, and oracles which promised them all prosperity, and at last had met with an unhappy end, while not one of their gods had stood by to warn them of the impending wrath of heaven; while one alone who had pursued an entirely opposite course, who had condemned their error, and honored the one Supreme God during his whole life, had formal I him to be the Saviour and Protector of his empire, and the Giver of every good thing. Reflecting on this, and well weighing the fact that they who had trusted in many gods had also fallen by manifold forms of death, without leaving behind them either family or offspring, stock, name, or memorial among men: while the God of his father had given to him, on the other hand, manifestations of his power and very many tokens: and considering farther that those who had already taken arms against the tyrant, and had marched to the battle-field under the protection of a multitude of gods, had met with a dishonorable end (for one of them had shamefully retreated from the contest without a blow, and the other, being slain in the midst of his own troops, became, as it were, the mere sport of death (4)); reviewing, I say, all these considerations, he judged it to be folly indeed to join in the idle worship of those who were no gods, and, after such convincing evidence, to err from the truth; and therefore felt it incumbent on him to honor his father's God alone.

CHAPTER XXVIII.

ACCORDINGLY he called on him with earnest prayer and supplications that he would reveal to him who he was, and stretch forth his right hand to help him in his present difficulties. And while he was thus praying with fervent entreaty, a most marvelous sign appeared to him from heaven, the account of which it might have been hard to believe had it been related by any other person. But since the victorious emperor himself long afterwards declared it to the writer of this history, when he was honored with his acquaintance and society, and confirmed his statement by an oath, who could hesitate to accredit the relation, especially since the testimony of after-time has established its truth? He said that about noon, when the day was already beginning to decline, he saw with his own eyes the trophy of a cross of light in the heavens, above the sun, and bearing the inscription, CONQUER BY THIS. At this sight he himself was struck with amazement, and his whole army also, which followed him on this expedition, and witnessed the miracle.

CHAPTER XXIX.
He said, moreover, that he doubted within himself what the import of this apparition could be. And while he continued to ponder and reason on its meaning, night suddenly came on ; then in his sleep the Christ of God appeared to him with the same sign which he had seen in the heavens, and commanded him to make a likeness of that sign which he had seen in the heavens, and to use it as a safeguard in all engagements with his enemies.

CHAPTER XXX.
AT dawn of day he arose, and communicated the marvel to his friends: and then, calling together the workers in gold and precious stones, he sat in the midst of them, and described to them the figure of the sign he had seen, bidding them represent it in gold and precious stones. And this representation I myself have had an opportunity of seeing.

CHAPTER XXXI.
Now it was made in the following manner. A long spear, overlaid with gold, formed the figure of the cross by means of a transverse bar laid over it. On the top of the whole was fixed a wreath of gold and precious stones; and within this, the symbol of the Saviour's name,

two letters indicating the name of Christ by means of its initial characters, the letter P being intersected by X in its centre: and these letters the emperor was in the habit of wearing on his helmet at a later period. From the cross-bar of the spear was suspended a cloth, a royal piece, covered with a profuse embroidery of most brilliant precious stones; and which, being also richly interlaced with gold, presented an indescribable degree of beauty to the beholder. This banner was of a square form, and the upright staff, whose lower section was of great length, bore a golden half-length portrait of the pious emperor and his children on its upper part, beneath the trophy of the cross, and immediately above the embroidered banner.

The emperor constantly made use of this sign of salvation as a safeguard against every adverse and hostile power, and commanded that others similar to it should be carried at the head of all his armies.

CHAPTER XXXII.

These things were done shortly afterwards. But at the time above specified, being struck with amazement at the extraordinary vision, and resolving to worship no other God save Him who had appeared to him, he sent for those who were acquainted with the mysteries of His doctrines, and enquired who that God was, and what was intended by the sign of the vision he had seen. They affirmed that He was God, the only begotten Son of the one and only God: that the sign which had appeared was the symbol of immortality, and the trophy of that victory over death which He had gained in time past when sojourning on earth. They taught him also the causes of His advent, and explained to him the true account of His incarnation. Thus he was instructed in these matters, and was impressed with wonder at the divine manifestation which had been presented to his sight. Comparing, therefore, the heavenly vision with the interpretation given, he found his judgment confirmed; and, in the persuasion that the knowledge of these things had been imparted to him by Divine teaching, he determined thenceforth to devote himself to the reading of the Inspired writings.

Moreover, he made the priests of God his counselors, and deemed it incumbent on him to honor the God who had appeared to him with all devotion. And after this, being fortified by well-grounded hopes in Him, he hastened to quench the threatening fire of tyranny.

Edict of Milan

It was granted by Emperor Constantine the Great in the West and Licinius Augustus in the East in 313 granting religious freedom throughout the Roman Empire. In addition, the Edict of Milan ordered the restitution of property confiscated from Christians.

"When I, Constantine Augustus, as well as I, Licinius Augustus, fortunately met near Mediolanurn (Milan), and were considering everything that pertained to the public welfare and security, we thought, among other things which we saw would be for the good of many, those regulations pertaining to the reverence of the Divinity ought certainly to be made first, so that we might grant to the Christians and others full authority to observe that religion which each preferred; whence any Divinity whatsoever in the seat of the heavens may be propitious and kindly disposed to us and all who are placed under our rule. And thus by this wholesome counsel and most upright provision we thought to arrange that no one whatsoever should be denied the opportunity to give his heart to the observance of the Christian religion, of that religion which he should think best for himself, so that the Supreme Deity, to whose worship we freely yield our hearts) may show in all things His usual favor and benevolence. Therefore, your Worship should know that it has pleased us to remove all conditions whatsoever, which were in the rescripts formerly given to you officially, concerning the Christians and now any one of these who wishes to observe Christian religion may do so freely and openly, without molestation. We thought it fit to commend these things most fully to your care that you may know that we have given to those Christians free and unrestricted opportunity of religious worship. When you see that this has been granted to them by us, your Worship will know that we have also conceded to other religions the right of open and free observance of their worship for the sake of the peace of our times, that each one may have the free opportunity to worship as he pleases; this regulation is made we that we may not seem to detract from any dignity or any religion.
Moreover, in the case of the Christians especially we esteemed it best to order that if it happens anyone heretofore has bought from our treasury from anyone whatsoever, those places where they were

previously accustomed to assemble, concerning which a certain decree had been made and a letter sent to you officially, the same shall be restored to the Christians without payment or any claim of recompense and without any kind of fraud or deception, Those, moreover, who have obtained the same by gift, are likewise to return them at once to the Christians. Besides, both those who have purchased and those who have secured them by gift, are to appeal to the vicar if they seek any recompense from our bounty, that they may be cared for through our clemency. All this property ought to be delivered at once to the community of the Christians through your intercession, and without delay. And since these Christians are known to have possessed not only those places in which they were accustomed to assemble, but also other property, namely the churches, belonging to them as a corporation and not as individuals, all these things which we have included under the above law, you will order to be restored, without any hesitation or controversy at all, to these Christians, that is to say to the corporations and their conventicles: providing, of course, that the above arrangements be followed so that those who return the same without payment, as we have said, may hope for an indemnity from our bounty. In all these circumstances you ought to tender your most efficacious intervention to the community of the Christians, that our command may be carried into effect as quickly as possible, whereby, moreover, through our clemency, public order may be secured. Let this be done so that, as we have said above, Divine favor towards us, which, under the most important circumstances we have already experienced, may, for all time, preserve and prosper our successes together with the good of the state. Moreover, in order that the statement of this decree of our good will may come to the notice of all, this rescript, published by your decree, shall be announced everywhere and brought to the knowledge of all, so that the decree of this, our benevolence, cannot be concealed." Lactantius (De Mort. Pers., ch. 48)

The Nicene Creed (325). Jesus, God and the Holy Spirit. The Trinity

The purpose of a creed is to act as a yardstick of correct belief. The creeds of Christianity have been drawn up at times of conflict about doctrine: acceptance or rejection of a creed served to distinguish believers and deniers of a particular doctrine or set of doctrines. For that reason a creed was called in Greek a σύμβολον, a word that meant half of a broken object which, when placed together with the other half, verified the bearer's identity. The Greek word passed through Latin "symbolum" into English "symbol", which only later took on the meaning of an outward sign of something. The Nicene Creed was adopted in the face of the Arian controversy. Arius, a Libyan preacher, had declared that although Jesus Christ was divine, God had actually created him, and "there was when he was not," also worded by others of the era "there was once when he was not" and "he was made out of nothing."This made Jesus less than the Father and contradicted the doctrine of the Trinity. Arius's teaching provoked a serious crisis. The Nicene Creed of 325 explicitly affirms the divinity of Jesus, applying to him the term "God". The 381 version speaks of the Holy Spirit as worshipped and glorified with the Father and the Son. The Athanasian Creed describes in much greater detail the relationship between Father, Son and Holy Spirit. The Apostles' Creed makes no explicit statements about the divinity of the Son and the Holy Spirit, but, in the view of many who use it, the doctrine is implicit in it.

> We believe in one God, the Father Almighty, the maker of heaven and earth, of things visible and invisible.
> And in one Lord Jesus Christ, the Son of God, the begotten of God the Father, the Only-begotten, that is of the essence of the Father.
> God of God, Light of Light, true God of true God, begotten and not made; of the very same nature of the Father, by Whom all things came into being, in heaven and on earth, visible and invisible.
> Who for us humanity and for our salvation came down from heaven, was incarnate, was made human, was born perfectly of the holy virgin Mary by the Holy Spirit.
> By whom He took body, soul, and mind, and everything that is in man, truly and not in semblance.
> He suffered, was crucified, was buried, rose again on the third day, ascended into heaven with the same body, [and] sat at the right hand of the Father.

He is to come with the same body and with the glory of the Father, to judge the living and the dead; of His kingdom there is no end.

We believe in the Holy Spirit, in the uncreated and the perfect; Who spoke through the Law, prophets, and Gospels; Who came down upon the Jordan, preached through the apostles, and lived in the saints.

We believe also in only One, Universal, Apostolic, and [Holy] Church; in one baptism in repentance, for the remission, and forgiveness of sins; and in the resurrection of the dead, in the everlasting judgement of souls and bodies, and the Kingdom of Heaven and in the everlasting life.[1]

The 'Decretum Gelasianum de libris recipiendis et non recipiendis' (4th century a.d.)

HERE BEGINS THE COUNCIL OF ROME UNDER POPE DAMASUS "ON EXPLAINING THE FAITH"

I. It was said:
1. Firstly the seven-fold Spirit which remains in Christ should be discussed:
the spirit of wisdom: 'Christ the power and wisdom of God'. the spirit of understanding: 'I will give you understanding, and I will instruct you in the way you will go'.
the spirit of counsel: 'And his name is called the messenger of great counsel'.
the spirit of virtues: as above, 'The power of God and the wisdom of God'.
the spirit of knowledge: 'Because of the eminence of the knowledge of the apostle of Christ Jesus'. the spirit of truth: 'I am the way the life and the truth'.
the spirit of the fear of God: 'The fear of the Lord is the beginning of wisdom'.

2. However the dispensation of Christ has a name of many forms:

God, who is spirit;
the word, who is God;
the Son, who is only-begotten of the Father;
the man, who was born of the virgin;
the priest, who offered himself as a sacrifice;
the shepherd, who is the guard;
the worm, who rose from the dead;
the mountain, which is strong;
the way, which is straight;
the harbour, which one may pass through into life;
the lamb, which was slain;
the stone, which is the cornerstone;
the master, who is the bringer of life;
the sun, which is the illuminator;
the true, which is of the Father;
the life, which is the creator;
the bread, which is dear;
the Samaritan, who is the guard and the merciful;
the Christ, who is the anointed one;
Jesus, who is the saviour;
God, who is from God;
the messenger, who was sent;
the bridegroom, who is the mediator;
the vine, by whose own blood we are redeemed;
the lion, who is king;
the rock, which is the foundation;
the flower, which is chosen;
the prophet, who revealed the future.

3. For the Holy Spirit is not of the Father only or of the Son only, but of the Father and the Son; for it is written: 'He who delights in the world, the Spirit of the Father is not in him'; again it is written; 'However anyone who does not have the Spirit of Christ, does not belong to him'. So the Holy Spirit is understood to be called of the Father and the Son, [and] of whom the Son himself in the gospel says that the Holy Spirit 'proceeds from the Father' and 'he will receive from me and he will make known to you'.

II. Likewise it was said:

Now indeed the issue of the divine scriptures must be discussed, which the universal Catholic church receives or which it is required to avoid.

1. THIS IS THE ORDER OF THE OLD TESTAMENT:

Genesis	one book
Exodus	one book
Leviticus	one book
Numbers	one book
Deuteronomy	one book
Joshua	one book
Judges	one book
Ruth	one book
Kings	four books
Chronicles	two books
150 Psalms	one book
Three books of Solomon	
proverbs	one book
ecclesiastes	one book
song of songs	one book
The same of Wisdom	one book
ecclesiasticus	one book

2. LIKEWISE THE ORDER OF THE PROPHETS:

Isaiah	one book
Jeremiah	one book
with Cinoth i.e. his lamentations	
Ezechiel	one book
Daniel	one book
Hosea	one book
Amos	one book
Micah	one book

Joel	one book
Obadiah	one book
Jonah	one book
Nahum	one book
Habbakuk	one book
Zephaniah	one book
Haggai	one book
Zechariah	one book
Malachi	one book

3. LIKEWISE THE ORDER OF THE HISTORIES:

Job	one book
Tobit	one book
Esdras	two books
Ester	one book
Judith	one book
Maccabees	two books

4. LIKEWISE THE ORDER OF THE SCRIPTURES OF THE NEW TESTAMENT which the holy and catholic Roman church upholds and is venerated:

Four books of the Gospels

according to Mathew	one book
according to Mark	one book
according to Luke	one book
according to John	one book
Likewise the acts of the apostles	one book
The letters of the apostle Paul in number fourteen	
to the Romans	one letter
to the Corinthians	two letters
to the Ephesians	one letter

to the Thesalonians	two letters
to the Galatians	one letter
to the Philippians	one letter
to the Colossians	one letter
to Timothy	two letters
to Titus	one letter
to the Philemon	one letter
to the Hebrews	one letter
Likewise the apocalypse of John	one book
Likewise the canonical [catholic] letters in number seven	
of the apostle Peter	two letters
of the apostle James	one letter
of the apostle John	one letter
of the other John the elder	two letters
of the apostle Judas the Zealot	one letter

HERE ENDS THE CANON OF THE NEW TESTAMENT.

III. Likewise it was said:
HERE BEGINS THE DECRETAL 'ON BOOKS TO BE RECEIVED AND NOT TO BE RECEIVED' WHICH WAS WRITTEN BY POPE GELASIUS AND SEVENTY MOST ERUDITE BISHOPS AT THE APOSTOLIC SEAT IN THE CITY OF ROME

1. After all these [writings of] the prophets and the evangelical and apostolic scriptures which we discussed above, on which the catholic church is founded by the grace of God, we also have thought necessary to say what, although the universal catholic church diffused throughout the world is the single bride of Christ, however the holy Roman church is given first place by the rest of the churches without [the need for] a synodical decision, but from the voice of the Lord our saviour in the gospel obtained primacy: 'You are Peter,' he said, 'and upon this rock I shall build my church and the gates of hell shall not prevail against it; and to you I give the keys of the kingdom of heaven, and whatever you shall bind upon Earth shall be bound also

in heaven and whatever you release upon Earth shall also be released in heaven'.

2. In addition there is also the presence of the blessed apostle Paul, 'the chosen vessel', who not in opposition, as the heresies jabber, but on the same date and the same day was crowned in glorious death with Peter in the city of Rome suffering under Nero Caesar; and equally they made the above-mentioned holy Roman church special in Christ the Lord and gave preference in their presence and veneration-worthy triumph before all other cities in the whole world.

3. Therefore first is the seat at the Roman church of the apostle Peter 'having no spot or wrinkle or any other [defect]'.

However the second place was given in the name of blessed Peter to Mark his disciple and gospel-writer at Alexandria, and who himself wrote down the word of truth directed by Peter the apostle in Egypt and gloriously consummated [his life] in martyrdom.

Indeed the third place is held at Antioch of the most blessed and honourable apostle Peter, who lived there before he came to Roma and where first the name of the new race of the Christians was heard.

IV. And although 'no other foundation can be established except that which has been established, Christ Jesus', however for edification likewise the holy Roman church after the books of the Old and New Testaments which we have enumerated above according to the canon also does not prohibit the reception of these writings:

1. the holy synod of Nicaea of 318 fathers chaired by the Emperor Constantine the Great,

at which the heretic Arius was condemned; the holy synod of Constantinople chaired by Theodosius the senior Augustus, at which the heretic Macedonius escaped his deserved condemnation;

the holy synod of Ephesus, at which Nestorius was condemned with the consent of the blessed pope Caelestinus chaired by Cyril of Alexandria in the magistrate's seat and by Arcadius the bishop sent from Italy;

the holy synod of Chalcedon chaired by Marcian Augustus and by Anatolius Bishop of Constantinople, at which the Nestorian et Eutychian heresies together with Dioscorus and his sympathisers were condemned.

but also if there are councils hitherto held by the holy fathers of lesser authority than those four, we have decreed [that] they must be both

kept and received. Here added below is on the works of the holy fathers, which are received in the catholic church.
Likewise the works of blessed Caecilius Cyprian the martyr and Bishop of Carthage;
likewise the works of blessed Gregory Nanzanensis the bishop;
likewise the works of blessed Basil Bishop of Cappadocia;
likewise the works of blessed John Bishop of Constantinople;
likewise the works of blessed Theophilus Bishop of Alexandria;
likewise the works of blessed Cyril Bishop of Alexandria;
likewise the works of blessed Bishop Hilary of Poitiers;
likewise the works of blessed Ambrosius Bishop of Milan;
likewise the works of blessed Augustine Bishop of Hippo;
likewise the works of blessed Jerome the priest;
likewise the works of blessed Prosper a most religious man;
3. likewise the letter of blessed pope Leo sent to Flavian Bishop of Constantinople, of which text however if any portion is disputed and it is not that anciently received by all, let it be anathema;
likewise the works and every treatise of all the orthodox fathers, who deviated in nothing from the common [teaching] of the holy Roman church, neither separated from its faith or worship but remained in communion by the grace of God to the last day of their life, we decree are to be read;
likewise the decretal/official letters, which blessed popes gave for the consideration of various fathers at various times from the city of Rome, are to be upheld reverently;
4. likewise the deeds of the holy martyrs, who are glorious from the manifold tortures on the rack and their wonderful triumphs of steadfastness. Who of the catholics doubts that most of them would be enduring still in agonies with their full strength but would bear it by the grace of God and the help of everyone? but according to old custom by the greatest caution they are not read in the holy Roman church, because the names of those who wrote are not properly known and separate from unbelievers and idiots or [the accounts] are thought less attached to the order of events than they should have been; for instance the [accounts of] Cyricus and Julitta, like Georgius and the sufferings of others like these which appear to have been composed by heretics. On account of this, as it was said, so that no pretext for casual mockery can arise, they are not read in the holy Roman church. However we venerate together with the aforesaid

church all the martyrs and their glorious sufferings, which are well known to God and men, with every devotion;

likewise the lives of the fathers Paul, Antony and Hilarion which with all the hermits described by that blessed man Jerome we receive with honour;

likewise the acts of blessed Silvester bishop of the apostolic seat, although the name of him who wrote [them] is unknown, [but] we know to be read by many catholics however in the city of Rome and because of the ancient use of the multitude this is imitated by the church;

likewise the writings on the finding of the cross and certain other novel writings on the finding of the head of the blessed John the Baptist are romances and some of them are read by catholics; but when these come into the hand of catholics, the saying of Paul the blessed apostle should be <considered> first: 'prove all things, hold fast to what is good'.

likewise Rufinus, a most religious man, work many books of ecclesiastical works, also some interpreting the scriptures; but since the venerable Jerome noted that he took arbitary liberties in some of them, we think those [acceptable] which we know the aforesaid blessed Jerome thought [acceptable]; and not only those of Rufinus, but also [those] of anyone whom that man often remembered for his zeal for God and for the religion of faith criticised.

likewise some works of Origen, which the blessed man Jerome does not reject, we receive to be read, but we say that the rest with their author must be refused.

likewise the chronicle of Eusebius of Caesarea and the books of his church history, however much he fell flat in the first book of his narration and [although he also] afterwards wrote one book in praise and to excuse Origen the schismatic, however on account of his narration of remarkable things, which are useful for instruction, we do not say to anyone that it must be refused.

likewise we praise Orosius a most erudite man, who wrote a very necessary history for us against the calumnies of the pagans and and with marvellous brevity.

likewise the paschal work of that venerable man Sedulius, which was written in heroic verses [hexameters], we give preference to with manifest praise.

likewise the laborious work of Iuvencus we nevertheless do not spurn but are amazed by.

V. The remaining writings which have been compiled or been recognised by heretics or schismatics the Catholic and Apostolic Roman Church does not in any way receive; of these we have thought it right to cite below a few which have been handed down and which are to be avoided by catholics:

LIKEWISE A LIST OF APOCRYPHAL BOOKS
firstly we confess that the synod of Sirmium called together by Constantius Caesar the son of Constantine through the Prefect Taurus is damned then and now and for ever.

the Itinerary in the name of Peter the apostle, which is called the nine books of the holy Clement	apocryphal
the Acts in the name of the apostle Andrew	apocryphal
the Acts in the name of the apostle Thomas	apocryphal
the Acts in the name of the apostle Peter	apocryphal
the Acts in the name of the apostle Philip	apocryphal
the Gospel in the name of Mathias	apocryphal
the Gospel in the name of Barnabas	apocryphum
the Gospel in the name of James the younger	apocryphum
the Gospel in the name of the apostle Peter	apocryphum
the Gospel in the name of Thomas which the Manichaeans use	apocryphum
the Gospels in the name of Bartholomew	apocrypha
the Gospels in the name of Andrew	apocrypha
the Gospels which Lucianus forged	apocrypha
the Gospels which Hesychius forged	apocrypha
the book on the infancy of the saviour	apocryphus
the book of the nativity of the saviour and of Mary or the midwife	apocryphus
the book which is called by the name of the Shepherd	apocryphus
all the books which Leucius the disciple of the devil made	apocryphi

the book which is called the Foundation	apocryphus
the book which is called the Treasure	apocryphus
the book of the daughters of Adam Leptogeneseos	apocryphus
the cento on Christ put together in Virgilian verses	apocryphum
the book which is called the Acts of Thecla and Paul	apocryphus
the book which is called Nepos's	apocryphus
the books of Proverbs written by heretics and prefixed with the name of holy Sixtus	apocryphus
the Revelation which is called Paul's	apocrypha
the Revelation which is called Thomas's	apocrypha
the Revelation which is called Stephen's	apocrypha
the book which is called the Assumption of holy Mary	apocryphus
the book which is called the Repentance of Adam	apocryphus
the book about Og the giant of whom the heretics assert that after the deluge he fought with the dragon	apocryphus
the book which is called the Testament of Job	apocryphus
the book which is called the Repentance of Origen	apocryphus
the book which is called the Repentance of holy Cyprian	apocryphus
the book which is called the Repentance of Jamne and Mambre	apocryphus
the book which is called the Lots of the apostles	apocryphus
the book which is called the grave-plate (?) of the apostles	apocryphus
the book which is called the canons of the apostles	apocryphus
the book Physiologus written by heretics and prefixed with the name of blessed Ambrose	apocryphus
the History of Eusebius Pamphilii	apocrypha
the works of Tertullian	apocrypha
the works of Lactantius also known as Firmianus	apocrypha
the works of Africanus	apocrypha
the works of Postumianus and Gallus	apocrypha

the works of Montanus, Priscilla and Maximilla	apocrypha
the works of Faustus the Manichaean	apocrypha
the works of Commodian	apocrypha
the works of the other Clement, of Alexandria	apocrypha
the works of Thascius Cyprianus	apocrypha
the works of Arnobius	apocrypha
the works of Tichonius	apocrypha
the works of Cassian the Gallic priest	apocrypha
the works of Victorinus of Pettau	apocrypha
the works of Faustus of Riez in Gaul	apocrypha
the works of Frumentius Caecus	apocrypha
the cento on Christ stitched together from verses of Virgil	*apocryphum*
the Letter from Jesus to Abgar	apocrypha
the Letter of Abgar to Jesus	apocrypha
the Passion of Cyricus and Julitta	apocrypha
the Passion of Georgius	apocrypha
the writing which is called the Interdiction of Solomon	apocrypha
all amulets which are compiled not in the name of the angels as they pretend but are written in the names of great demons	apocrypha

These and those similar ones, which Simon Magus, Nicolaus, Cerinthus, Marcion, Basilides, Ebion, Paul of Samosata, Photinus and Bonosus, who suffered from similar error, also Montanus with his obscene followers, Apollinaris, Valentinus the Manichaean, Faustus the African, Sabellius, Arius, Macedonius, Eunomius, Novatus, Sabbatius, Calistus, Donatus, Eustasius, Jovianus, Pelagius, Julian of Eclanum, Caelestius, Maximian, Priscillian from Spain, Nestorius of Constantinople, Maximus the Cynic, Lampetius, Dioscorus, Eutyches, Peter and the other Peter, of whom one disgraced Alexandria and the other Antioch, Acacius of Constantinople with his associates, and what also all disciples of heresy and of the heretics and schismatics, whose names we have scarcely preserved, have taught or compiled, we acknowledge is to be not merely rejected but eliminated from the whole Roman Catholic and Apostolic Church and with their authors and the followers of its authors to be damned in the inextricable shackles of anathema forever.

The Codex Theodosianus. On Religion, 4th Century CE

C. Th. XV.xii.1: Bloody spectacles are not suitable for civil ease and domestic quiet. Wherefore since we have proscribed gladiators, those who have been accustomed to be sentenced to such work as punishment for their crimes, you should cause to serve in the mines, so that they may be punished without shedding their blood. Constantine Augustus.
C. Th. XVI.v.1: It is necessary that the privileges which are bestowed for the cultivation of religion should be given only to followers of the Catholic faith. We desire that heretics and schismatics be not only kept from these privileges, but be subjected to various fines. Constantine Augustus.
C. Th. XVI.x.4: It is decreed that in all places and all cities the temples should be closed at once, and after a general warning, the opportunity of sinning be taken from the wicked. We decree also that we shall cease from making sacrifices. And if anyone has committed such a crime, let him be stricken with the avenging sword. And we decree that the property of the one executed shall be claimed by the city, and that rulers of the provinces be punished in the same way, if they neglect to punish such crimes. Constantine and Constans Augusti.
C. Th. XVI.vii.1: The ability and right of making wills shall be taken from those who turn from Christians to pagans, and the testament of such an one, if he made any, shall be abrogated after his death. Gratian, Valentinian, and Valens Augusti.
C.Th. XI.vii.13: Let the course of all law suits and all business cease on Sunday, which our fathers have rightly called the Lord's day, and let no one try to collect either a public or a private debt; and let there be no hearing of disputes by any judges either those required to serve by law or those voluntarily chosen by disputants. And he is to be held not only infamous but sacrilegious who has turned away from the

service and observance of holy religion on that day. Gratian, Valentinian and Theodosius Augusti.

C.Th. XV.v.1: On the Lord's day, which is the first day of the week, on Christmas, and on the days of Epiphany, Easter, and Pentecost, inasmuch as then the [white] garments [of Christians] symbolizing the light of heavenly cleansing bear witness to the new light of holy baptism, at the time also of the suffering of the apostles, the example for all Christians, the pleasures of the theaters and games are to be kept from the people in all cities, and all the thoughts of Christians and believers are to be occupied with the worship of God. And if any are kept from that worship through the madness of Jewish impiety or the error and insanity of foolish paganism, let them know that there is one time for prayer and another for pleasure. And lest anyone should think he is compelled by the honor due to our person, as if by the greater necessity of his imperial office, or that unless he attempted to hold the games in contempt of the religious prohibition, he might offend our serenity in showing less than the usual devotion toward us; let no one doubt that our clemency is revered in the highest degree by humankind when the worship of the whole world is paid to the might and goodness of God. Theodosius Augustus and Caesar Valentinian.

C. Th.XVI.i.2: We desire that all the people under the rule of our clemency should live by that religion which divine Peter the apostle is said to have given to the Romans, and which it is evident that Pope Damasus and Peter, bishop of Alexandria, a man of apostolic sanctity, followed; that is that we should believe in the one deity of Father, Son, and Holy Spirit with equal majesty and in the Holy Trinity according to the apostolic teaching and the authority of the gospel. Gratian, Valentinian and Theodosius Augusti.

C. Th. XVI.v.iii: Whenever there is found a meeting of a mob of Manichaeans, let the leaders be punished with a heavy fine and let those who attended be known as infamous and dishonored, and be shut out from association with men, and let the house and the dwellings where the profane doctrine was taught be seized by the officers of the city. Valentinian and Valens Augusti.

Bibliography

Bettenson, H., ed. The Early Christian Fathers. Oxford University Press, 1969.

_____. The Later Christian Fathers. Oxford University Press, 1969.

Quasten, J. and J.C. Plumpe, eds. Ancient Christian Writers. London: Longmans, 1946-75.

Roberts, A. and J. Donaldson, eds. Ante-Nicene Christian Library, ed. Edinburgh: T&T Clark, 1867-72.

Schaff, P. and H. Wace, eds. A Select Library of Nicene and Post-Nicene Fathers of the Christian Church. Oxford, 1887-92.

Chadwick, Henry and G. R. Evans, eds. Atlas of the Christian Church. New York, N.Y.:Facts on File Publications, 1987.

Cornell, Tim and John Matthews. Atlas of the Roman World. New York, N.Y.: Facts on File, 1982.

Cross, F. L. and E. A. Livingstone, eds. The Oxford Dictionary of the Christian Church. Oxford University Press, 1974.

Eusebius of Caesarea, The History of the Church from Christ to Constantine (=The Ecclesiastical History).

Ferguson, Everett, ed. Encyclopedia of Early Christianity. New York: Garland Publishing, Inc., 1990.

Jones, A. H. M. Prosopography of the Later Roman Empire. Cambridge University Press, 1971-1992.

Quasten, J., Patrology. 3 volumes. Westminster, Maryland: Newman Press, 1962-4.

Young, F. From Nicaea to Chalcedon: A Guide to the Literature and its Development. Philadelphia: Fortress Press, 1983.

Barnes, Timothy D. Athanasius and Constantius: Theology and Politics in the Constantinian Empire. Cambridge: Harvard University Press, 1993.

_____. Constantine and Eusebius. Cambridge: Harvard University Press, 1981.

Brown, Peter. Authority and the Sacred: Aspects of Christianisation of the Roman World. Cambridge University Press, 1995.

_____. Body and Society: Men, Women, and Sexual Renunciation in Early Christianity. New York: Columbia University Press, 1988.

_____. The Cult of the Saints: Its Rise and Function in Latin Christianity. University of Chicago Press, 1981.

_____. The Making of Late Antiquity. Cambridge: Harvard University Press, 1978.

_____. Power and Persuasion in Late Antiquity: Towards a Christian Empire. University of Wisconsin Press, 1992.

_____. The World of Late Antiquity. New York: Harcourt Brace Jovanovich, 1971.

Cameron, Averil. Christianity and the rhetoric of empire: the development of Christian discourse. Berkeley: University of California Press, 1991.

_____. The later Roman empire. Cambridge, Mass.: Harvard University Press, 1993.

_____. The Mediteranean World in Late Antiquity, AD 395-600. New York:Routledge, 1993.

Chadwick, Henry. The Early Church. The Pelican History of the Church, vol. 1; Penguin Books, 1967.

Comby, Jean. How to Read Church History, vol. 1. New York: Crossroad, 1989.

Fowden, Garth. Empire to Commonwealth: Consequences of Monotheism in Late Antiquity. Princeton, New Jersey: Princeton University Press, 1993.

Fox, Robin Lane. Pagans and Christians. San Francisco: Harper, 1986.

Frend, W. H. C., The Early Church. London, SCM, 1982.

_____. The Rise of Christianity. Philadelphia: Fortress Press, 1984.

Hazlett, Ian, ed. Early Christianity: Origins and Evolution to A.D. 600. Nashville:Abingdon Press, 1991.

Holum, Kenneth. Theodosian Empresses: Women and Imperial Dominion in Late Antiquity. Berkeley: University of California Press, 1982.

Kelly, J. N. D. Early Christian Creeds. 3rd revised edition. Longman, 1972.

_____. Early Christian Doctrines. 5th revised edition. New York: Harper & Row, 1978.

MacCormack, Sabine. Art and Ceremony in Late Antiquity.

MacMullen, Ramsay. Christianizing the Roman Empire A.D. 100-400. Yale University Press, 1984.

Markus, R. A. The End of Ancient Christianity. New York: Cambridge University Press, 1990.

Pelikan, J. The Christian Tradition: A History of the Development of Doctrine. Volume 1:The Emergence of the Catholic Tradition (100-600). University of Chicago Press, 1971.
Ramsay, B. Beginning to Read the Fathers. Mahwah, New Jersey: Paulist Press, 1985.
Trimmingham, J. S., Christianity among the Arabs in Pre-Islamic Times. London, 1979.
Wilken, Robert L. The Christians as the Romans Saw Them. Yale University Press, 1984.
James Charlesworth (ed.), The Old Testament Pseudepigrapha (1983 New York, two volumes)
John J. Collins, The scepter and the star. The Messiahs of the Dead Sea scrolls and other ancient literature (1995 New York)
Craig Evans, Jesus and his contemporaries. Comparative studies (1995 Leiden)
Israel Finkelstein & Neil Asher Silberman, The Bible Unearthed. Archaeology's New Vision of Ancient Israel and the Origin of Its Sacred Texts (2001 New York)
Israel Knohl, The Messiah before Jesus. The Suffering Servant of the Dead Sea Scrolls (2000 Berkeley)
A. Schalit, 'Die Erhebung Vespasians nach Josephus, Talmud und Midrasch: Zur Geschichte einer messianischen Prophetie' in Aufstieg und Niedergang der Römischen Welt 2.2 (1975) 208-327
Gershom Scholem, Sabbatai Sevi: the Mystical Messiah (1973 Princeton)
Michael Wise, The first Messiah. Investigating the Savior before Jesus (1999 San Francisco)
Ben Witherington, The Christology of Jesus (1990 Philadelphia)

ENCICLOPEDIA BRITANICA   http://www.britannica.com/
ENCICLOPEDIA CATOLICA
    http://www.enciclopediacatolica.com/
THE JEWISH ENCICLOPAEDIA   www.jewishenciclopaedia.com

www.ingramcontent.com/pod-product-compliance
Lightning Source LLC
Chambersburg PA
CBHW050556170426
43201CB00011B/1711